Lon

CALIFORNIA

Alexis Averbuck, Alison Bing, Shawn Forno,
Ryan Ver Berkmoes, Wendy Yanagihara

IDAHO

NEVADA

OREGON

CALIFORNIA

Yosemite &
the Sierra Nevada 142

Bishop

Kings Canyon
National Park

Mono
Lake

Mammoth
Lakes

Yosemite
National
Park

Thrilling Lake Tahoe
138

South Lake Tahoe

Goose
Lake

Alturas

Susanville

Truckee

Lake
Tahoe

Sierra Nevada

Sonora

Volcanic
California 114

The Capital City: Sacramento 136

Eagle
Lake

Lassen
Volcanic
National
Park

Mt Shasta

Redding

Chico

Sutter
Creek

Stockton

San Joaquin River

Weed

Red Bluff

Davis

Sacramento River

Sacramento Valley

Yosemite
4½hrs

Oakland

Palo Alto

San Jose

Coast Range

Clear
Lake

Calistoga

Santa Rosa

Monterey
3hrs

Santa Cruz

Klamath River

Crescent
City

Eureka

Arcata

Redwood
National Park

Northern California &
the Redwood Coast 94

Leggett

Mendocino

Napa Valley &
Sonoma 70

San Francisco &
the Bay Area 38

Above Dolores Park (p52), San Francisco.

Wendy Yanagihara
@ *@wendyyanagihara*

Though Wendy savors the simple pleasures of Santa Barbara like tasting local wine and hiking front-country trails, some of her most magical adventures have been stand-up paddleboarding when dolphins glide alongside or great white sharks cruise below.

Contents

Above Lifeguard tower, Santa Monica (p209).

EPIC
EPICURIAN

California is the epicenter of good eating in the United States, if not the world. Where else is the natural bounty fresher or more varied, the kitchen creativity more boundary-pushing or the flavors and textures more international?

New wines and brews have been developed at California's cultural crossroads for centuries, too. Get adventurous with the latest food trends, from hip food halls to Cal-Japanese tasting menus to indigenous cooking.

Left Food at the Ferry Building, San Francisco. **Right** Fruit at San Francisco Ferry Building Farmers Market. **Below** Baja-style fish taco.

→ FARM-TO-TABLE PIONEERS

With farmers as neighbors and seafood and foraged ingredients fresh from its beaches and forests, cooks bring California's roots and modern-day fresh harvests to the plate.

VAUNTED VINEYARDS

Raise a toast to California's wine-producing regions pioneering sustainable practices. Experience blooming biodynamic orchards, sun-dappled organic olive groves and lazy bicycle rides to LEED-certified tasting rooms.

↑ CALIFORNIA MEXICAN

Burritos and tacos are a staple of the food scene, especially in San Francisco (try La Palma Mexicatessen), LA and San Diego, where the humble Baja-style fish taco is a local obsession.

Best Culinary Experiences

▶ Duck inside the 19th-century ferry terminal in San Francisco for a showcase of top artisanal food producers. (p48)

▶ Dive into the country's top Asian restaurants from SF's embarrassment of riches to modern Steep in LA. (p48; p208)

▶ Get fancy at restaurants like Benu or SingleThread. (p69; p78)

▶ Sup on Mexican specialties at SoCal taco stands, the town of Salinas, or at Sonoma's El Molino. (p78)

CALIFORNIA'S WILD FACTS

Acres of red-wood forest 110,000

Miles of coastline 840

Rivers 100-plus

Highest peak The Sierra Nevada's Mt Whitney at 14,494ft

BIG
NATURE

In California, Mother Nature has been as prolific as Picasso in his prime. Blissful beaches, unspoiled wilderness, big-shouldered mountains, trees as tall as the Statue of Liberty, lakes as blue as sapphires – this land is an intoxicating mosaic that has inspired visionaries, artists and wanderers for centuries. Go and plunge in to create memories sure to last a lifetime.

Left Sequoia National Park (p152). **Right** View from Glacier Point (p147), Yosemite National Park. **Below** Black bear, Yosemite National Park (p146).

→ YOSEMITE TIPS

Feeling so small has never felt grander than in Yosemite. To achieve maximum wonder, stop at Glacier Point under a full moon or drive high-country Tioga Rd.

DON'T MISS: RANGING THE REDWOODS

The state is swathed in magnificent redwoods from Big Sur to Sequoia and Kings Canyon then north to the Oregon border where groves rule the road.

↑ WILDING OUT

Unique creatures great and small inhabit California's diverse ecosystems – from elephant seals and gray whales to elk, black bears and mountain lions.

Best Nature Experiences

▶ Hit the all-season adventure hub and lake extraordinaire at Tahoe. (p138)

▶ Explore otherworldly Lassen Volcanic National Park – a mosaic of lava, craters and mud pots. (p115)

▶ Gawk at massive stands of old-growth California coastal redwoods at Redwood National & State Parks. (p103)

▶ Twist your way through narrow canyons, zoom across crackled salt flats and touch the lowest point in North America in Death Valley. (p231)

COASTAL QUICK HITS

Public beaches 420-plus

Gray whale migration January through March

Rules Many beaches don't allow fires, smoking, dogs, glassware or, alas, nudity

COASTAL
PLEASURES

Life's a beach in California, and so much more. When the coastal fog lifts, the state's 840 miles of shoreline truly earn their 'golden' moniker. Find family fun in La Jolla, ogle world-class surfers in Huntington Beach, mingle with eccentrics in Venice Beach, cuddle at sunset in a Big Sur cove or find yourself on the stunning Lost Coast Trail.

HOLBOX/SHUTTERSTOCK ©

→ SURF CITY USA

Even if you never set foot on a board, you should, like, totally check out Huntington and Newport Beach. Surfing defines California pop culture, from street slang to movies and fashion.

Left Venice Beach (p202), Los Angeles. **Right** Huntington Beach Pier (p214). **Below** Harbor seal, Channel Islands (p168).

DON'T MISS: BIG SUR

Cradled by mossy redwood forests, the rocky Big Sur coast is a mystical place. Search out hidden waterfalls and hot springs and watch for endangered California condors while scrambling along sea cliffs.

RIGHT: JOE BELANGER/SHUTTERSTOCK ©
LEFT: XAVIER ARNAU/GETTY IMAGES ©

↑ CHANNEL ISLANDS NATIONAL PARK

Commune with coral-reef creatures and giant colonies of seals and sea lions while hiking, snorkeling or kayaking around the uninhabited Channel Islands, SoCal's version of the Galapagos.

Best Coastal Experiences

▶ Dive into endless summer at Santa Monica and Venice with a solar-powered Ferris wheel and soul-stirring sunsets. (p202)

▶ Escape San Francisco's buzz at Baker Beach, fronting the Pacific with the picture-perfect Golden Gate Bridge.

▶ Drive between the Lost Coast and gigantic redwoods to world-wonder Prairie Creek Redwoods State Park. (p103)

▶ Marvel in the marine sanctuary of Monterey Bay, hugging Santa Cruz, Monterey and Carmel. (p122)

Avenue of the Giants
Raw redwood brilliance

The incredible 32-mile road at Humboldt Redwoods State Park is canopied by the world's tallest trees, some of which were seedlings during the Roman Empire. The best time is in the morning when sunlight glints off dew-drenched ferns.

🚗 *2½hrs north of Mendocino*
▶ p103

PACIFIC OCEAN

Pacific Coast Highway
World-class ocean views

No matter if you follow the entire 656 miles or just a short stretch of coast-hugging Hwy 1, you'll hit the Insta jackpot. Posing options include dramatic sea cliffs, sun-soaked surfing towns, playful harbor seals and the Golden Gate Bridge.

🚗 *runs from SoCal at I-5 to Hwy 101 in Leggett*
▶ p120

PERFECT
ROAD TRIPS

▬▬ Road-tripping is the ultimate way to experience California, so fill the gas tank and buckle up for unforgettable drives through scenery that tugs at your heart and soul. Get ready for memory-making encounters as you wheel past sensuous vineyards, humbling redwood forests, epic desert expanses, endless miles of coastal highway and skytouching Sierra Nevada peaks. Just make sure that rental car has unlimited miles – you'll need 'em all.

Santa Ynez Valley
Winding wineries

Watch the 2004 Oscar-winning *Sideways,* then sip soft pinot noir *in situ* on a tour of these sylvan hillsides quilted with oaks, olive trees and endless rows of vineyards.

🚗 *45min northwest of Santa Barbara via Hwy 154*
▶ p174

Arcata
Eureka
Lassen Volcanic National Park
Redding
Susanville
Lost Coast
Red Bluff
Leggett
Coast Ranges
Chico
Sacramento Valley
Mendocino
Nevada City
Calistoga
Santa Rosa
Davis
Sacramento
Sonoma
Point Reyes
Berkeley
Stockton
San Francisco
Oakland
Palo Alto
San Jose
Santa Cruz
Monterey Bay
Monterey
Diablo Range
Big Sur
Cambria
San Luis Obispo

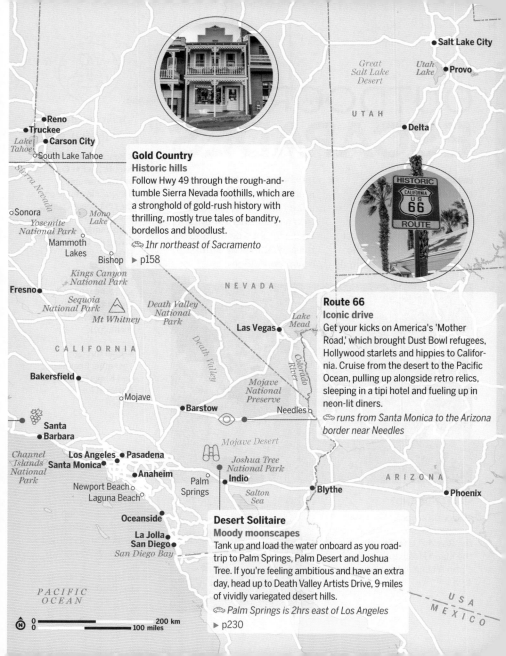

● Salt Lake City

Great Salt Lake Desert

Great Salt Lake

Utah Lake

● Provo

UTAH

● Reno
● Truckee
Lake Tahoe ● Carson City
○ South Lake Tahoe

● Delta

Sierra Nevada

○ Sonora
Yosemite National Park
Mono Lake
Mammoth Lakes
Bishop ○
Kings Canyon National Park

Fresno ●

Sequoia National Park
△ Mt Whitney

Death Valley National Park

NEVADA

Las Vegas ●

Lake Mead

CALIFORNIA

Bakersfield ●

○ Mojave

Death Valley

Mojave National Preserve

Colorado River

● Barstow ◉

Needles ○

● Santa Barbara

Channel Islands National Park

Los Angeles ● Pasadena
Santa Monica ●
● Anaheim
Newport Beach ○
Laguna Beach ○

Mojave Desert

Palm Springs
Joshua Tree National Park
● Indio

Salton Sea

● Blythe

ARIZONA

● Phoenix

Oceanside ●

La Jolla ●
San Diego ●
San Diego Bay

PACIFIC OCEAN

USA
MEXICO

Gold Country
Historic hills
Follow Hwy 49 through the rough-and-tumble Sierra Nevada foothills, which are a stronghold of gold-rush history with thrilling, mostly true tales of banditry, bordellos and bloodlust.

🚗 *1hr northeast of Sacramento*
▶ p158

Route 66
Iconic drive
Get your kicks on America's 'Mother Road,' which brought Dust Bowl refugees, Hollywood starlets and hippies to California. Cruise from the desert to the Pacific Ocean, pulling up alongside retro relics, sleeping in a tipi hotel and fueling up in neon-lit diners.

🚗 *runs from Santa Monica to the Arizona border near Needles*

Desert Solitaire
Moody moonscapes
Tank up and load the water onboard as you road-trip to Palm Springs, Palm Desert and Joshua Tree. If you're feeling ambitious and have an extra day, head up to Death Valley Artists Drive, 9 miles of vividly variegated desert hills.

🚗 *Palm Springs is 2hrs east of Los Angeles*
▶ p230

Ⓝ 0 ___ 200 km
   0 ___ 100 miles

OUTDOOR
ESCAPADES

An irresistible combo of forests, mountains, ocean and desert, California's outdoors is nothing short of extraordinary and the menu of options seemingly inexhaustible. Make memories while hiking in a fairytale forest, plunging into a glistening mountain lake, clambering around massive dunes or schussing down epic slopes.

Best Outdoor Experiences

▶ **Beachcomb in remote Shelter Cove or tackle an epic backpacking route on the Lost Coast.** (p98)

▶ **Go snorkeling and diving off Catalina Island.** (p200)

▶ **Explore craters, spatter cones and lava tubes at Lava Beds National Monument.** (p115)

▶ **Hike through Yosemite, Sequoia, and Kings Canyon National Parks.** (p150)

→ CITY-BOUND?

California's cities offer great escapes. In San Francisco, walk the Golden Gate Bridge to hike the Marin Headlands. In LA, climb Mt Lee to the Hollywood sign.

★ **HOT SOAKS**

Leave a little extra time to hot-spring-hop in Northern California – from Calistoga on up to Harbin, Vichy and Orr.

Top left Snorkeling off Catalina Island. **Bottom left** View from, Marin Headlands, San Francisco. **Right** Hollywood Walk of Fame.

LEFT: JUSTIN LEWIS/GETTY IMAGES ©, BOTTOM: IOANA CATALINA E/SHUTTERSTOCK ©

LIGHTS, CAMERA...

More movies are made in California than in any other state.

Hollywood was founded in 1887. The first movie to be made there in 1911 is called *In Old California*.

Best Movie Experiences

▶ Snap a selfie at Grauman's Chinese Theatre in Hollywood, then duck inside for one of the largest IMAX screens in the world. (p196)

▶ Scout film settings like Death Valley or Armstrong Woods for *Star Wars,* Bodega for *The Birds* and San Juan Bautista for *Vertigo.*

▶ Find your favorite celebrity on the Hollywood Walk of Fame. (p196)

MOVIE
MAGIC

To Shakespeare all the world may have been a stage, but in California, it's actually more of a film set. And although movies were born in France, they certainly came of age in Hollywood. Even without any celebrities to snare your stare, you can still stand in their footprints, look behind the scenes on a studio tour or hop on a bus to see where the stars live.

SERGIO TB/SHUTTERSTOCK ©

CITY
LIFE

California's cities have more flavors than a jar of jelly beans. They will seduce you with a cultural kaleidoscope that spans the arc from art museums, architectural showpieces and vibrant theater to tantalizing food scenes and high-octane nightlife.

Best City Experiences

▶ Push boundaries in scene-stealing San Francisco. (p38)

▶ Contrast Los Angeles' beaches and celebutantes with its rich cultural diversity. (p178)

▶ Take it easy in San Diego – grab a fish taco and hit the beach. (p220)

▶ Immerse yourself in Santa Barbara's architecture. (p170)

▶ Explore fascinating cities like San Luis Obispo, Oakland and Sacramento. (p136)

QUIRKY
CALI

California is full of cultural surprises. SoCal's deserts and the North Coast deliver a disproportionate share of offbeat attractions, but wild LA and bohemian SF are also jam-packed with memorable spots. Sculpture gardens, houses built of bottles, a museum dedicated to crocheted animals, dinosaurs by the freeway – it's all in California's unconventional DNA.

Best Offbeat Experiences

▶ Tour the cool-cat communities from Sea Ranch to Mendocino. (p106)

▶ Explore LA's Broad Museum and La Brea Tar Pits. (p190; p194)

▶ Shake your rump at lavish drag shows and dance parties at San Fran's Oasis. (p45)

▶ Plan ahead for Coachella, where headliners, indie acts and DJs gather near Palm Springs. (p232)

→ SEBASTOPOL

Stroll the patchouli-filled farmers market in this eccentric Sonoma County town and don't miss Florence Ave, lined with Patrick Amiot's witty yard sculptures.

★ **HEARST CASTLE**

Book an unforgettable tour of William Randolph Hearst's hilltop estate with its sparkling Neptune Pool, interiors lavishly decorated in European antiquities and jewels, and stunning sunsets.

Far left Haight St (p66), San Francisco. **Above left** Sea Ranch Chapel (p107). **Left** Kale harvest, Sebastopol.

LEFT TANGENT IMAGEZ/SHUTTERSTOCK © (DESIGNER: JAMES HUBBELL), BOTTOM: HUTCH AXILROD/GETTY IMAGES ©

↘ Pride Month

California celebrates LGBTIQ+ pride for the entire month of June, especially in San Francisco, which sets the global standard.

Peak summer season across California runs from Memorial Day in late May to Labor Day in early September.

↓ July 4

Cities and towns large and small across California celebrate America's Independence Day with parades, festivals and fireworks.

↓ Southern California Beaches

From Santa Barbara to San Diego, the nearly continuous ribbon of beaches is thronged and the Pacific is warm.

JUNE

Average daytime max: 71°F
Days of rainfall: 0
(San Francisco)

JULY

California in
SUMMER

California State Fair

Pie-eating contests, craft-beer competitions, championship hogs, carnival rides and much more draw a million people to Sacramento in late July.

📍 Sacramento

▶ calexpostatefair.com

↖ Comic-Con International

Not just for comic-book fans, this enormous convention in San Diego covers pop culture, sci-fi and anime. Look for celebs aplenty.

📍 San Diego

▶ comic-con.org

↑ Outside Lands

San Francisco's Summer of Love roots underpin this music and comedy bacchanalia that takes over Golden Gate Park in August.

📍 San Francisco

▶ sfoutsidelands.com

CALIFORNIA PLAN BY SEASON

Average daytime max: 83°F
Days of rainfall: 0 (Los Angeles)

AUGUST

Average daytime max: 107°F
Days of rainfall: 0
(Palm Springs)

Demand for accommodation across much of California peaks during summer. Book tours and overnight adventures in advance at lonelyplanet.com/activities/california.

🧳 Packing Notes

Bring a warm layer for cold and clammy coastal fog in the morning.

Early autumn is a spectacular time on the Northern California coast, with summertime fog in retreat and balmy days the norm.

→ Monterey Jazz Festival

Traditional, fusion, cross-cultural and iconic local West Coast–style jazz are played in September at one of the world's great music festivals.

📍 Monterey

▶ montereyjazzfestival.org

⟍ Wine Country Colors

Vineyards erupt in an ocean of golden, orange and magenta hues throughout the fall from Napa and Sonoma to Paso Robles.

Wine Country Festivals

Vineyards big and small across the state celebrate the fall harvest with gala tastings and celebrations, most held outside.

SEPTEMBER

Average daytime max: 77°F
Days of rainfall: 1 (Big Sur)

OCTOBER

California in
FALL

Halloween

Spooks and ghosts can be found statewide, but head to West Hollywood for a day-long carnival of flamboyantly extreme costumes.

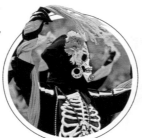

↗ Día de los Muertos

November 2 is the Day of the Dead, when Mexican culture honors deceased relatives. Look for candlelight processions, festivals and decorated altars.

Unpredictable November storms can blanket the Sierras in snow, giving winter sports fans an early start to the ski season.

Average daytime max: 77°F
Days of rainfall: 2 (Napa)

NOVEMBER

Average daytime max: 77°F
Days of rainfall: 0 (Death Valley)

↙ National Parks

October is an ideal month to visit national parks, from Sequoia and Kings Canyon to Death Valley. Crowds and temperatures are moderate.

 Packing Notes

Temps across California are moderate to warm, with cool nights.

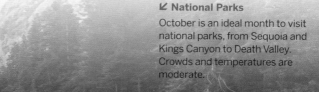

↘ Whale-Watching

Gray whales follow the coast south to their winter home in Baja all December and January. Whale-watching tours depart from many harbors.

It's peak ski season from Thanksgiving through February. Avoid the weekend throngs by hitting the slopes midweek.

↓ Tournament of Roses Parade

The smell of posies pervades the air on New Year's Day in Pasadena for this long-running parade of lavish floats and celebrities.

📍Pasadena

▶ tournamentofroses.com

DECEMBER

Average daytime max: 58°F
Days of rainfall: 7 (San Francisco)

JANUARY

California in
WINTER

Parades of Lights

Skippers decorate boats and yachts of all shapes and sizes for holiday-season parades in major Southern California marinas.

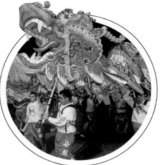

↙ Lunar New Year

The biggest date on the Chinese calendar sparks fireworks, parades and festivities, with the largest in San Francisco's Chinatown.

See the Salmon Run

A few creeks in Marin County still have salmon runs in January. Ask the rangers at Muir Woods and Point Reyes for tips.

Winter is a wonderful time in Death Valley and Joshua Tree National Parks, and the Mojave Desert; mild temperatures are made for hiking.

FEBRUARY

Average daytime max: 44°F
Days of rainfall/snowfall: 6
(Lake Tahoe)

Average daytime max: 69°F
Days of rainfall: 4 (Los Angeles)

← Awards Season

Hollywood marches from one awards ceremony to the next in February right up to the crowning spectacle, the Academy Awards.

 Packing Notes

Bring rain gear as in nondrought years Pacific storms can roll through.

CALIFORNIA PLAN BY SEASON

↘ Wildflowers

California's hillsides erupt in carpets of colors that draw crowds to parks statewide. Polychromatic wildflowers burst forth in oranges, purples and more.

↓ Coachella Valley Music & Arts Festival

For two weekends in April, top headliners, indie sensations, cult DJs and more take the stages at this enormous festival near Palm Springs.

● Palm Springs

▶ coachella.com

Spring Celebrations

Town and cities shed any winter doldrums with food and drink festivals statewide. Grab a craft beer or a newly released wine.

MARCH

Average daytime max: 81°F
Days of rainfall: 1 (Palm Springs)

APRIL

California in
SPRING

San Francisco International Film Festival

Hundreds of indie films premiere at one of the world's oldest film festivals. That guy seated next to you might be named Coppola.

📍 San Francisco

▶ sffilm.org

→ Cinco de Mayo

It can seem like half the cars in the state are decked out to celebrate Mexican independence and culture on May 5.

← Bay to Breakers

Tipsy trippers, bare-assed streakers, determined amateurs and even big-time pros make the dash through a partying San Francisco in May.

📍 San Francisco

▶ capstoneraces.com/ bay-to-breakers

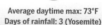

MAY

Average daytime max: 68°F
Days of rainfall: 4 (Santa Cruz)

Average daytime max: 73°F
Days of rainfall: 3 (Yosemite)

↓ Colorful Road Trips

Emerald hills make every stretch of Hwy 1 from Big Sur to the north coast a wonder of seasonal rebirth under dazzling skies.

Early May is the ideal time to take in Yosemite – snow is melting, waterfalls are surging and crowds are few.

 Packing Notes

Bring layers for late rains, early highs and lingering lows.

SAN FRANCISCO & NORTHERN CALIFORNIA
Trip Builder

TAKE YOUR PICK OF MUST-SEES AND HIDDEN GEMS

San Francisco is a trip. Cruise through its free-form cultural and cutting-edge realities. Going further, around the bay great communities like Berkeley brim with allure. Napa and Wine Country offer languid days amid the vineyards, while the North Coast is nature's stage for pounding Pacific drama and soaring redwoods.

🗺 Trip Notes

Hub towns San Francisco, Napa, Mendocino

How long Allow two weeks.

Getting around Get around San Francisco on its web of public transportation; use trains, ferries and buses for the Bay Area; get a car for Wine Country and the North Coast.

Tips If you have a car in San Francisco, never leave *anything* visible inside. Elsewhere, use public transportation, ride apps and tours to avoid wine-tasting and driving.

Lost Coast

Mendocino
Explore salt-sprayed and wave-tossed Mendocino, the perfect North Coast village, where idiosyncratic is the norm amid cliffside walks and natural – and creative – diversions.
🕐 ½–1 day

PACIFIC OCEAN

Sonoma
Sip fine local wines and sample exquisite regional fare amid adobe walls and red-tile roofs in Sonoma, one of California's oldest towns.
🕐 1 day

San Francisco Days & Nights
Seek out adventure by day *and* night in San Francisco, where uninhibited expression is the rule rather than the exception.
🕐 2–4 days

Ⓝ
0 ———— 100 km
0 ———— 50 miles

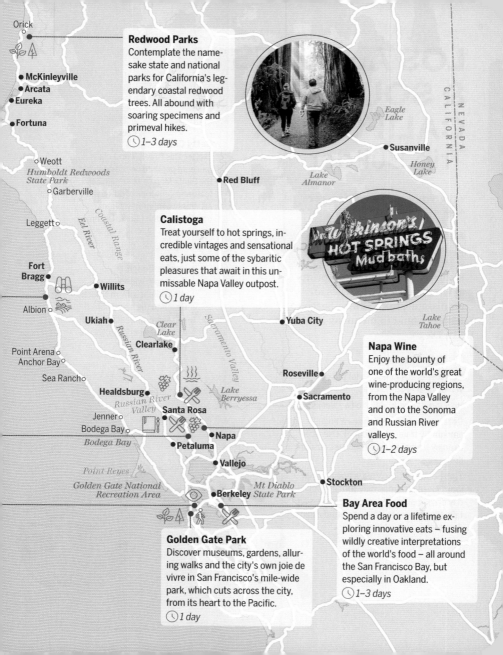

Redwood Parks

Contemplate the namesake state and national parks for California's legendary coastal redwood trees. All abound with soaring specimens and primeval hikes.

🕐 *1–3 days*

Calistoga

Treat yourself to hot springs, incredible vintages and sensational eats, just some of the sybaritic pleasures that await in this unmissable Napa Valley outpost.

🕐 *1 day*

Napa Wine

Enjoy the bounty of one of the world's great wine-producing regions, from the Napa Valley and on to the Sonoma and Russian River valleys.

🕐 *1–2 days*

Bay Area Food

Spend a day or a lifetime exploring innovative eats – fusing wildly creative interpretations of the world's food – all around the San Francisco Bay, but especially in Oakland.

🕐 *1–3 days*

Golden Gate Park

Discover museums, gardens, alluring walks and the city's own joie de vivre in San Francisco's mile-wide park, which cuts across the city, from its heart to the Pacific.

🕐 *1 day*

Orick
McKinleyville
Arcata
Eureka
Fortuna
Weott
Humboldt Redwoods State Park
Garberville
Leggett
Fort Bragg
Willits
Albion
Ukiah
Clear Lake
Clearlake
Point Arena
Anchor Bay
Sea Ranch
Healdsburg
Jenner
Bodega Bay
Bodega Bay
Point Reyes
Golden Gate National Recreation Area
Berkeley
Coastal Range
Eel River
Russian River
Russian River Valley
Santa Rosa
Napa
Petaluma
Vallejo
Red Bluff
Lake Almanor
Susanville
Eagle Lake
Honey Lake
CALIFORNIA
NEVADA
Sacramento Valley
Yuba City
Lake Tahoe
Roseville
Sacramento
Lake Berryessa
Stockton
Mt Diablo State Park

LOS ANGELES & SOUTHERN CALIFORNIA
Trip Builder

TAKE YOUR PICK OF MUST-SEES AND HIDDEN GEMS

▬▬▬ There's more to see in LA than in most countries. The famous sights just keep coming, from the Hollywood sign to the footprints at Grauman's. The beaches are unmissable, from Venice Beach to Balboa Island to the many strands of San Diego.

🗺 Trip Notes

Hub towns Los Angeles, Hollywood, Venice Beach, San Diego

How long Allow 10 days to two weeks.

Getting around You can see a huge amount by train, bus and foot. Use a car to enjoy traffic jams and connect obscure dots.

Tips Southern California is huge – what looks close on a map may turn into an all-day driving ordeal. Clump your sights, eg take the subway to Hollywood and explore it on foot.

Getty Center
Explore this (free!) world-class museum perched on the edge of the Santa Monica Mountains and featuring centuries of European art and sweeping views from downtown to the Pacific Ocean.
🕐 ½–1 day

Venice Beach
Go people-watching at Venice Beach, from Muscle Beach to the boardwalk. If you like your beaches with a dash of weirdness, this is your place.
🕐 1 day

Los Padres National Forest

California Aqueduct

Angeles National Forest

Santa Clarita ●

San ● Fernando

Santa Monica ●

Santa Monica Bay

San Pedro Channel

Outer Santa Barbara Channel

San Nicolas Island

San Clemente Island

PACIFIC OCEAN

0 ———— 50 km
0 ———— 30 miles

Hollywood

Plunge right into the Hollywood glam, a defining part of what makes LA great. Studios, stars and the silver screen have shaped Southern California.
🕐 *1 day*

Los Angeles

Go carless and enjoy destinations great and small, from hip Silver Lake to downtown icons and on to oddities like the La Brea Tar Pits.
🕐 *2–4 days*

Mojave Desert

CALIFORNIA

Angeles National Forest

San Bernardino National Forest

● **Pasadena**

San Bernardino ●
Redlands ●

● **Moreno Valley**

Buena Park

● **Corona**

Long Beach

● **Anaheim**

Santa Ana Mountains

Sunset Beach
● **Santa Ana**

● **Irvine**

Huntington Beach

San Clemente ○

Balboa Island & Peninsula

Glimpse old Orange County at Balboa Island. Stroll the boardwalk, revel in tasty snacks that are bad for you, play arcade games and beat the summer heat in the surf.
🕐 *½ day*

Salton Sea

Gulf of Santa Catalina

Oceanside ●
Carlsbad ●

● **Escondido**

Encinitas ●

Anza-Borrego Desert State Park

San Diego River

La Jolla ●

San Diego ●

San Diego Bay

Catalina Island

Take a quick ferry ride to Catalina, the ultimate Southern California day trip. The quaint island has chill island vibes, a 1930s casino and no traffic.
🕐 *1–2 days*

San Diego's Balboa Park

Wander around sprawling Balboa Park with its 65-plus miles of trails, 16 museums, dozens of shops, stalls, restaurants and attractions like the world-famous San Diego Zoo.
🕐 *1–2 days*

USA
MEXICO

CENTRAL COAST & SANTA BARBARA
Trip Builder

TAKE YOUR PICK OF MUST-SEES AND HIDDEN GEMS

Touring California's Central Coast is a dream of outstanding scenery, winding drives and unexpected surprises. Catch a whale's breach on the Monterey Bay, hike to a hidden waterfall near Big Sur and sip a superb wine in sunny Santa Barbara.

🗺 Trip Notes

Hub towns Santa Cruz, Monterey, San Luis Obispo, Santa Barbara

How long Allow one week to 10 days.

Getting around This is car country, which is the only way to travel the unmissable stretches of Hwys 1 and 101.

Tips Do like local residents and be prepared for cold, clammy, coastal fog on summer mornings. Spring and fall bring great weather and smaller crowds.

Monterey Bay   Moss Landing

Pacific Grove

Carmel-by-the-Sea

Santa Lucia Range

Monterey
Stroll the craggy shore of Monterey, which anchors Pacific Grove and Carmel, for tide pools and crashing waves. It also has an unmissable aquarium and whale-watching tours on its namesake bay.
🕐 *1–2 days*

Big Sur
Consider this: is Big Sur a place or a state of mind? Its waterfalls, hidden beaches and surreal beauty can seem like a dream. But cruising legendary Hwy 1, you'll thrill to the reality.
🕐 *1–2 days*

Santa Barbara Wine Country
Drive Hwy 154 deep into the Santa Ynez Valley to the heart of Santa Barbara's Wine Country, where fabulous merlots are just the beginning.
🕐 *1 day*

0
0
100 km
50 miles

Santa Cruz

Find out why there's no better beach town than Santa Cruz. Surfers catch rides on Monterey Bay sets while fun seekers hit the boardwalk, roller coaster, walkable downtown and more.

🕐 1–2 days

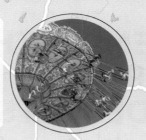

Paso Robles

Discover why Paso Robles rivals the Napa Valley for the quality of its vineyards. The town is set amid wildflower-flecked hills that nurture both grapes and the building blocks of great gastronomy.

🕐 1 day

Pismo Beach

Enjoy the northern outpost of Southern California beach culture – Pismo's famous swath of sand is a four-season pleasure ground of coastal fun.

🕐 1 day

Santa Barbara

Don't miss superb food, drinks, walks, water sports and much more in this coastal city, where romantic Spanish Colonial Revival–style architecture rules and the main drag ends at the beach.

🕐 1–3 days

Santa Cruz Island

Explore this wild and windswept island, home to whales, sharks and more wildlife on land and sea. Just off the Santa Barbara coast, it's the most accessible of the Channel Islands.

🕐 1 day

Hollister

Pinnacles National Park

Coast Ranges

Soledad

Los Padres National Forest

King City

Gorda

Hwy 1

Lake Nacimiento

Cholame

San Simeon

Cambria

Morro Bay

Morro Bay

Los Osos

San Luis Obispo

Los Padres National Forest

San Luis Obispo Bay

Guadalupe

Santa Maria

PACIFIC OCEAN

San Rafael Mountains

Los Padres National Forest

Ventucopa

Santa Ynez Valley

Los Alamos

Los Olivos

Santa Ynez

Lompoc

Hwy 154

Santa Barbara Channel

Channel Islands National Park

San Miguel Island

Santa Rosa Island

Kings Canyon National Park

Sequoia National Park

San Joaquin Valley

California Aqueduct

YOSEMITE, THE SIERRAS & THE DESERTS
Trip Builder

TAKE YOUR PICK OF MUST-SEES AND HIDDEN GEMS

Yosemite National Park is the obvious draw for the Sierra Nevada mountains, where natural wonders abound among California's highest peaks. But just a short drive south are low-lying deserts with names like Death Valley and arresting, stark beauty. Find city pleasures in Lake Tahoe, Palm Springs and Sacramento.

🗺 Trip Notes

Hub towns Sacramento, Lake Tahoe, Palm Springs

How long Allow one to two weeks.

Getting around California's eastern spine – the mountains and deserts – is car country. You'll need the freedom to explore mile after mile of sensational scenery.

Tips Many mountain roads close due to winter conditions (which can last from November through May); summer can make the deserts dangerous for casual travelers.

Redwood National Park

Arcata ●

Lassen Volcanic National Park

Redding ● **Red Bluff**

Sacramento
Stop over at the state capital of the world's fifth-largest economy, which celebrates California's history and art while offering great food and drink that epitomize this diverse state.
🕐 *1 day*

● Chico

Santa Rosa ● **Sonoma**

Stockton ●

San Francisco ●

Yosemite National Park
Be wowed by America's grandest national park with one extraordinary sight after another: from wonders shaped in granite to waterfalls plunging down sheer cliffs, from alpine meadows to trout-filled creeks.
🕐 *1–3 days*

● **San Jose**

● **Santa Cruz**

Monterey Bay
Monterey ○

Cambria ○

Big Sur

PACIFIC OCEAN

0 ___ 200 km
0 ___ 100 miles

Lake Tahoe

Peer into the indigo depths of Lake Tahoe, then take in the surrounding tree-cloaked mountains. In summer hop on the trails, in winter hit the slopes.

🕐 1–2 days

Great Salt Lake Desert

UTAH

Eastern Sierras

Drive Hwy 395 as it follows the eastern flank of the Sierras through forgotten frontier towns, scenic oddities like Mono Lake and historic shrines like Manzanar National Historic Site.

🕐 1–2 days

Truckee

Nevada City

● **Carson City**

○ South Lake Tahoe

NEVADA

Sonora ○

Mono Lake

● Mammoth Lakes

CALIFORNIA

○ Bishop

Sierra Nevada

Hwy 395

Death Valley National Park

Explore the lowest place in North America and the hottest place in the world at this sun-blasted bowl of minimalist beauty hard by the Nevada border in Southern California.

🕐 1 day

● **Fresno**

Manzanar National Historic Site

San Joaquin Valley

Diablo Range

Death Valley

Las Vegas

Lake Mead

Colorado River

ARIZONA

○ Paso Robles

○ Morro Bay

San Luis Obispo

Bakersfield

Hwy 395

○ Mojave

○ Mojave

● **Barstow**

Mojave National Preserve

Needles ○

Joshua Tree National Park

See otherworldly trees and wild rock formations spanning the stark horizons of this national park, which comes alive with springtime wildflowers and cactus blossoms.

🕐 1 day

Santa Barbara

Santa Barbara Channel

Channel Islands National Park

Santa Monica Bay

Mojave Desert

● **Los Angeles**

● Anaheim

Long Beach

● **Indio**

Salton Sea

Blythe ●

Kings Canyon & Sequoia National Parks

Celebrate astonishing geography and extraordinary trees in these two neighboring parks. Myriad trails offer hikes long and short across the best of the Sierra Nevada mountains.

🕐 1–2 days

Palm Springs

Visit art museums, year-round outdoor cafes, golf courses aplenty and mid-century design gems at this desert resort – a hard place to leave any time, especially in winter.

🕐 1–2 days

USA

MEXICO

7 Things to Know About
CALIFORNIA

INSIDER TIPS TO HIT THE GROUND RUNNING

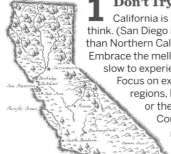

1 Don't Try to See it All

California is way bigger than you think. (San Diego is closer to El Paso, TX, than Northern California!) Don't rush. Embrace the mellow vibes and take it slow to experience the real California. Focus on exploring a few neighboring regions, like LA to Santa Barbara or the Bay Area and Wine Country.

▶ For trip builders, see p26 and individual cities and regions

2 Wear a Tee, Pack a Jacket

Don't believe everything you see in the movies. California gets plenty of sun, but the 'June gloom' marine layer and coastal breezes can cause temperatures to plummet. Even in summer. There are wild temperature swings many days, often with freezing temperatures at night. Pay attention to elevation (especially in the desert!), and pack pants and a light jacket. You can always spot a tourist shivering in shorts and a T-shirt.

3 Drive-Throughs are Good

California has excellent cuisine, but you don't need to go to a top-end restaurant to have a great meal. Pull into a drive-through for authentic Mexican food or mouthwatering smash burgers.

4 Measure Distance in Minutes, not Miles

Traffic can happen anywhere, anytime. That's why locals tell you how long it takes to get somewhere, not how far away it is. Plan accordingly.

▶ For more on getting around, see p244

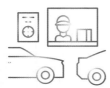

5 California is Diverse

Not everyone in California starts their day shredding gnarly waves. In fact, California is home to more farmers than Kansas. There's a massive difference in lingo, culture, lifestyle, food and climate between Northern and Southern California and the Inland Empire. There's literally something for everyone here – from rodeos to poetry readings. You're sure to find people who share your passion.

6 Local Lingo Quirks

Names for places and roads change as you move up the coast, so double-check your directions to stay on course. In Southern California locals call the main highway 'PCH' (Pacific Coast Hwy). Up north people call it 'Hwy 1.'

Southern Californians say 'the' before a freeway name (eg take 'the' 405 to 'the' 5). Northern Californians don't. 'Hella' is a very Northern Californian way to say 'very.' 'No worries' is the unofficial slogan of California. Everyone says it.

'The Valley' can refer to wildly different places across California. In LA, 'the Valley' usually refers to the San Fernando Valley, north of LA, but it can also mean the San Gabriel Valley, which is east of the city on the way to the desert – and a big difference in terms of driving times. There's also the Central Valley, and, of course, Silicon 'Valley.' Make sure you're headed to the right one!

7 You Have to Drive

Uber and BART (high-speed transit) are decent ways to get around San Francisco, but that's the exception to the rule. If you want to explore the rest of California, you have to drive. Get a car with good gas mileage, air-conditioning, cruise control and comfy seats.

Read, Listen, Watch & Follow

 READ

Hollywood (Charles Bukowski; 1989) No one captures LA's glitter and grit like Bukowski.

Slouching Towards Bethlehem (Joan Didion; 1968) A time capsule of California in the 1960s.

East of Eden (John Steinbeck; 1952) The California that came before Hollywood and Silicon Valley.

The Joy Luck Club (Amy Tan; 1989) A story of Chinese immigrants trying to make a life in San Francisco.

  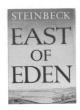 

 LISTEN

California (Phantom Planet, pictured; 2002) We dare you not to roll down the windows and sing along to this California anthem.

Route 66 (Bobby Troup; 1946) Get in the mood to cruise the coast with the ultimate road-trip song about California's iconic highway.

California Love (2Pac; 1995) This West Coast hip-hop anthem from Dre and Pac is a California playlist auto-include.

California Dreamin' (The Mamas and the Papas; 1965) Absolutely perfect for your first (or 50th) visit to the coast.

PETER KRAMER/STAFF/GETTY IMAGES ©

Headgum Podcast Network
Choose from dozens of shows like *Gilmore Guys* or *No Joke*.

WATCH

Swingers (1996, pictured top right) A struggling comedian and his actor friends try to make LA feel like home.

La La Land (2016, pictured bottom right) A Hollywood musical love letter to LA.

The Big Lebowski (1998) Laid-back and clueless, Jeff Bridges' 'the Dude' is the unofficial mascot of California.

The Californians (*Saturday Night Live*) This comedy sketch is a spot-on depiction of driving in California.

Orange County (2002) Story of an Orange County surfer on a quest to attend Stanford.

UNITED ARCHIVES GMBH/ ALAMY STOCK PHOTO ©

PICTORIAL PRESS LTD/ ALAMY STOCK PHOTO ©

FOLLOW

Yosemite National Park
(@yosemitenps) Outdoor inspiration and epic views.

Kate Voegele
(@katevoegele) LA-based singer-songwriter.

Tobin James Cellars
(tobinjames.com) The most popular winery you've never heard of.

Getty Museum
(@gettymuseum) LA's best art gallery.

Venice Beach Skatepark
(@venicebeach.skatepark) Peak SoCal.

SAN FRANCISCO & THE BAY AREA

FREE EXPRESSION | INNOVATION | LGBTQ+ CULTURE

**Experience
San Francisco
and the Bay
Area online**

SAN FRANCISCO & THE BAY AREA
Trip Builder

Fog lifts over the Golden Gate Bridge, revealing new horizons. The city that launched free speech, the internet, gay and trans rights, organic cuisine, fortune cookies and biotech is onto its next idea. Go ahead: join a parade, or a start-up, or a parade start-up.

Relax or get active at **Golden Gate Park**, San Francisco's mile-wide wild streak (p62)
(⏱ 2–4hr

Let your free-spirited side out on and around **Haight St** (p67)
⏱ ½ day

Mountain Lake

THE RICHMOND

California St

Geary Blvd

Turk Blvd

Presidio Ave

Divisadero St

Masonic Ave

UPPER HAIGHT

Fell St

The Panhandle

Oak St

Buena Vista Park

COLE VALLEY

25th Ave

Fulton St

Golden Gate Park

Stow Lake

Lincoln Way

7th Ave

THE SUNSET

0   1 km
0   0.5 miles

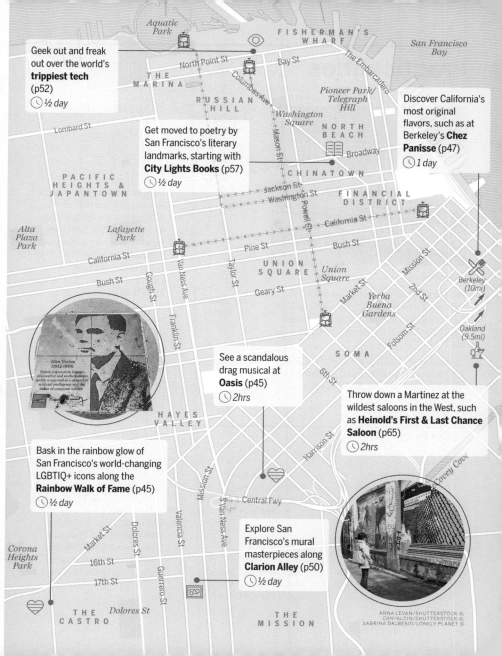

Geek out and freak out over the world's **trippiest tech** (p52)
⏱ ½ day

Get moved to poetry by San Francisco's literary landmarks, starting with **City Lights Books** (p57)
⏱ ½ day

Discover California's most original flavors, such as at Berkeley's **Chez Panisse** (p47)
⏱ 1 day

Alan Turing (1912–1954)
British cryptanalyst, logician, philosopher and mathematician widely recognized as a pioneer of artificial intelligence and the father of computer science

See a scandalous drag musical at **Oasis** (p45)
⏱ 2hrs

Throw down a Martinez at the wildest saloons in the West, such as **Heinold's First & Last Chance Saloon** (p65)
⏱ 2hrs

Bask in the rainbow glow of San Francisco's world-changing LGBTIQ+ icons along the **Rainbow Walk of Fame** (p45)
⏱ ½ day

Explore San Francisco's mural masterpieces along **Clarion Alley** (p50)
⏱ ½ day

ANNA LEVAN/SHUTTERSTOCK ©,
CANYALCIN/SHUTTERSTOCK ©,
SABRINA DALBESIO/LONELY PLANET ©

Practicalities

SAN FRANCISCO INTERNATIONAL

KAREN DESJARDIN/GETTY IMAGES ©

ARRIVING

San Francisco Airport (SFO) The Bay Area's main airport is a 30- to 45-minute drive south of San Francisco (rideshares $40 to $65 off-peak, plus tip) or 20 to 30 minutes to San Francisco by BART ($10).

Oakland Airport (OAK) Take BART from OAK to San Francisco (45 minutes, $11) or rideshares (40 to 60 minutes, $45 to $80 off-peak plus tip).

HOW MUCH FOR A

Burrito
$9

Drag show ticket
$5–$50

Historic cocktail
$12

GETTING AROUND

Muni Streetcar and bus schedules vary; the fare is $3 cash or $2.50 with a reloadable Clipper card (also good for BART and ferries). Cable cars are frequent, slow and scenic, 6am to 12:30am daily. The fare is $8 per ride, or get a Muni Passport ($24 per day, $13 with MuniMobile app).

Bicycle Cyclists love Golden Gate Park, but San Francisco hills require nerve and muscle. Lyft offers bike-sharing with electric-hybrid options and citywide pickup/drop-off.

BART High-speed transit to/from East Bay, San Francisco (downtown and Mission), SFO and Millbrae (Caltrain transfer station); rides from $2.50.

WHEN TO GO

DEC-FEB
Low-season rates, brisk but rarely cold days and Lunar New Year fireworks

MAR-MAY
Film fests, farmers markets and Hunky Jesus contests signal spring

JUN-AUG
Festivals, parades and Pride make up for high-season rates and chilly afternoon fog

SEP-NOV
Blue skies, free concerts, reasonable hotel rates and flavor-bursting harvest cuisine

EATING & DRINKING

Ever since the gold rush, Bay Area diners have enjoyed three distinct advantages: California sunshine, inventive chefs and drunken sailors. Competitive chefs reinvent award-winning seasonal, multicultural menus daily – for a sneak peek at specials, browse San Francisco farmers markets. Order whatever dish credits local producers on the menu, and you'll become a locavore – the Bay Area's honorary title for people who prefer eating food within 100 to 200 miles of its origin. Toast your achievement with citrus-infused gold-rush cocktails.

Best only-in-SF flavors
Nari (p49)

Must-try Martinez
Comstock Saloon (p65)

CONNECT & FIND YOUR WAY

Wi-fi Hot spots abound in the birthplace of the internet and smartphone – #SFWiFi offers free access. Check with your mobile provider about data and roaming charges.

Navigation San Francisco is 7x7 miles, laid out on a wonky but simple grid. The Bay Area is well mapped by Google and Apple (both headquartered here).

WHERE TO STAY

San Francisco hotels are notoriously expensive – but with advance planning, you can stay in romantic Victorian B&Bs, chic boutique hotels or bargain waterfront hostels.

Neighborhood	Pro/Con
The Marina & Fisherman's Wharf	Family-friendly motels, overpriced hotels and bargain waterfront hostels.
The Haight & Hayes Valley	Charming Victorian B&Bs, sometimes with shared bathrooms.
Downtown & SoMa	Smart boutique hotels and boring chains. Avoid Tenderloin residence-hotels.
North Beach & Chinatown	Old Italian inns and boho hostels. Not quiet, but fun.
The Mission & Castro	Apartment shares are prime for summer fun, but scarce.
Japantown & Pacific Heights	Book hilltop inns and Japantown's mid-century-modern hotels ahead.

GREEN GUIDELINES

To achieve sustainability goals, SF mandates recycling and composting, and bans plastic bags. Use SF-designed Baggu reusable bags to avoid 25¢ bag surcharges.

MONEY

Cash is rarely used, except for tips. Credit cards and locally invented digital payment methods (including Apple Pay, Square, PayPal, Google Pay and Stripe) are widely accepted.

01 DRAG
Across SF

LGBTIQ+ CULTURE | ENTERTAINMENT | CIVIL RIGHTS

Nowhere does drag quite like San Francisco. Between shows, drag queens, kings and nonbinary royals run for office, fundraise for public health and win civil rights victories with false eyelashes and true courage. Trust San Francisco's beloved *RuPaul's Drag Race* star and community activist Honey Mahogany when she says: you don't want to miss our next act.

LYNN FRIEDMAN/SHUTTERSTOCK ©

🖼 How to

DIY drag Score size 12 heels at Community Thrift, rock San Francisco-designed Piedmont Boutique drag couture and create lewks with notions from Cliff's Variety.

Drag in the park Pride is spectacular but

Easter Sunday is iconic, thanks to the Sisters of Perpetual Indulgence, San Francisco's order of glitter drag nuns. The Sisters throw community fundraisers in Dolores Park, including the Egg Hunt, Easter Bonnet Competition and all-gender Foxy Mary & Hunky Jesus Contest.

JUSTIN SULLIVAN /STAFF/GETTY IMAGES ©

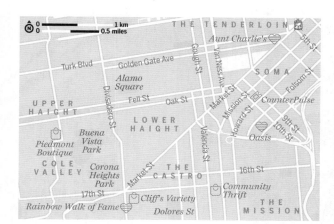

Top left Dharma Gettin', Sisters of Perpetual Indulgence. **Bottom left** Roxy Brooks-Lords performing at Oasis.

San Francisco drag dates from the gold rush, when theatrical shorthand for 'dressed as girl' applied to anyone defying gender norms. When the city tried to ban gender-nonconforming dress in 1863, the community banded together for safety. By the 1940s, Tenderloin's theater district 'queens' hotels' housed 600 trans San Franciscans, and drag shows were well-established – yet police harassment persisted. So in 1961, WWII veteran and drag hostess José Sarria became the first out gay American to run for public office, pledging to stop antigay harassment.

Sarria narrowly lost election – but instead of accepting defeat, she declared herself Empress of San Francisco. Her Imperial Drag Court became a fundraising powerhouse in the AIDS epidemic, establishing lifesaving care and prevention protocols. Follow **Rainbow Walk of Fame**'s rainbow-lit plaques honoring LGBTIQ+ trailblazers from **José Sarria Court** to **Castro Theatre**, featuring drag stars and LGBTIQ+ **Frameline Film Fest**.

San Francisco's all-gender drag revues perpetually push boundaries. SF's legendary Cockettes scandalized New York in 1972 with 'Tinsel Tarts in a Hot Coma' – a psychedelic blur of glitter beards, nudity and spectacularly uncoordinated 47-person chorus lines featuring eight-months-pregnant Sweet Pam Tent. Today drag cabaret venue **Oasis** keeps audiences gagging with scandalous original musicals like *Shit & Champagne,* and hilarious live-action *Star Trek* episodes featuring Honey Mahogany as Commander Uhura. As drag king Leigh Crow's impeccable Captain Kirk would say: brace for impact.

Transgender Cultural District

The Tenderloin has the highest concentration of trans people in the world, but it isn't some trans-Disneyland. Historically, it's a containment zone for poverty, marginalized people and criminalized commerce. Police took bribes to look the other way, from Prohibition onward – so antigay laws weren't always enforced. The first LGBTIQ+ uprising was 1966 Compton's Cafeteria Riot, when trans women fought police harassment at Turk and Taylor, where we hold our **Riot Party**. Down the block you'll find drag Hot Boxx Girls at **Aunt Charlie's**, **GLIDE** doing incredible work for housing stability, comedy at **PianoFight**, **CounterPulse** art-house theater – plus unsung heroes running Covid-test sites, opening businesses and providing neighbors in need with groceries.

■ Recommended by **Honey Mahogany,** *Oasis star, Compton's Transgender Cultural District cofounder and the nation's first African American trans woman Democratic Committee chair.* @honeymahogany

02 The Bay's Boldest
FLAVORS

CHEFS | SUSTAINABILITY | FLAVORS

Tell food-obsessed Bay Area friends you're in town, and immediately they will start planning your menu: dim sum, chaat and tacos, leisurely lunches and bayfront brunches, plus daring dinners by award-winning chefs. But with this list, you've got all that covered already.

Above Cheese Board Collective. **Right** Pasticcini from Chez Panisse.

SAN FRANCISCO & THE BAY AREA EXPERIENCES

How to

Getting here Hop BART to/from San Francisco's downtown/ Mission, Berkeley and Oakland.

Chef's secrets Find inspiration in Rainbow Food Cooperative's bulk organic aisles, compile app platters at Bi-Rite and equip pop-ups at Chinatown's Wok Shop.

À la mode Follow Mission crowds to Garden Creamery for organic Hawaiian-inspired flavors (sesame-butter mochi, mmm), Humphrey Slocombe for freaky flavors like Secret Breakfast (bourbon and cornflakes) and Bi-Rite Creamery for salted caramel that tastes like sunny Ocean Beach days.

Berkeley's 'gourmet ghetto' At **Chez Panisse**, trailblazing chef/owner Alice Waters has redefined good food with local, organic farmers since 1971. Seasonal, sensational menus (downstairs) and à la carte dishes (upstairs) are artfully casual, not simple: every ingredient is scrupulously sourced and prepared for flavor that 'brings people to their senses,' as chef Waters says. Taste zesty winter fennel and tangerine salad, and you'll get why the Obamas invited Waters to commandeer their healthy school lunch initiatives. Try Sonoma duck with peak-summer Mission figs, and you'll understand how Waters inspired the global Slow Food movement. Across the street is another gourmet go-to since 1971: **Cheese Board Collective**, serving seasonally inspired sourdough pizzas.

UC Berkeley's brain food How does UC Berkeley keep protest movements going and Nobel Prizes coming? Grad students swear by **Vik's Chaat**, where A+ dishes include decadent *cholle bature* (spicy chickpeas scooped with puffy flatbread) and masala dosa (lentil-flour crepes with spiced potatoes). California cuisine has deep roots on campus at **Cafe Ohlone**, celebrating indigenous food-ways with local oysters and black-oak-acorn soup among 'singing trees' playing Ohlone music. No Berkeley education is complete without **Great China** graduation banquets of crackling roast duck and toe-tingling, cumin-braised lamb.

San Francisco taste sensations Hope you're hungry: SF has the most restaurants and star chefs per capita of any US city. Try **Good Mong Kok**, where fragrant shrimp *har gow* and other classic dim sum are packed to enjoy in Portsmouth Sq. Golden Gate Bridge views are upstaged at **Greens** by vegetarian fare reinvented by Katie Reicher and a pan-theon of women star chefs since 1979, using ingredients from organic, Zen Buddhist **Green Gulch Farm**.

Lunch options are endless at **Ferry Building farmers market**, with 100-plus purveyors of

✖️ Oakland's Breakout Stars

Oakland serves megawatt flavor for every palate and budget, from $3 to $300. Taco traditionalists queue at the techie-sounding **Taqueria El Paisa@.com** counter for classic $3 carnitas tacos loaded with *nopales* (cactus), sweet onion, radish and *escabeche* (spicy pickled carrots) – then immedi-ately rejoin the line for slow-cooked *tripa* (beef tripe) tacos. **Commis** looks like an art gallery and its food tastes like an edible California landscape paint-ing – wildflowers grace bergamot-infused scallops, and puddles of California caviar top creamy taro root (menu $200, wine pairings $100).

📖 Edible Education

What should you eat for dinner, and why? *Omnivore's Dilemma* author Michael Pollan tackles juicy questions in 'Edible Education' YouTube lectures, hosted by Alice Waters' nonprofit **Edible Schoolyard** and featuring guests from *Salt Fat Acid Heat* author Samin Nosrat to *Stuffed and Starved* author Raj Patel.

organic, local produce and gourmet foods. At Ferry Building's **Slanted Door**, James Beard Award–winning chef Charles Phan delights diners with signature Dungeness crab cellophane noodles.

Get Palestinian-Californian comfort food hot from the oven at **Reem's Mission** – especially chef/owner Reem Assil's 'Pali-Cali' flatbread with sumac-laced chicken and caramelized onions. At **La Palma Mexicatessen**, *tortilleras* (tortilla-makers) hand-make organic *huaraches* (stuffed masa) and *pupusas* (filled corn tortillas). **Good Good Culture Club** packs extra good vibes into chef Kevin Keovanphang's turmeric-coconut-brined Petrale sole and carafes of California wine – plus a 20% flat fee shared among staff in lieu of tips.

At Japantown's **Nari**, chef/owner Pim Techamuanvivit will rock your world with Thai-Californian signatures like oysters with water-beetle mignonette and *kapi plah* (fermented shrimp paste) with Meyer-lemon sass. Romance is served at **Rich Table**, where star chefs/owners Sarah and Evan Rich create unexpectedly perfect combos like porcini doughnuts and burrata funnel cake.

Left Roasted quail, Commis. **Above top** Pork bun from Good Mong Kok. **Above** Slanted Door.

03 Magnificent MURALS

ART | HERITAGE | LANDMARKS

▬▬▬ Love changed the landscape when modern-art power couple Frida Kahlo and Diego Rivera rekindled their romance in 1930s San Francisco. While Frida painted her first commissions, Diego completed colorful, controversial murals. See the landmark artworks they created and inspired, from SFMOMA showstoppers to mural-lined Mission alleys.

ROHAN VAN TWEST/ALAMY STOCK PHOTO ©

🗺️ How to

Getting around Hop the Powell–Mason cable car from North Beach to Downtown, then BART to the Mission.

When to go Murals included in this itinerary are open to the public 10am to 5pm Friday to Monday.

Cost Free. But if you like what you see, consider donating to Precita Eyes to commission more murals.

Photos Allowed for noncommercial purposes. When you post on social media, please credit the muralists and nonprofits that commission and preserve murals.

📷 An Open-Air Gallery

Muralistas make bold statements at **Clarion Alley** (pictured), an open-air gallery curated by Clarion street-artists' collective. Few murals survive tests of time and taggers – notable exceptions include Megan Wilson's daisy-covered *Tax the Rich* and Tanya Wischerath's portraits of San Francisco's trans-rights trailblazers as saints.

SAN FRANCISCO & THE BAY AREA EXPERIENCES

01 Diego Rivera Gallery's *The Making of a Fresco Showing the Building of a City* is Rivera's 1931 love letter to San Francisco, featuring the artist admiring workers building the city.

02 Coit Tower's Rivera-inspired murals capture Depression-era San Francisco, from speakeasies and soup kitchens to police confronting protestors. Authorities tried to censor these murals, but San Franciscans voted to preserve them.

03 Rivera's *Pan American Unity* fresco in **SFMOMA**'s lobby shows California and Mexico linked by freedom struggles. Upstairs, Kahlo's 1931 wedding portrait is worth admission.

05 The **Women's Building** has served SF since 1979 – and women muralists graced this landmark with murals featuring feminists and goddesses weaving the fabric of community.

04 Since the 1970s, **Balmy Alley** muralists have celebrated Latinx heritage and freedom movements here, from Kahlo homages to Lucía González Ippolito's *Women of the Resistance*.

San Francisco Bay

FISHERMAN'S WHARF

Bay St
Chestnut St
Greenwich St
Columbus Ave
NORTH BEACH
Broadway
Van Ness Ave
Taylor St
Kearny St
NOB HILL
Lafayette Park
Alta Plaza Park
California St
Bush St
UNION SQUARE
Powell St BART MUNI Station
CIVIC CENTER
Market St
Mission St
Howard St
Folsom St
3rd St
4th St
SOMA
S Van Ness Ave
10th St
Central Fwy
16th St Mission BART Station
16th St
18th St
Potrero Ave
Valencia St
Mission St
Harrison St
THE MISSION
24th St
24th St Mission BART Station
Bernal Heights Park
Glen Canyon Park
GLEN PARK

N 0 | 0
2 km
1 miles

04 Totally Trippy TECH

PSYCHEDELIA | TECHNOLOGY | EXPERIMENTS

You may think you know San Francisco from social media – invented here, after all – but this town is full of inventions far too freaky for smartphones. Virtual reality can't quite do San Francisco's psychedelic, precision-engineered immersive experiences justice – you just have to be here.

How to

Getting around Conquer hills with San Francisco's steampunk cable cars – virtually unchanged since 1873, with hand-pulled brakes and no seatbelts. Grab a leather hand strap: you're in for a wild ride.

Reinvent reality When reality seems less than ideal, join San Francisco nonprofit Code for America to crowdsource new approaches to bike safety, homeless shelters, public health and more at Civic Hack Nights (Wednesdays 6:30pm). Tech experience isn't required – diverse, multidisciplinary perspectives strengthen ideas.

When you reach for your smartphone, consider this: most social media, search engines, apps and cloud platforms you're using were invented within 50 miles of SF. This tech boom wasn't launched in Silicon Valley boardrooms, but at one blowout party in North Beach's **Longshoremen's Union Hall**.

The 1966 Trips Festival promoted by **San Francisco Mime Troupe** manager Bill Graham featured music by the Warlocks and *One Flew Over the Cuckoo's Nest* author Ken Kesey, hired by the CIA to test psychoactive drugs intended to create the ultimate soldier. Kesey spiked Trips Festival punch with government-issue

LSD in the parking lot, under **Beniamino Bufano's St Francis statue** – and the rest is hippie history.

Bill Graham launched **Fillmore Auditorium**, the Warlocks became the Grateful Dead, and San Francisco Mime Troupe still performs in **Dolores Park**. But festival organizer and *Whole Earth Cat-*

◎ Mind-Expanding Experiments

Exploratorium Can you stop time, sculpt fog or make sand sing? San Francisco's hands-on laboratory of science and human perception invites you to experiment. Physicist Frank Oppenheimer founded the Exploratorium in 1969, after leaving the atom bomb Manhattan Project to promote science in the public interest.

The Interval The bar-cafe HQ for nonprofit Long Now Foundation invites long-term thinking with Brian Eno's fourth-dimensional art and excellent Old Tom Collins cocktails.

Audium Since 1967, Stan Shaff and his son Dave have performed original compositions on a trippy instrument: an auditorium with 176 floor-to-ceiling speakers, blending urban sounds into meditative 'room compositions.'

alog founder Stewart Brand had the longest, strangest festival trip: he hallucinated a computer shrunk to palm-size, bringing machine power to the people. Forty years later, Steve Jobs thanked him for the inspiration.

In a converted SF temple, **Internet Archive** volunteers have cataloged 616 billion web pages and digitized *Whole Earth Catalogs,* Grateful Dead tapes and more for posterity, not profit. Meanwhile, Stewart Brand's **Long Now Foundation** imagines a future where technology isn't judged by downloads, but by long-term impact – Long Now's YouTube channel hosts free seminars.

Above Exploratorium.

Boom to Bust & Back

THE HIGHS AND LOWS OF BOOMTOWN LIVING

Grab your slippery wooden seat as your cable car careens downhill: that's how boomtown living feels. From the gold rush to dot-com crash, giddy booms and spectacular busts are San Francisco's defining moments. But who comes out ahead and who pays the price?

CHRONICLE/ALAMY STOCK PHOTO ©

Dreams & Schemes

From mercury mining to biotech, SF booms are hailed as 'the next gold rush' – but the original gold rush is a cautionary tale. San Francisco was a Mexican encampment on Ohlone land when the first permanent residence was built by Juana Briones, California-born multiracial dairy farmer and mother of 11, including two Ohlone orphans. She was SF's first start-up founder, with side hustles as town midwife and international trader – until Mexico lost California to the US in 1848.

By then, Juana's dairy covered SF's northern waterfront, and she co-owned ranches with Ohlone neighbors. Women could own property under Mexican law, but not under US law c 1848 – so Juana had to protect her interests against unscrupulous speculator Samuel Brannan.

Brannan was publishing SF tabloids when he heard rumors of gold 120 miles away. To sell newspapers, Brannan convinced fellow Mormons to provide a gold nugget 'for the church,' swearing secrecy. Instead he ran through Portsmouth Sq, yelling, 'Gold on the American River!'

Brannan's scheme backfired. Everyone left SF to pan for gold. His newspaper folded – there was no one around to read, write or print it. But Brannan bought every available shovel, pick and pan for his general store. With his profits, Brannan snapped up real estate from Juana – who had legal bills to pay – becoming SF's biggest landowner.

Newspapers republished Brannan's tales of 'gold mountains' near San Francisco. Within a year, 25,000 prospectors arrived – including refugees and escaped slaves dreaming of fresh starts. After grueling voyages, many

Above left Samuel Brannan. **Above middle** Portsmouth Sq in 1891. **Above right** Juana Briones.

arrived sick and broke, only to find slim pickings. Latecomers discovered gold claims were already staked by Native American, Mexican, Chinese, Peruvian and Chilean miners. When disputes erupted, Brannan cashed in, selling bullets for $50 each.

Changing Fortunes

Under US law, women couldn't testify in court, so their claims were routinely rejected. Juana appealed all the way to the US Supreme Court, which finally determined women could own property. But gaining legal title took Juana 15 more years.

> 25,000 prospectors arrived – including refugees and escaped slaves. After grueling voyages, many arrived sick and broke, only to find slim pickings.

Meanwhile, Brannan hired mercenaries to colonize Hawaiian islands – but his militia was tossed out. Brannan loaned his militia to Mexican revolutionary Benito Juarez to assassinate Mexico's colonial Emperor Maximilian. Brannan was promised 361,000 acres in Mexico's Sonora state – but Sonora's native Yaqui weren't consulted, and civil war erupted.

After Juana's Supreme Court victory granting women property rights, Brannan's wife Anna divorced him for alcoholism, winning the largest divorce settlement in US history. She moved to Paris, investing fortunes in Comstock silver mines – and went bust. Anna returned to SF, where she lived among friends until age 93. When Brannan died destitute, his children refused to buy a gravestone. Today SF's Brannan St runs past SoMa start-ups to the county jail.

◎ Remembering Juana Briones

California Historical Society recognizes Juana Briones as San Francisco's *fundadora* (founder), and gold-rush memoirs praise her for caring for destitute miners and helping sailors escape indentured servitude. Yet the Washington Square Park plaque honoring her omits her singular achievement: sacrificing 31 years and her fortune to defend women's property rights, so that her daughters and future generations of women could live independently. In a town where gold, silver and tech stocks come and go, courage remains the only lasting currency – and in that respect, Juana left behind an absolute fortune.

05 Poetry in
THE AIR

FREE SPEECH | POETRY | BOOKS

'The air was soft/ the stars so fine/ the promise of every cobbled alley so great...' Jack Kerouac typed these words in San Francisco, and today this *On the Road* quote is inscribed in the alley named after him. Spend a day looking at San Francisco through a poet's eyes, and you'll see what he means.

Above City Lights Books.
Right Beat Museum (p58).

HORST FRIEDRICHS/ALAMY STOCK PHOTO ©

JENNY JONES/ALAMY STOCK PHOTO ©

How to

Getting around Hop the Powell–Mason cable car to North Beach and take BART to the Mission.

Free poetry SF Main Public Library keeps inspiration flowing with free Koret Auditorium readings, multilingual poetry at the International Center and letterpress chapbooks in Book Arts.

Poetic peaks Summit Russian Hill parks named for George Sterling, who dubbed SF 'the cool, grey city of love,' and Ina Coolbrith, Poet's Corner founder and Mark Twain's mentor.

How Poetry Fought the Law & Won

Words were a dangerous business in the 1950s, when library books were often banned, Hollywood screenwriters were blacklisted and comedians got arrested for swearing in North Beach nightclubs – but poet Lawrence Ferlinghetti founded **City Lights Books** anyway. City Lights' affordable paperback Pocket Poets series brought poetry to the people, sparking the Beat Poetry movement.

Number four in the series was Allen Ginsberg's epic *Howl and Other Poems* (1956), an instant sensation that got Ferlinghetti and City Lights manager Shigeyoshi Murao arrested for publishing poetry with homoerotic content. They fought the charges not on technicalities but on artistic merits, and won a landmark free speech victory. Celebrate your right to read freely in City Lights' **Poetry Room** – *Howl* is available in 24 languages.

Streetcorner Poetry

North Beach's **Beat Museum** preserves 1000-plus Beat-era relics like butterflies in glass cases, including Allen Ginsberg's typewriter and Diane di Prima's collected *Revolutionary Letters*. When San Francisco named Ferlinghetti its first Poet Laureate in 1998, he proposed another tribute to Beat poets: a dozen streets named after politicians, renamed after poets.

As befits the Beat poet and haiku translator, **Kenneth Rexroth Alley** is a short, poignant, trilingual back alley linking Chinatown apothecaries and North Beach delis. Peaceful **Bob Kaufman Alley** was named for the legendary Black Buddhist spoken-word poet frequently jailed for 'resisting arrest' in verse. He took a 12-year vow of silence until the Vietnam War ended, when he walked into a North Beach cafe and recited his poem *All Those Ships That Never Sailed*.

📖 Mission Poetry

You'll hear Mayan blessings in **Balmy Alley** for **Flor y Canto Literary Festival**, Brazilian music at **Carnaval**, and Paseo Poético poetry at *panaderías* (bakeries) and **Brava Theater**. **Mission Cultural Center**'s Día de los Muertos Aztec dances aren't performances – they're prayers. Collectively owned **Adobe Books** and **Medicine for Nightmares** host multilingual readings, and Precita Eyes' mural honors Alfonso Texidor, poetry editor for bilingual *El Tecalote*. Juana Alicia's **Mission Library** mural is a flowering *nopal* (cactus) – a resistance symbol on a library built by capitalist Andrew Carnegie. What could be more poetic?

■ **By Alejandro Murguía,** *SF Poet Laureate, Mission Cultural Center for Latino Arts cofounder, and San Francisco State University Latinx Studies Professor.*

📖 Prison Poetry

Visitors, immigrants and refugees carved 220 poems protesting their treatment at **Angel Island Immigration Station** (1910–1946). Five hundred thousand people were interrogated, detained and deported here – Asians were refused entry under the racist Asian Exclusion Act (1882–1943). **Detention Barracks Museum** preserves their indelible words (aiisf. org/poems-and-inscriptions).

Renaming streets remains a work in progress. 67 years before poet Maya Angelou received the US Presidential Medal of Freedom, she was hired as San Francisco's first Black woman streetcar conductor. It's fitting that T-line streetcar bells and Bay foghorns will sound along **Maya Angelou Way** in the new Mission Rock residential development. You can almost hear her voice, invoking the powers of the tides in her poem 'Still I Rise.'

Bookish Valencia Street

At nonprofit writing center **826 Valencia**, you'll find sea-themed literary anthologies in the Pirate Supply Store, angelfish acting out in the Fish Theater and kids scribbling their first poems at after-school programs. Load up on chapbooks, magazines and comics at **Dogeared Books**, **Needles and Pens** and **Mission Comics**, and take your haul to **Radio Habana Social Club** or **Café la Bohème** to strike up spirited conversations with local poets – if you see Poet Laureate Alejandro Murguía, say hi.

Left Carnaval. **Above top** Carved poem, Angel Island Immigration Station. **Above** Dogeared Books.

06 Come Out & PLAY

LGBTIQ+ | PRIDE | JOY

It doesn't matter where you're from or who your daddy is: San Francisco welcomes you home with flags flying. Do you love a parade? So do the million people who converge here for Pride – and once you know where to go, you'll find circuit parties, leather kinkfests and fabulous fundraisers for LGBTIQ+ rights here year-round.

SHEILA FITZGERALD/SHUTTERSTOCK ©

🗺 How to

Getting around Hop vintage F-line streetcar to the Castro and Compton's Transgender Cultural District, J Church to Dolores Park, and 14 Mission bus to SoMa leather bars and Bernal Heights lesbian hangouts. If you stay too long at the party, nonprofit Homobile will get you home safely.

Stay healthy To play safe, get pre-exposure prophylaxis (PrEP) at STRUT community center. Lyon-Martin Health Services provides primary care for women, trans and nonbinary folk regardless of ability to pay.

OLIVERDELAHAYE/SHUTTERSTOCK ©

SAN FRANCISCO & THE BAY AREA EXPERIENCES

Far top left Pride. **Bottom left** 'Gay Beach,' Dolores Park. **Near left** Folsom St Fair.

Gay all day, every day You don't have to stay up late to be out, loud and proud in SF. Flag-flying crowds are an absolute joy throughout June **Pride** month, at Sunday afternoon Castro 'tea dances' (a WWII euphemism for gay parties) and any sunny day at **Dolores Park**'s 'Gay Beach.' Rainy days call for matinees at **Castro Theatre**'s LGBTIQ+ Frameline Film Fest and Roxie's SF Queer Film Fest.

Club nights When the music's right, the rainbow glow of SF dance floors is probably visible from space. Drag dynamo Juanita More's euphoric dance parties include BeatPig at **Powerhouse**, Princess at **Oasis** and disco benefits galore. Comfort and Joy throws Castro's neon-lit Glow street fair and brings blissful Radical Faerie energy to Sprung circuit parties. Doja Cat meets Drake on the dance floor in drag at **Rickshaw Stop**'s Bootie Mashup, while bathhouse anthems make the Tubesteak Connection at **Aunt Charlie's**. After 2am last call, the night's getting started at **EndUp**.

SoMa leather scene Bring your kink to SF's landmark Leather & LGBTQ Cultural District, where public spankings and cheap beer are mere appetizers at **Folsom St Fair** and **Dore Up Your Alley Fair**. Thirsty bikers hit **Hole in the Wall Saloon**, where 1970s erotica seems tame once you've been to the bathroom. At **Powerhouse** Underwear Tuesdays, Bare Chest Thursdays and Speedo Fridays, less is definitely more.

 Best Backyard Scenes

El Rio SF's flirtiest patio is also the most diverse, with good times had by all since 1978 – especially at Mango lesbian nights, Salsa Sundays, Red Hot Burlesque and Hard French afternoon soul.

SF Eagle A leather landmark for Sunday BBQ beer busts and well-earned back-patio sunburns since 1981.

Wild Side West When it opened in 1962, haters tried to get the lesbians to leave by throwing old toilets in the bar's backyard – now they're rebelliously repurposed as flower pots in the sunny beer garden.

07 Golden Gate **PARK**

GARDENS | ANIMALS | ARTS

Welcome to San Francisco's mile-wide wild streak, with surprises at every turn – massive free concerts, miniature yacht regattas, outer space portals, buried art treasures, chatty penguins and hushed redwood groves. When you find your bliss and/or the bison, you've done the park justice.

FILEDIMAGE/SHUTTERSTOCK ©

How to

Getting here Bicycle the Wiggle route or hop the N Judah streetcar.

When to go Starting around noon, you've got a four-hour window before fog rolls in.

Peak picnic On sunny September weekends,

grand pianos mysteriously appear in San Francisco Botanical Gardens. Welcome to Flower Piano, where professional pianists serenade plants and park-goers with nature-inspired jazz, tango, ragtime, classical and original works. BYO burrito for truly inspired picnics.

TERRY SMITH STUDIOS/ALAMY STOCK PHOTO ©

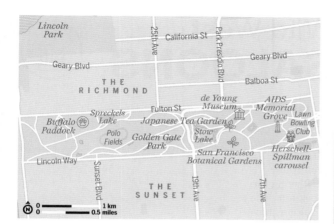

Top left Stow Lake. **Bottom left** Cyclists near the Buffalo Paddock.

When New York's Central Park architect Frederick Law Olmsted balked at transforming 1013 acres of windswept dunes into the world's largest developed park, **Golden Gate Park** plans fell to young engineer William Hammond Hall. He insisted that instead of planned casinos, racetracks and a plaster igloo village, the park should showcase nature – including **Stow Lake**, **San Francisco Botanical Gardens**, **Conservatory of Flowers** and a dedicated **Buffalo Paddock**. Today this urban preserve includes 7.5 miles of bicycle trails, 12 miles of equestrian trails, three fly-casting pools, 21 tennis courts, four soccer fields – and not a single fake igloo.

East side The wild rumpus starts with year-round drum circles at **Hippie Hill** and toddlers clinging for dear life onto 1914 **Herschell-Spillman carousel** ponies. Sweater-clad dandies gather at historic **Lawn Bowling Club** and meditators mellow in contemplative **AIDS Memorial Grove**. On Sundays, John F Kennedy Dr closes to traffic around 9th Ave, where you can groove with roller-disco skaters and join free Lindy Hop lessons.

West side Watch turtles paddle past miniature racing yachts on **Spreckels Lake**, try your hand at handball courts, make offerings behind the baseball diamond at hilltop pagan altars made from repurposed Spanish monastery stones, and free your mind at free concerts in the **Polo Fields** – site of 1967's hippie Human Be-In. At the **Buffalo Paddock**, thank San Francisco's resident bison for sharing the wild West with you.

🌿 Surreal Scenery

de Young Museum
Explore world wonders, from millennium-old Inuit sculpture to Masami Teraoka's monumental sumi-ink screens capturing the AIDS epidemic as it unfolded. Dreamers cloud-watch in James Turrell's outdoor **Skyspace**.

California Academy of Sciences Butterflies flit around **Osher Rainforest Dome**, octopuses roam **Steinhart Aquarium** and **African Hall** penguins waddle winsomely. Thursday NightLife features cocktails and **Planetarium** shows.

Japanese Tea Garden
Since 1894, this five-acre garden has blushed pink with cherry blossoms and red with maple leaves. **Hagiwara Bonsai Grove** honors the heroic gardeners who survived WWII internment camps and restored this mini-marvel. After **Zen Garden** meditation, enjoy fortune cookies – invented for the **Tea House**.

08 Wild West **SALOONS**

HAPPY HOUR | COCKTAILS | TROUBLE

▬▬▬ Tonight you're gonna party like it's 1899. Back then, San Francisco had some 3000 saloons plus 2000 'blind pigs' (speakeasies), all vying for attention with signature cocktails. The city's swaggering Western saloons have survived fires and earthquakes, brawls and busts – and today they're roaring back to life, with historically accurate gin cocktails and whiskey concoctions.

🗺 **How to**

Getting around Hop the Powell–Mason cable car to North Beach and BART to the Mission.

Buying a round Cocktails cost $8 to $14, plus tip: $1 per beer, $2 per cocktail. Cash tips are preferred.

SF's best speakeasy Under the Tenderloin 'Anti-Saloon League' sign, mutter 'books' to be ushered into Bourbon and Branch's 'Library' speakeasy.

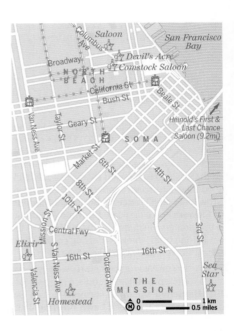

Gold-rush dandies were shaken down for gold dust in North Beach's notorious Devil's Acre saloon district. San Franciscans have dressed down to party at **Saloon** since 1861 – when fire swept SF in 1906, patrons allegedly saved Saloon by dousing it with hooch. Victorian boozehounds once relieved themselves at **Comstock Saloon**'s bar trough. **Comstock's** cocktails remain potent as ever, and ragtime bands entertain bathroom lines. At **Devil's Acre**, enemies Call a 'Treuse – a knockout punch of chartreuse, vermouth, egg white and 'gold-rush bitters.'

Many 19th-century sailors started happy hour with smiles and shots – and awoke days later, indentured to Patagonia-bound ships. Now that shady barkeeps are no longer offloading unconscious sailors onto passing ships, revelers can relax portside at 1899-vintage **Sea Star**, where

JAMES KIRKIKIS/SHUTTERSTOCK ©

🍸 Best Historic Cocktails

Comstock Saloon Martinez
According to San Francisco legend, this precursor to the modern martini was invented when a gun-toting cowboy demanded a drink to tide him over on the ferry to Martinez. Comstock's would do the trick.

Bourbon & Branch
Pisco punch The original citrus-spiked Pisco punch invented c 1853 had a secret ingredient – possibly nutmeg or cocaine, probably bitters? Bourbon & Branch isn't telling.

Elixir's Golden Hydrant
Named for the sole functioning hydrant (now painted gold) that saved the Mission during the 1906 Great Earthquake and Fire, this cocktail features jalapeño-spiked tequila and smoky mezcal quenched with wild lime – $2 goes to NorCal fire relief.

Alicia Walton's friendly crew serves mean hot toddies. Bartenders remain reassuringly gruff at **Heinold's First & Last Chance Saloon**, slinging whiskey to Oakland port arrivals since 1884.

To survive Prohibition, saloons got creative. **Homestead** served soda with shots in secret table compartments – today the 120-year-old saloon openly serves gin-spiked Corpse Revivers. There's been a saloon where **Elixir** stands since 1858, though it passed as a soda fountain during Prohibition – notice the discreet women's entrance inside the bathroom.

Above Heinold's First & Last Chance Saloon.

09 Free-Spirited FRISCO

COUNTERCULTURE | STREET ART | FREEDOM

'Don't call it Frisco.' This command attributed to San Francisco's eccentric self-appointed Emperor Norton may be the only law that's stuck in unruly San Francisco. Go on: break that bogus rule. Now you can relate to free thinkers who've lived, loved and dreamed freely in San Francisco – and pick up where they left off.

SVETLANASF/SHUTTERSTOCK ©

🗺 How to

Getting around Get a MUNI Passport to take the cable car to/from Chinatown and hop the 7 Haight bus.

Cost The best things in life are still free, but donations keep the good vibes and creativity flowing.

Free shows Follow smoke signals to Sharon Meadow for 4:20 festivities on April 20, folk-rock out at October's Hardly Strictly Bluegrass and catch free classical shows at Stern Grove Festival.

HUANGCOLIN/SHUTTERSTOCK ©

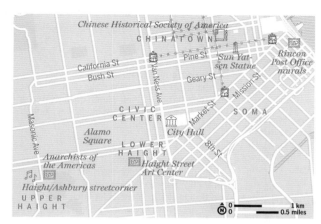

Chinese Historical Society of America

CHINATOWN

California St
Bush St
Pine St
Sun Yat-sen Statue
Geary St
Van Ness Ave
Rincon Post Office murals

CIVIC CENTER
SOMA
Mission St
Market St

Masonic Ave
Alamo Square
City Hall
8th St
LOWER HAIGHT
Anarchists of the Americas
Haight Street Art Center
Haight/Ashbury streetcorner
UPPER HAIGHT

N 0 — 1 km
0 — 0.5 miles

Top left Haight/Ashbury street corner. **Bottom left** Hardly Strictly Bluegrass Festival.

Freewheeling San Francisco comes alive in **Rincon Post Office murals**, from bordellos to ruthless railroad barons. Artist Anton Refregier made 92 changes to appease McCarthyist censors – but he had the last word, dedicating his final 1948 mural to free speech. This proved prophetic in 1957, when **City Lights Books** won its landmark free-speech case.

Celebrate free expression at Chinatown's **Li Po**, hosting spirited debates of art and politics for 70-plus years. If tonight's ideas seem revolutionary, you should've visited Chinatown c 1911, when Sun Yat-sen plotted China's revolution at 36 Spofford Alley. **Chinatown Alley Tours** and **Chinese Historical Society of America** highlight Chinatown's legacy of resistance, while Beniamino Bufano's Sun Yat-sen statue observes rebel skateboarders in **Old St Mary's Square**.

The '60s counterculture hub was Haight St, where psychedelic posters are screen-printed at **Haight Street Art Center** and trailblazing cannabis dispensaries sell weed legally (18-plus, ID required). At **Haight/Ashbury street corner**, musicians jam and the clock always reads 4:20 – aka 'international bong hit time,' a Bay Area term coined c 1971. 1967's Summer of Love celebrated free love, free food and free music – catch those vibes at **Haight St Fair**, neighborhood nonprofits and **Hippie Hill** drum circles.

At **City Hall**, you're free to join protests and cheer on couples getting married alongside Harvey Milk's statue in the **Rotunda**, where same-gender weddings were legalized in 2004. You could get hitched here too – or stay fancy-free in Frisco.

The Haight's Best Street Art

Evolution Rainbow Joana Zegri's 1967 Cole St mural shows evolution as a work in progress, from the Pleistocene era through the Age of Aquarius.

Healthcare is a right Haight-Ashbury Free Clinic has championed the motto painted at 558 Clayton since the 1960s, setting public health standards.

Anarchists of the Americas Since 1976, volunteer-run Bound Together Anarchist Book Collective has supplied freethinkers with radical ideas – and kept Emma Goldman looking sharp in this mural.

Banksy's masked rat Atop Red Victorian commune at 665 Haight St, Banksy's masked plague rat points the way forward through epidemics of HIV/AIDS, Covid and opioid abuse.

Listings

BEST OF THE REST

🎵 Classy Date Nights

SFJAZZ

Witness extraordinary main-stage collaborations by US and global jazz legends from Argentina to Yemen, and hear fresh takes on classic jazz albums and poets riffing with jazz combos in the Joe Henderson Lab.

San Francisco Symphony

Musical maverick Esa Pekka-Salonen sets the tempo for contemporary classical, with Grammy-winning San Francisco Symphony, musical guests ranging from Renee Fleming to Metallica, and SoundBox emerging-artist showcases. Nab $20 terrace seats and sit right behind the musicians.

San Francisco Opera

Cheers for premieres of classics and San Francisco-original operas, from Grammy-winning *The (R)Evolution of Steve Jobs* to Pulitzer Prize–winner Nilo Cruz's *El Último Sueño de Frida y Diego* (Frida and Diego's Last Dream). Score $26 balcony seats to appreciate David Hockney's sets and Eun Sung Kim's musical direction.

✂ Dim Sum with a Difference

Mister Jiu's $$

In a landmark 1880s Chinatown banquet hall, chef Brandon Jew reinvents banquets with ingenious Chinese-Californian signatures: house-cured Sichuan-pepper charcuterie, Dungeness crab spring rolls and Stemple Creek sirloin fried rice.

State Bird Provisions $$

Carts zoom between tables laden with California-inspired, dim-sum-sized 'provisions' like cumin lamb dumplings, pork-belly citrus salad and the namesake dish: buttermilk-brined Wolf Ranch quail nested on sweet-and-sour onions. Book 30 days ahead or line up before 5pm for walk-ins.

Dragon Beaux $$

Hong Kong meets Vegas at San Francisco's most decadent Cantonese restaurant, with premium teas and sharp service. Say yes to cartloads of succulent roast duck and pork belly, and creative dumplings like XO brandy-laced shrimp in spinach wrappers.

🖼 Immersive Art Shows

SFMOMA

Take on SFMOMA's sprawling collection from the top, jumping into top-floor art installations, navigating Olafur Eliasson's One-Way Color Tunnel and taking selfies with Bay Area artists' murals, with breathers at the outdoor terrace sculpture garden and cafe.

Asian Art Museum

Travel across Asia without ever leaving San Francisco, surrounded by 18,000 artworks spanning 6000 years. Ground-floor galleries showcase contemporary artists and timeless ideas, from Kolkata-based Jayashree Chakravarty's maps of personal space to shape-shifting disguises by San Franciscan artist Carlos Villa.

Museum of the African Diaspora

Take your own personal journey through epic stories of diaspora: start with Maya Angelou's riveting video of slave narratives, and emerge into powerful showcases of contemporary Black artists, including Cynthia Aurora Branvall's careworn, stained lace maps of America.

Contemporary Jewish Museum

Enter a blue-steel box miraculously balancing on one corner to discover fresh perspectives on Jewish culture, history, art and ideas, from Jim Henson's endearingly quirky, diverse world of Muppets to the radically casual style of San Francisco's own Levi Strauss.

 Culinary Creations

Benu $$$

Star chef/owner Corey Lee makes San Franciscan jaws drop with dazzling dishes that look like SFMOMA minimalist sculptures and burst with pan-Pacific flavor – lobster-stuffed sea cucumber, chrysanthemum-laced eel, barbecued quail with truffled XO brandy. Monumental 12-course dinners run $450 with tip, plus ingenious wine pairings.

Acquerello $$$

Even Tuscan traditionalists convert to Cal-Italian cuisine in this former chapel thanks to chef/owner Suzette Gresham's divine seasonal menus ($150 to $250) – truffled Roman artichoke gnocchi and olive-oil-poached black bass, amen. The anteroom where brides once steadied their nerves is lined with rare Italian vintages – *cin cin!*

Atelier Crenn $$$

The menu arrives in the form of a poem, and each exquisite dish by multistarred chef/owner Dominique Crenn is an ode to the coasts of Brittany and Sonoma – from oysters with rosé gelée to rosebud-shaped geoduck and *uni* (sea urchin roe) tart. Fourteen-course menus run $400; for casual dates, hit cozy next-door Bar Crenn for sumptuous bar bites.

Alamo Sq Park.

 Smooch-Worthy Views

Bay Lights

San Francisco's best light show dazzles from dusk until dawn, with 25,000 LED lights twinkling across 500ft Bay Bridge suspension cables in never-repeating patterns. San Francisco artist Leo Villareal's installation is equally mesmerizing from atop Russian Hill or below near Embarcadero's Pier 24.

Alamo Square Park

Graceful 'Painted Lady' Victorian mansions have housed bordellos, jazz speakeasies and hippie communes, and survived elegantly intact – especially east-end 'Postcard Row' (aka the *Full House* backdrop) and northwest-corner Westerfield mansion, where Kenneth Anger filmed satanic tower rituals.

Coastal Trail

Pick up the freshly restored trail near Sutro Baths ruins and head around the Lands End bluffs for pine-framed Pacific views, with glimpses of shipwrecks at low tide and Golden Gate Bridge panoramas.

Scan to find more things to do in San Francisco and the Bay Area online

NAPA & SONOMA

WINE | NATURE | RESILIENCE

Experience Napa and Sonoma online

Feast on tide pools of
sensational seafood at
SingleThread (p78)
🚗 *2hrs from San Francisco*

Wallow in bubbling volcanic
mud, drink bubbly, repeat in
Calistoga (p74)
🚗 *1½hrs from San Francisco*

Healdsburg

*Austin Creek State
Recreation Area*

*Lake
Berryessa*

Russian River Valley

*Bothe-Napa Valley
State Park*
St Helena

Napa River

*Lake
Hennessey*

● **Guerneville**

○ Graton

**Santa
Rosa**

*Annadel
State Park* ○ Kenwood

○ Rutherford
○ Oakville

Yountville

Napa Valley

Toast nature's
glorious comeback
in **Sonoma Valley**
(p82)
🚗 *1¼hrs from San
Francisco*

○ Sebastopol

○ Freestone

○ Glen Ellen

Follow your bliss down
the Bohemian Highway to
Occidental (p89)
🚗 *1½hrs from San Francisco*

Find out why it's
called the Wild
West in **Downtown
Sonoma** (p91)
🚗 *1hr from San
Francisco*

Sonoma

Sonoma Valley

● **Napa**

Eat and drink like a
rock star in **Down-
town Napa** (p77)
🚗 *1hr from San
Francisco*

NAPA &
SONOMA
Trip Builder

In a single day in Napa, you can wallow in
volcanic mud, see priceless art and drift away in
a hot-air balloon. Or head to Sonoma to wander
thousand-year-old redwoods and eat the meal of your
life. Also: there's wine.

0 20 km
0 10 miles

Practicalities

ARRIVING

Plane/ferry Charles M Schultz-Sonoma County Airport (STS) serves Santa Rosa. For Napa, take San Francisco Bay Ferry to Vallejo and transfer to Napa Valley Vine bus 11.

FIND YOUR WAY

Cell coverage is variable, so download maps before you go. Wi-fi is free at most hotels, B&Bs and cafes.

MONEY

Bring cash for farmers market purchases and tips for housekeeping, cafes and bartenders.

WHERE TO STAY

Area	Pro/Con
Napa	Victorian B&Bs have character. New hotels downtown are pricey.
Calistoga	Spa hotels and cottage inns. Rare spa deals on weekdays.
Russian River	Cabins for outdoor weekends and gay getaways.
Healdsburg	Boutique inns near top restaurants and wine tasting. Priced accordingly.

EATING & DRINKING

Wine Country menus are guided by the seasons. Look for winter citrus and Dungeness crab, spring lamb and tender greens, summer berries and wild salmon, fall heirloom tomatoes and steak – plus wine all the time.

Best picnic supplies
Sebastopol Farmers Market (p89; pictured top left)

Must-try wine and food pairings
Robert Sinskey Vineyards (p92; pictured bottom left)

GETTING AROUND

Car/motorcycle To reach Napa from San Francisco (1½ to two hours), take Hwy 101 to 12/121E, then follow Hwy 29N. For Sonoma, take Hwy 101N to Santa Rosa (one to two hours) or Healdsburg (1½ to two hours). For Sonoma Valley, take Hwy 37E to Hwy 121N.

Bus Take Sonoma County Transit buses ($1.50 to $5) or Napa Valley Vine bus 10 ($1.60).

| **JAN-MAR** Flowering cover-crops grace bargain spa getaways | **APR-MAY** Enjoy sunshine and vineyard tours before the crowds arrive | **SEP-OCT** Crush means crunch time at wineries, plus harvest fair fun | **NOV-DEC** Kick back with locals at film festivals and holiday events |

10 BUBBLES
for Your Troubles

BUBBLY | MUD BATHS | HOT SPRINGS

Take the edge off the week/year/decade with Napa's scientifically unproven but utterly delightful stress remedy: a wallow in bubbling volcanic mud, chased with a glass of local bubbly. For 8000 years, the indigenous Wappo people enjoyed geothermal baths in Nilektsonoma, now called Calistoga – and why argue with time-honored tradition when it feels this good? Bottoms up.

STEPHEN SAKS PHOTOGRAPHY/ALAMY STOCK PHOTO ©

🗺 How to

When to go Weekdays offer more availability and spa package deals. Napa can get too hot for mud baths June to September – but outdoor pools are a treat.

Sabrage Bust open a bottle of bubbly with a saber sword, and you'll feel like a victorious and very fancy pirate. Healdsburg's Breathless Wines shows you how in a sabrage session ($75) that includes Breathless' top-notch Sonoma sparkling wine. Huzzah!

CHARLES O'REAR/GETTY IMAGES ©

Top left Indian Hot Springs. Bottom left Mud bath, Dr. Wilkinson's.

Legendary speculator Sam Brannan saw gold in northern Napa's bubbling black mud, promoting **Calistoga** as California's signature spa resort – and by 1873, he'd lost a fortune trying to make it happen. Today, Brannan's dream seems to have come true at **Indian Hot Springs**, where guests shuffle from mud baths ($135) to an Olympic-sized, outdoor hot-spring-fed pool (access with treatment $50), then onto **Sam's Social Club** for bubbly at bathrobed happy hours. Across the street, **Dr. Wilkinson's** 1952 spa-motel offers de-stress sessions in mineral-water pools, extra-squishy mud baths ($239) and 'beer brew' (hops-infused mineral bath, $199) – plus **House of Better**'s hearty-yet-healthy Southwestern fare paired with sparkling wine or fizzy watermelon kombucha.

Muddy mysteries, clarified What makes Calistoga mud so special? Never mind the dubious health claims – just stick your feet in and find out. That natural warmth and squishiness comes from volcanic ash, peat and mineral spring water. If you're wondering why some mud baths cost more, maybe it's silkier mud with higher volcanic ash content... or maybe it's marketing. Mud-bath treatments usually involve a tub of aromatic mud, a mineral-water soak, then a blanket-wrap session ($130 to $190). Check for deals midweek from lodging sites and **Calistoga Visitors Center**.

Family-friendly spa resorts Most spa treatments are adults-only, but mineral hot-springs pools keep kids entertained while adults unwind at 1947 **Calistoga Motor Lodge and Spa** and best-value **Roman Spa Hot Springs**.

Best Bubbly Tastings

Iron Horse Celebrate milestones at this scenic Sonoma hilltop bar with sparkling wines served at White House inaugurations from Carter to Obama – plus special cuvées celebrating first responders, LGBTIQ+ Pride and ocean conservation (tasting $30).

Domaine Carneros Champagne house Taittinger makes excellent bubbly in Napa's Carneros marshlands, keeping this hilltop chateau popping with sparkling flights ($40 to $60) and Bubbles and Bites pairings ($95).

Schramsberg Enter estate caves to glimpse top-secret Champagne-method riddling and racking, then taste *tête de cuvées* (best of the vintages) at this Napa Green–certified, enchanted 1862 Calistoga winery (tour and tasting $80).

11 Culinary
ALL-STARS

STAR CHEFS | FEASTS | CLASSES

In Wine Country, you can see where chefs source ingredients, acquire kitchen skills and buy cookbooks to re-create signature dishes. Chefs know you'll come back for more, because once seasonal inspiration is served to you on a platter, you'll need to taste what's next on Wine Country's ever-changing menu.

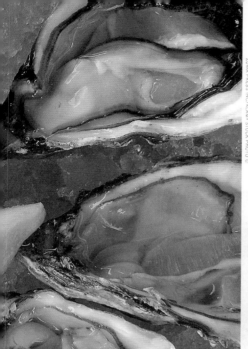

🐚 How to

When to go Book fine dining one to two months ahead. For walk-ins, arrive before or after the lunch/dinner rush.

Come hungry Hike, bike or kayak solo, take a bicycle tasting tour with Getaway Adventures or Napa Valley Bike Tours, or join Active Wine Adventures for art walks and mountain hikes.

Taste-test culinary student exams The Culinary Institute of America at Greystone's Gatehouse Restaurant serves sumptuous meals cooked by chefs-in-training (three courses $40, four courses $50, sommelier pairings $35-$45).

Farm Fare with Global Flair

Ever since the gold rush, Wine Country's signature dishes have been casually multilingual, combining local ingredients with shipping-route flavors from the Pacific Rim to the Mediterranean. At Sonoma's **FolkTable**, *Top Chef*'s Casey Thompson's down-home cosmopolitan food includes truffled hand pies and slow-braised pork with peanut hoisin and pickled pineapple. Ex-Momofuku chef Nick Tamburo's wood-fired menu for Yountville's **North Block** is peak NorCal, from sourdough pizzas with duck sausage to miso-slathered grilled trout with sea beans. Try a little of everything at **Oxbow Market**: **Hog Island** oysters mignonette, **C Casa** duck-confit tacos, **Eiko's** hamachi sushi bonbons, **Bar Lucia**'s sparkling wine and **Ritual Coffee** espresso.

🎓 Make Your Own Feast

Downtown Napa's **Culinary Institute of America at Copia** offers drop-in cooking classes, demos, documentaries and star-chef panels too spicy for TV. Hit free **Chuck Williams Culinary Arts Museum** upstairs; buy **Marketplace** gadgets and signed cookbooks downstairs.

Above left Oysters, Oxbow Market, Hog Island. **Left** Bar Lucia. **Above right** Latte, Ritual Coffee

Since Wine Country belonged to Spain and Mexico before joining the US, Mexican and Southern European cuisines are deeply rooted here. Sonoma's best lunches are served on **El Molino Central**'s picnic tables – including banana-leaf-wrapped tamales slathered in Zoraida's mother's tangy red mole. **Tasca Tasca** serves Portuguese tapas feasts celebrating the sea, gardens and land of Sonoma, from Dungeness crab empanadas to goat stew with heirloom potatoes. Geyserville's **Diavola Pizza** serves decadent oven-roasted vegetables with NorCal's finest wood-fired, life-saving pies – when fires raged nearby, Diavola stayed open to make free pizza for firefighters.

Destination Dining

Planets and Michelin stars mysteriously align over **Healdsburg** and **Yountville**, Western stagecoach stops transformed into global dining destinations. The most spectacular meal in California and quite possibly a lifetime awaits at **SingleThread**, where twinkly-eyed servers reveal your first course: a driftwood log festooned

The Making of Legendary Meals

Sonoma yields crops year-round, but I especially enjoy early-season produce that points to the bounty ahead – tender shoots of asparagus, green garlic, flowering sweet peas.

We're proud to serve elegant, versatile wines from our neighbors at **Liocco**, **Reeve**, **Bloodroot** and **Marine Layer** – and of course beer from **Russian River Brewing**.

Working closely with **Sonoma Family Meal** and **Farm to Pantry**, we've fed neighbors through floods, fires and a pandemic. When people visit Sonoma to support local farmers and makers and back a good food system, that's important – we're so grateful.

 ■ By Katina Connaughton, *farmer and floral designer, SingleThread and Little Saint @lumberjackieo*

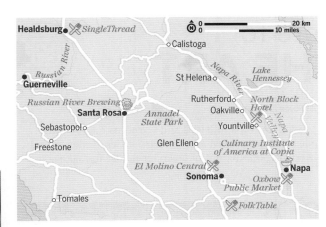

Left California-grown asparagus.
Below SingleThread, Healdsburg.

with forest moss, meadow wildflowers and ceramic dishes of pristine Pacific seafood – all sublime, especially silken Dungeness crab *chawanmushi* (egg custard). This edible Sonoma landscape is followed by 10 equally poetic seasonal courses, ranging from vineyard 'cover crop' grains to foraged-morel dashi – a tour de force of nature and invention. In Yountville's historic saloon, **French Laundry** dazzles through nine opulent, original courses, from 'oysters and pearls' (oyster-caviar custard) to 'doughnuts and coffee' (cappuccino semifreddo). To discover their secret ingredients, visit Yountville's **French Laundry Gardens**, and book food-craft and floristry workshops at SingleThread's working farm.

Hyperlocal Sensations

Wine Country excels at laid-back, hyperlocal fare. SingleThread farmer Katina Connaughton and chef-husband Kyle celebrate plant-based food and community at **Little Saint**, and chef Dustin Valette crafts **Valette** tasting menus from wagon-loads of **Healdsburg Farmers Market** finds: crispy-skin bass with Preston farro, Skyhill Farms honey-brined pork chops. St Helena's **Charter Oak** serves still-bubbling dishes family-style – from petrale sole poached in Mendocino seaweed butter to slow-smoked short ribs sliding drunkenly off the bone into Napa cabernet-grape saba.

12 Here for
THE ART

SCULPTURE | ART INSTALLATIONS | WINERIES

███ If you know where to look on Napa hillsides and Carneros marshlands, you'll find contemporary masterpieces tucked away in barn attics, underground art installations, and censored art popping out of lavender fields. To make sense of it all, try some wine.

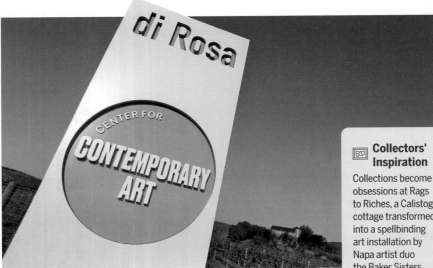

NAPA VALLEY REGISTER VIA ZUMA WIRE/ALAMY STOCK PHOTO ©

🗺 Trip Notes

Getting here To navigate hillsides around Carneros and Napa, you'll need a car – or a bicycle, helmet and serious calf muscles.

Time to contemplate Book visits in advance, and build in extra time. Contemporary art aims to provoke, so leave room to react, process and discuss afterwards – ideally over wine.

Pack a picnic Napa zoning rules limit winery picnics, but di Rosa Center allows picnics in sculpture-filled meadows.

🖼 Collectors' Inspiration

Collections become obsessions at Rags to Riches, a Calistoga cottage transformed into a spellbinding art installation by Napa artist duo the Baker Sisters. Deco teapots pour out fountain pens in the parlor, while the den's lined with psychedelic Fillmore posters and rare vinyl from owner/collector Gary Himelfarb's reggae-album-producing days.

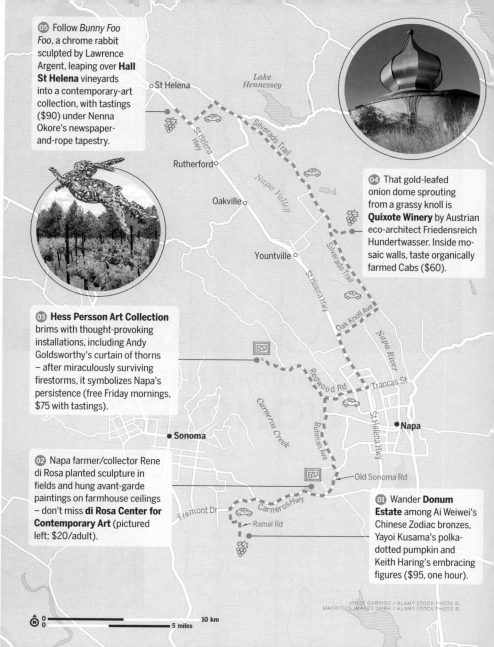

05 Follow *Bunny Foo Foo*, a chrome rabbit sculpted by Lawrence Argent, leaping over **Hall St Helena** vineyards into a contemporary-art collection, with tastings ($90) under Nenna Okore's newspaper-and-rope tapestry.

04 That gold-leafed onion dome sprouting from a grassy knoll is **Quixote Winery** by Austrian eco-architect Friedensreich Hundertwasser. Inside mosaic walls, taste organically farmed Cabs ($60).

03 **Hess Persson Art Collection** brims with thought-provoking installations, including Andy Goldsworthy's curtain of thorns – after miraculously surviving firestorms, it symbolizes Napa's persistence (free Friday mornings, $75 with tastings).

02 Napa farmer/collector Rene di Rosa planted sculpture in fields and hung avant-garde paintings on farmhouse ceilings – don't miss **di Rosa Center for Contemporary Art** (pictured left; $20/adult).

01 Wander **Donum Estate** among Ai Weiwei's Chinese Zodiac bronzes, Yayoi Kusama's polka-dotted pumpkin and Keith Haring's embracing figures ($95, one hour).

St Helena
Lake Hennessey
Rutherford
Napa Valley
Oakville
Yountville
Silverado Trail
St Helena Hwy
Oak Knoll Ave
Napa River
Trancas St
Redwood Rd
Carneros Creek
Burnam Ave
St Helena Hwy
Napa
Sonoma
Old Sonoma Rd
Fremont Dr
Carneros Hwy
Ramal Rd

0 10 km
0 5 miles
N

13 Sonoma's Natural WONDERS

PARKS | REDWOODS | WINES

Sonoma's pristine wooded parklands and historic terraced vineyards have survived floods and fires amazingly intact. Forward-thinking ecologists and first responders have preserved Sonoma Valley panoramas and protected West Sonoma's ancient redwoods for all to enjoy.

🗺️ How to

Getting around Cars get around faster – but nature would probably prefer if you bicycle around Sonoma Valley, and follow biking trails to the redwoods from Santa Rosa.

When to go Hiking gets hot in Sonoma Valley between June and September, while redwoods keep their cool.

Conservation in progress Sonoma's natural splendors are protected by volunteer firefighters and maintained by park volunteers – support their efforts by heeding fire advisories and make their day by saying thanks.

NAPA & SONOMA EXPERIENCES

Valley of the Moon

Sonoma Valley's Hwy 12 follows the footsteps of Miwok, Pomo and Wintun people, who dubbed this enchanted place 'Valley of the Moon.' Vines thrive under extinct volcano **Mt St Helena**, but wouldn't grow on abandoned quarries. So decades ago, Jane Davenport Jansen and dedicated conservationists planted 25-acre **Quarryhill Botanical Garden** with Asian magnolias, lilies and maples – including species now endangered elsewhere.

Conservation isn't new here, as you'll see at **Jack London State Park**. He wrote the world's longest-running bestseller, *Call of the Wild* – but Jack London (1876–1916) claimed his greatest work was rescuing this 1400-acre preserve from early settlers' slash-and-burn farming. **Beauty Ranch** remains as Jack left it, cowboy hat hanging by his desk – Jack's widow, editor

🌿 Botany Breakthroughs

Sonoma horticulturist Luther Burbank (1849–1926) cultivated 800 hybrid plant species for sustainability and delight, including California's tastiest fruits and vegetables. You'll find early experiments still thriving at **Luther Burbank Home & Gardens** and **Gold Ridge Experiment Farm**.

Above left View of the valley beneath Mt St Helena. **Left** Jack London State Park. **Above right** Luther Burbank Home & Gardens

and fellow writer Charmian Kittredge London, donated their estate to the public. Take the ruggedly romantic hiking trail from **Wolf House** ruins to **House of Happy Walls** – check the bookshop for Charmian's riveting memoirs and Jack's rejection letters from publishers.

Sonoma ecologists have preserved 13,000 acres of Sonoma Valley as parkland, though purple-brown burn hillside scars reveal where volunteer firefighters battled recent fires. To assist regrowth, stick to volunteer-restored trails at panoramic **Sugarloaf Ridge Park**.

Mighty Redwoods

Nothing puts life into perspective like walking among Western Sonoma's giant redwoods. Hard to believe that in the 1870s, lumber companies clear-cut centuries-old redwoods around **Occidental** and **Guerneville** (nicknamed 'Stumptown') – until changes of heart rescued ancient groves.

Lumber baron Colonel Armstrong couldn't bring himself to chop down millennium-old redwoods near Guerneville, and with his

⚖ Where Drinking Comes Naturally

Horse & Plow The chickens are used to admirers flocking here for sunny afternoons of hard cider and easy living among heirloom apple trees.

Porter Creek Vineyards From family vineyards originally cultivated in 1978 and Demeter-certified in 2003, Alex Davis crafts elegant, sustainable pinot noir and chardonnay featured at tool-shed tastings ($30).

Preston On Lou Preston's biodynamic farmstead, taste satiny viognier and spicy zinfandel, and picnic under walnut trees (tasting $35).

Unti Vineyards Sun-drenched Dry Creek Valley looks and tastes like Tuscany, thanks to Mitch Unti's organically farmed, crisp white fiano, and sangiovese to rival Super Tuscans (tasting $25).

MELISSA KUHNELL/ROBERTHARDING/GETTY IMAGES ©

NAPA & SONOMA EXPERIENCES

Far left Porter Creek Vineyards. **Left** Armstrong Redwoods State Natural Reserve. **Below** Canoe trip, Russian River.

daughters preserved 500-plus acres as **Armstrong Redwoods State Natural Reserve**. Outside Occidental, 48-acre **Grove of the Old Trees** was also owned by lumber-mill magnates who were convinced to sell the grove to conservation nonprofits. You can still see blue marks on towering trees once earmarked for lumberyards – now thriving in this designated 'Forever Wild' conservation site.

Sonoma residents are standing by their redwoods through climate change, volunteering to tend habitats and fight parkland fires. But redwoods also have their own emergency response system: they send distress signals via interconnected root systems and supportive fungi, and release flame-retardant tannins in their bark to contain fire. So redwoods have survived to sprout new growth in fire-damaged Armstrong Woods, providing fresh perspectives for generations to come.

FAR LEFT: ANDREW MONTGOMERY/LONELY PLANET ©, LEFT: VIVU/SHUTTERSTOCK ©

Redwood Adventures

Zipline through the redwood canopy at 30mph and rappel down to the forest floor with **Sonoma Canopy Tours** – it's thrilling and eco-educational for ages 10 and above, plus tour proceeds provide outdoor education camp scholarships to at-risk kids. In summer drift through redwoods in a canoe with **Russian River Adventures**.

14 Cult
REDS

RARE WINES | TASTINGS | TOURS

Napa cabernet is a fine choice on any wine list – but have you tried Sonoma pinot noirs, Napa zinfandels and rogue cab francs? Wine Country is brimming with reds you won't find elsewhere, because the entire production is snapped up by top restaurants and wealthy collectors. But with the right intel, you can drink them all without robbing a bank. Red-y when you are.

ROBERT FRIED/ALAMY STOCK PHOTO ©

🗺 How to

When to go For relaxed tastings, go November to April. It gets hot and packed between May and July, and wineries are busy with crush August to October.

Book ahead Zoning laws prohibit Napa wineries from taking drop-ins, and small wineries don't always have staff to spare from winemaking duties.

Winery overview Napa is even more breathtaking when morning mists lift from vineyards on hot-air balloon flights with Aloft (rides $270 per adult), followed by a convivial brunch with mimosas ($28).

BILL MARSH ROYALTY FREE PHOTOGRAPHY/ ALAMY STOCK PHOTO ©

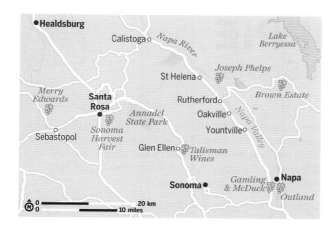

Top left Frog's Leap. **Bottom left** Wine bottles, Joseph Phelps.

Napa cabs Napa Valley was cowboy country until local wine-makers won a 1976 Paris wine competition. Climate change makes cabernet harder to produce in hot valleys, but as they say in Napa: adversity makes wine taste better. Now **Joseph Phelps**' definitive Oakville cabernets share limelight with wine-maker Ashley Hepworth's Insignia blends. Howell Mountain cabs fetch upwards of $1000 – don't miss **Piña** winemaker Anna Monticelli's affordable standout.

Downtown Napa's indie hits Toast Napa's all-zin flights at **Brown Estate**, Napa's first African American–owned winery. Go all-natural at **Outland**, or go rogue with **Gamling & McDuck**'s 'Do Not Sneak This Wine into Movie Theaters' cab franc.

Sonoma's pinot power Sonoma's oldest vines survived Prohibition, producing 'communion wine.' But Pinot Noir vines suffered from viruses in the 1970s, until trailblazing enologist **Merry Edwards** treated them with heat. Toast her legacy at Merry Edwards, and taste **Sonoma Harvest Fair**'s pinot Double Gold winners. For pinots with cult followings, take **Talisman Wines**' library pinot flights, and join Laura Carpenter Carpenter for epic **Carpenter** coastal pinot tastings.

🍇 Truly Fun Wine Tours

Tres Sabores Your tail-wagging welcome committee are founder/winemaker Julie Johnson's dogs, who gently herd you around Napa's most enchanted vineyards. See where winemaking magic happens under olive trees and drink in valley views over Napa's best zin.

Sutro wine Hike vineyards with fifth-generation farmer/winemaker Alice Sutro, and you'll taste local landscape features in your wineglass. Chalk Hill gives Sutro sauvignon blanc mineral notes, while mist-swirled treelines lend aromatic mystery to Sutro cabernet.

Frog's Leap Vineyard cats pose while human hosts supply witty banter and insights you can taste in organically farmed wines. Sauvignon blanc is the critical darling, but the merlot might make you boogie in the barn.

15 HIPPIE
Hot Spots

MAKERS | MUSIC | ORGANICS

If you're enjoying Sonoma's scenery, thank the hippies. When freethinkers headed back to the land here in the 1960s, they planted biodiverse crops without pesticides and founded maker movements that flourish today. Enjoy organic food and cannabis, jam with musicians, throw down with ceramists and find inspiration along the Bohemian Highway.

JUDEAND/SHUTTERSTOCK ©

🗺 How to

Farm-to-spliff dispensaries Meet the Sonoma trailblazers behind California's legalization efforts at Solful, featuring outdoor-farmed, organic, biodynamic cannabis in joints, gummies, body butter and beer. Say hi(gh) to plants growing on-site at Flora Terra dispensary, offering organic, local, indie products.

Apple country Sonoma's original drink of choice was hard cider, and Sebastopol's varietal is celebrated at August's Gravenstein Apple Fair – and whenever Gravenstein pies emerge from the oven at Mom's Apple Pie.

HUTCH AXILROD/GETTY IMAGES ©

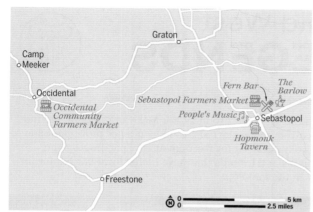

Sebastopol's maker scene Good vibes draw crowds to Sunday **Sebastopol Farmers Market**, where fiddlers slap, everyone boogies, and artists and activists share visions for a more creative, peaceful world. Drift into the **Barlow**, Sebastopol's apple-cannery sheds creatively repurposed into workshops for local indie makers, distillers and brewers – try **Pax Mahle**'s natural wines and **Spirit Works**' craft cocktails.

Brake for inspiration Follow your bliss down the **Bohemian Highway**, and you'll find fellow travelers among the redwoods in **Occidental**. Here at **Hinterland** and **Neon Raspberry**, you'll meet local talents behind recycled, organic and women-made art and design. **Altamont General Store** showcases ceramist Didem Mert and accessories artisan Angela Bohl, and invites you to throw down at Clayfolk workshops. Occidental celebrates the power of countercultural thinking every day – but especially **Fool's Day**, when a gloriously unruly parade takes all day to cover Occidental's four blocks.

Jam on Did you bring your dulcimer? No worries – just channel your inner folk-rocker and join jam sessions in progress for 40-plus years at **People's Music**, where you might spot Grateful Dead drummer Mickey Hart testing bongos. Hoedowns break out Fridays at **Occidental Community Farmers Market**, and on random sunny afternoons in front of **Bohemian Market**. Count on **HopMonk Tavern** for 'live beer and fresh music' – you can rock out with fellow singer-songwriters at Tuesday open mikes and catch the odd cameo by neighbor Tom Waits.

Top left Barlow, Sebastopol. **Bottom left** Organic farmer, Sebastopol.

🍴 Hippie Food, Reinvented

Fern Bar Come for laid-back 1970s fern-bar vibes inside a Barlow warehouse, stay for Sonoma-proud dishes – especially seasonal local trout with green garlic, or 'umami bomb' mushroom-cream broccolini on yeast-dusted sticky rice.

Ramen Gaijin One whiff and you'll know what the buzz here's about: spicy pork belly and smoky short ribs slumping into homemade noodles. Pair with Pliny the Elder and cap with black sesame-miso gelato.

Boon Eat + Drink Crista Luedtke's hyperlocal, organic comfort food has sustained Sonoma through fires and first dates with mycopia–mushroom mac-and-cheese, preserved Meyer lemon chicken, and her own excellent-value Perpetual Indulgence rosé.

16 Wild West **LEGENDS**

REBELS | RANCHERAS | RESILIENCE

Time-travel through the Wild West to meet the Mexican diplomat behind Wine Country, the drunk cowboys who started an independence movement and the civil rights pioneers who fundraised for freedom at epic parties. Get the inside scoop on debates, myths and legends that have fueled local bar banter for 150 years, and join history in the making.

ROBERT FRIED/ALAMY STOCK PHOTO ©

📸 **How to**

Getting around Carpooling lets you take the fast lane through highway traffic to Sonoma. Walking is the best way to see Downtown Sonoma and visit tasting rooms ringing Sonoma Plaza.

Picnic supplies Sonoma Plaza's Tuesday evening farmers market showcases local produce. Two blocks from the Plaza is The Patch, California's oldest urban farm, where neighbors grow pesticide-free produce for sale on the honor system – just weigh your haul and leave cash in the box.

ZUMA PRESS INC/ALAMY STOCK PHOTO ©

Far left Mission San Francisco Solano. **Left** General Vallejo's home. **Bottom left** Mary Ellen Pleasant's Grave, Napa Cemetery.

The Bear Flag Republic Miwok, Pomo, Wintun and Wappo people traded and thrived in Huichi (Sonoma) for millennia before the Spanish established **Mission San Francisco Solano** here – introducing measles and smallpox that decimated indigenous populations. When Spain lost California to Mexico in the 1830s, Mexico decided mission territory should revert to native control. That memo was somehow mislaid, and settlers snapped up mission lands.

Then one drunken night in 1846, partiers crashed **Sonoma's military barracks**, staggered into Mexican **General Vallejo's home** to guzzle his homemade brandy and proclaimed a breakaway republic. The next day, Sonoma awoke to epic hangovers in the new 'Bear Flag Republic,' under a flag featuring what looked like a wombat. The US military quelled the rebellion, and Vallejo became a US citizen and Sonoma's first state senator. Today around Sonoma's **historic town plaza**, a new bear flag features a grizzly in a fire helmet and hospital mask, saying: 'Thank you first responders.'

Mary Ellen Pleasant's history-making parties In the 1880s freed slave and self-made multimillionaire Mary Ellen Pleasant invited California's freewheeling elite to her Sonoma Valley Ranch for horse races and barnstorming dances. She used the proceeds and political capital she gained for civil rights initiatives – including the 25-year lawsuit that desegregated San Francisco streetcars in 1893. Today visitors can stay at Mary Ellen Pleasant's **Beltane Ranch**, and visit her **Napa Cemetery** gravestone honoring California's 'Mother of Civil Rights.'

✿ Toast Sonoma's Success Stories

Ceja Wine Country's most iconic romance started in Robert Mondavi's Napa vineyards, where young Pedro Ceja and Amelia Morán harvested grapes. Today their family pours heart and 55 years of winemaking expertise into every elegant bottle, including Ceja's signature red blend for French Laundry.

Robledo Taste the American dream at the winery built from the ground up by Reynoldo Robledo, who started as a farm worker in 1968 and became Sonoma's go-to vineyard expert. Reynoldo's kids run the family's Sonoma winery, dedicating Los Braceros red blends to Mexican farm workers who fed America through WWII. *¡Salud!*

Listings

BEST OF THE REST

Drink in these Views

Hanzell Vineyards

Chickens perch on pigs snoring in the vineyards at Hanzell, Sonoma's idyllic, organically farmed winery. Join cats in the stone barn overlooking Sonoma, and taste morning mists in cool-climate chardonnays and pinot noirs.

Soda Rock Winery

All hail Lord Snort, Sonoma artist Bryan Tedrick's recycled-metal boar, survivor of both Burning Man and Sonoma fires. Soda Rock's barn was rescued, and now hosts tastings of big-hearted zinfandel and merlot under Lord Snort's approving grin.

Porter-Bass

Fog swirls through redwoods above while Kitchen the cow meanders sunny vineyards below: if this hidden valley has you California dreaming, wait until you taste the biodynamic pinot noir and sauvignon blanc farmer Sue Bass and her winemaker son Luke gently coax from it.

Showtime

BottleRock Music Festival

Napa kicks off summer with a three-day music/food/wine festival featuring headliners like Janelle Monáe, P!nk and Metallica ($179 per day, $389 per three-day general admission).

Napa Valley Film Festival

Food and wine films are crowd-pleasers at Napa's five-day mid-November movie marathon. Stick around for food demos, wine receptions and appearances by stars like Geena Davis and Laurence Fishburne.

Sebastiani Theatre

Downtown Sonoma's community-run, 1934 Mission Revival cinema celebrates Sonoma's independent streak with art-house films, ecology-themed documentaries and live singer-songwriter concerts.

Wine & Food Pairings

House of Flowers

Picturesque pairings start with prized Sonoma Coast chardonnay and fennel-pollen sprinkled *gougères*, peaking with ridgetop pinot noir and black nori strewn with purple beets and yellow flowers.

Robert Sinskey Vineyards

Angel choirs seem to echo through this redwood-cathedral tasting room, where organic, biodynamic pinot and vin gris hit glory notes with chef Maria Helm Sinskey's flatbreads and estate-raised lamb.

La Luna Taqueria & Market

'Tacos y vinos' says the wine-fridge sign – an excellent suggestion at La Luna for 50-plus years. Pair fish tacos with Maldonado Farm Worker chardonnay and Elouan rosé with velvety *pollo adobado* (adobo-marinated chicken).

STERLING MUNKSGARD/SHUTTERSTOCK ©

BottleRock Music Festival.

Roadside Attractions

Chuck Gillet's Cyclops Iron Works

This lawyer-turned-artist, known to admiring neighbors as 'the maestro of mess,' has covered his Glen Ellen home-studio with delightful gargoyles, assembled from rusted farm tools and auto parts.

Patrick Amiot Junk Art

A cow rides a tractor, a rocket blasts off the lawn and a dinosaur grabs a red convertible for lunch: it's all happening on Florence Ave, in sculptures artist Amiot made for neighbors' yards from recycled junk.

Kool City Surf Shop

Under the 'Welcome to Monte Rio, Vacation Wonderland' sign, a skeleton casually leans on a Kool City surfboard, inviting you into this Quonset hut to score custom skateboards, tees and bowling pins reinvented as art.

The Morning After

Southside

Nothing 'soaks up the tannins' (read: fixes hangovers) like Southside's excellent coffee, chilaquiles with poached farm eggs, and avocado toast with smoked salmon and pepitas. Kids and pups chill on Southside's sunny patios in Carneros, Yountville and Napa.

Wild Flour Bread

Western Sonoma goes wild for organic artisan breads, sticky buns and mushroom *fougasse* glossy with olive oil, all hot from the brick oven. Loll on sunny, grassy lawns with coffee until you recover...or rejoin the line for seconds.

Les Pascals Patisserie

Everyone in Glen Ellen seems to have acquired a French accent since Pascale Merle and her husband, pâtissier Pascal Merle, started baking butter-glossed croissants, impeccable baguettes and savory quiches fresh daily.

Southside, Yountville.

Wine Country Style

Betty's Girl

When your Instagram following demands more than 'Wine Not?' tees, Kim Northrup gets you BottleRocking Napa's boho style: vintage cowboy boots, 1970s denim and flowy dresses Kim custom-makes from repurposed men's tuxedo shirts and antique lace. Bonus: Kim alters and ships.

Lolo's Consignment

Are heels slowing your roll through vineyards, or maybe you need a sweater for wine-cave tours? Crisis averted at Lolo's, where you can score mint secondhand cashmere and ditch stilettos for sleek sandals.

Gallery Lulo

Upgrade from predictable diamonds to wearable art – Lulo carries Emiko Oye's gemstone-studded Lego superhero cuff-bracelets, Tara Locklear's scuffed-skateboard statement necklaces, and silver-aura earrings by Sonoma's Karen Gilbert.

 Scan to find more things to do in Napa and Sonoma online

NORTHERN CALIFORNIA & THE REDWOOD COAST

BEACHES | WILDLIFE | AMAZING DRIVES

Experience Northern California and the Redwood Coast online

Crescent City

Hike among the world's oldest and tallest trees at **Redwood National Park** (p103)
🚗 3¾hr from Mendocino

Orick

Educate yourself about marijuana cultivation on a **Humboldt cannabis tour** (p100)
🚗 3hr from Mendocino

McKinleyville

Arcata

Eureka

Fortuna

Redding

Weott

Explore the mountainous **Lost Coast** on a backpacking adventure (p98)
🚗 3hr from Mendocino

Trinity River

Shasta-Trinity National Forest

Eel River

PACIFIC OCEAN

Leggett

Mendocino National Forest

Tahoe National Forest

Stroll wave-blasted bluffs and live large at swanky **Mendocino** (p112)
🚗 3hr from San Francisco

Fort Bragg

Willits

Elk

Ukiah

Clear Lake

Search for whale spouts from atop the historic **Point Arena Lighthouse** (p106)
🚗 1hr from Mendocino

Anchor Bay

Sea Ranch

Healdsburg

Bodega Bay

NORTHERN CALIFORNIA & THE REDWOOD COAST
Trip Builder

San Jose

Santa Cruz

Monterey

Big Sur
Los Padres National Forest

The jagged edge of the continent is wild and awe-inspiring. Craggy sienna cliffs tower over windswept beaches and rocky coves. Spectral fog fosters the world's tallest trees and shelters an outsider spirit, the country's most potent weed and idiosyncratic two-stoplight towns.

0 100 km
0 50 miles

Practicalities

ARRIVING

Arcata–Eureka Airport (flyacv.com) has regular services to San Francisco and LA, though expect cancellations due to fog. Crescent City's **Del Norte County Regional Airport** has one daily service (contourairlines.com) to Oakland.

FIND YOUR WAY

Zooming north on a schedule? Take Hwy 101, the faster, inland route, then cut over to the coast whenever you're ready to slow down.

MONEY

Camping, either car-camping or with a tent, will save you big bucks.

WHERE TO STAY

Place	Pro/Con
Mendocino	Standards are high and stylish; so are prices.
Ukiah	Inland stop with hot-spring resorts and bland chain hotels.
Sea Ranch	Surprisingly affordable to rent a house in low season.
Eureka	Good mix of delightful B&Bs and chain hotels.
Outdoors	Myriad state and national parks offer incredible camping.

EATING & DRINKING

Hippies headed back to the land here in the 1960s to find a more self-sufficient lifestyle, adopting Native Californian food ways and reviving Wild West traditions of making bread, cheese and beer from scratch in small batches. Early adopters of chemical-free farming, northerners innovate hearty, organic cuisine that satisfies the region's munchies.

Best road sandwich
Elk Store (p105; pictured top)

Must-try oysters
Humboldt Bay Provisions (p112)

GETTING AROUND

Car Hwy 1 is popular with cyclists, but otherwise, you'll really need a car to explore this region.

Bus and train
Neither Amtrak nor Greyhound serves cities on coastal Hwy 1. The brave can painstakingly piece together some bus travel. Check with Greyhound, Mendocino Transit Authority and, north of Mendocino County, the Redwood Transit System and Redwood Coast Transit.

Greenwood's

JUN-JUL
The driest season in the redwoods is spectacular for day hikes and big views

AUG-OCT
Warm weather and clear skies are ideal for hiking the Lost Coast

DEC-APR
Whales migrate off the coast

17 Explore the
COAST

CRAGGY COVES | CURIOUS HAMLETS | WHALE-WATCHING

The Sonoma and Mendocino coasts remain gloriously unspoiled, despite their easy proximity to the Bay Area. Their austere bluffs are some of the most spectacular in the country and the trip north gets more rewarding (and remote) with every passing mile. Where Hwy 1 cuts inland to join Hwy 101, the Lost Coast holds the state's best-preserved natural gifts.

How to

Getting around The drive between Bodega Bay and Fort Bragg takes three hours of daylight driving without stops. At night in the fog, it takes steely nerves and much, much longer. Plan accordingly.

Feeling peckish? The larger towns along Hwy 1 have a splendid choice of restaurants, particularly Mendocino and Fort Bragg. There are also organic markets where you can grab a sandwich for the road.

The drive Down south it's called the Pacific Coast Hwy, but northerners simply call it 'Hwy 1.' This fabulous coastal drive winds along isolated cliffs above the crashing surf and moody rocks, passing farms and fishing towns.

Use roadside pullouts to scan the horizon for migrating whales and stop off at historic **Point Arena Lighthouse**, the tallest on the US West Coast (tied with nearby Pigeon Point) at 115ft. Climb 145 steps for the jaw-dropping view.

The Lost Coast The North Coast's superlative backpacking destination is a grand stretch where narrow trails ascend the rugged peaks of the King Range. Ethereal mist hovers above roaring surf on volcanic beaches of black sand as majestic Roosevelt elk graze the forests. It became 'lost' when the highway system deemed it impassable in the mid-20th century.

⚓ Noyo Harbor

Noyo Harbor is the quintessential way to experience the Northern California coast. Take to the sea on a whale-watching boat, fishing charter or kayak tour. Landlubbers can enjoy the salty air and coastal sights as they stroll or cycle on the **Noyo Headlands Trail**. Check out the sea lions lounging on the green buoy or mind-surf the waves as they roll into Noyo Bay. To learn more about the waters and wildlife, visit the **Noyo Center for Marine Science**. Be sure to refuel after your adventures with locally caught seafood at a restaurant in the Noyo Harbor.

■ **Recommended by Cate Hawthorne,** *kayak instructor and guide,* Liquid Fusion Kayaking, Fort Bragg, @liquidfusionkayak

Far north At the 640-acre **Patrick's Point State Park** sandy beaches abut rocky headlands and easy access makes it a great bet for families. Climb rock formations, examine tide pools and listen to barking sea lions. **Sumêg** is a reproduction of a Yurok village, with hand-hewn redwood buildings where Native Americans gather for traditional ceremonies. In the native plant garden you'll find species for making traditional baskets and medicines.

Continuing north, the gorgeous campground at **Gold Bluffs Beach** sits between 100ft cliffs and the ocean.

Above Noyo Harbor

■ **With Amy Cirincione O'Connor,** *founder of Papa & Barkley Social cannabis lounge in Eureka*

Marijuana Capital of the World

WHAT'S THE TEA ON CALIFORNIA'S HOMEGROWN?

Two decades after legalizing medical cannabis, in 2016 California legalized marijuana for recreational use (aged 21-plus, with ID), with 56% of voters approving Proposition 64. This is changing the local economy and tourism, too, especially in the North Coast's Mendocino and Humboldt Counties. Find out firsthand – or through secondhand smoke.

Above left Cannabis plant.
Above middle Marijuana buds.
Above right Eel River.

How to

Mendocino's marijuana farms date from the '60s and an estimated one-fifth of Humboldt County's population farms its world-famous weed. So a good chunk of the economy here has run, for decades, as bank-less, tax-evading and cash only. This is starting to change, albeit slowly, thanks to local incentives aimed at drawing black-market farmers out of the forests and into the valleys now that recreational marijuana is – at least in California and some other US states – legal.

California's burgeoning legal cannabis industry has created a network of pot shops (aka dispensaries), weed tours and cannabis-friendly lodgings. Proponents of the movement say it's an economic boon that takes money out of the hands of drug cartels and puts it to good use as tax revenue. Opponents argue that legalization normalizes drug use, spurs dependency and can have adverse effects on teens and impoverished communities.

While the transition hasn't been easy (most farmers remain in the illegal market due to high regulatory fees and plummeting legal marijuana costs), there are safe and informative ways that visitors can learn about the local industry.

Get to Know Your Bud

For newbies, purchasing legal weed can be like walking into a fancy wine store and not knowing your sauvignon blanc from your cabernet sauvignon. Enter the folks at **Humboldt Cannabis Tours** (humcannabis.com) in Eureka, who can take you on educational visits to the best

local dispensaries – including **HPRC** (hprcdispensary.com), which sells pesticide-free cannabis products – or out to 'white-market' farms, where you'll learn about the growing cycle from the Emerald Triangle's longtime cannabis farmers.

Partake Like a Local

We talked to Amy Cirincione O'Connor, founder of **Papa & Barkley Social** (@papaandbarkleysocial) in Eureka, a premier cannabis lounge, and this is what she had to say:

'Cannabis is a great travel companion. Pre-rolls and gummies travel well and are convenient for microdosing, so you can relax and heighten your travel experience without getting stoned.

'For good vibes, the **Eel River** along the **Avenue of the Giants** is an incredible place to hike, swim or just hug the trees. The **Sequoia Park Zoo's Sky Bridge** is a series of suspension bridges that explore the redwood canopy. There is nothing else like it. Say hi to the otters while you're there!

'If the munchies hit, our favorite spot is **Cochina Mariposa** for authentic Mexican food in a unique setting, right on the golf course. I love the *tortas* and *agua fresca*. If you're looking for a more social experience, **Humboldt Farmers Markets** happen throughout the week, with the largest on Saturdays on the Arcata Plaza. It's a cannabis-friendly environment, with live music, amazing local produce and a real community hub. Of course, our favorite place to relax is at our Papa & Barkley Social Dispensary. We love sharing a joint with friends around the firepit, soaking in the sun and the vibes. Bonus points if you get a THC-infused massage in our spa while you're there. Full body high!'

ⓘ Stay Out of Trouble

Adult possession of up to 1oz of marijuana for recreational use is legal, but it's still against the law to use weed in public (fines are up to $500, as well as mandatory community-service and drug-education classes).

Driving under the influence of alcohol or drugs is illegal, as is carrying open containers of alcohol or marijuana, even empty ones, inside a vehicle. Store them in the trunk.

Best to heed the 'No Trespassing' signs you encounter, as local marijuana farmers don't take kindly to strangers wandering around.

For foreigners, conviction of any drug offense is grounds for deportation.

18 Land of Redwood **GIANTS**

TREES | HIKING | SASQUATCH

Congratulations, traveler: you've reached the land where the trees are so large that the tiny towns along the road seem like mini-dioramas. The scenery is pure drama: cliffs and rocks, legendary salmon runs, gargantuan trees, wild elk. Leave time to dawdle and bask in the haunting natural grandeur of it all.

LUCENTIUS/GETTY IMAGE ©

📷 **How to**

Where to go Redwood Coast Heritage Trails (visitredwoods.com) provides itineraries based around lighthouses, Native American culture, the timber and rail industries, and maritime life.

Plan ahead Ensure you've got a spot by reserving campsites in advance. Redwood National Park has no main entrance and only charges fees in some sections. To protect the Tall Trees Grove, visitor numbers are limited; get permits at the visitor centers in Orick and Crescent City.

STRUCTURED VISION/SHUTTERSTOCK ©

VIRRAGE IMAGES/SHUTTERSTOCK ©

Far left Fallen redwood, Humboldt Redwoods State Park. **Left** Redwood National Park. **Bottom left** Founders Grove, Humboldt Redwoods State Park.

Humboldt's oldest crop Don't miss the magical drive through Avenue of the Giants and California's largest redwood park, **Humboldt Redwoods State Park**, which covers 53,000 acres – 17,000 of which are old growth.

The park contains some of the world's most magnificent trees (three-quarters of the world's tallest 100 trees!). Stop at the quirky roadside shops along Hwy 101 before strolling agape through the primeval **Rockefeller Forest**, the world's largest grove of old-growth redwoods. The park has over 100 miles of trails for hiking, mountain biking and horseback riding. Other easy walks include short nature trails in **Founders Grove** and **Drury-Chaney Loop Trail** (with berry picking in summer). Challenging treks include popular **Grasshopper Peak Trail**, which climbs to the 3379ft fire lookout.

The far reaches Keep venturing north to wild **Redwood National Park**. Along the way, stop for a meal at Eureka's always-busy **Brick & Fire** and soak away any hiking aches at the **Finnish Country Sauna & Tubs** in the region's eclectic college town, Arcata.

Sleep out Try to spend a night in a tent under the hushing boughs. Then, as you gaze skywards, ponder that redwoods once covered thousands of square miles of coast here, before the mass logging around the turn of the 20th century (apparently 95% of the trees were felled). Fortunately, conservation measures now protect these magnificent giants that live for thousands of years.

Redwood National & State Parks

Hidden in the northwestern reaches of California's coast, **Redwood National Park** encompasses some of the world's tallest (up to 379ft) and most ancient trees (predating the Roman Empire by over 500 years), along with a luxuriantly verdant mix of coastal, riverine and prairie wildlands. The massive stands of old-growth coastal redwoods (*Sequoia sempervirens*), draped in moss and ferns, are managed in conjunction with three amazing neighboring state parks – **Prairie Creek Redwoods**, **Del Norte Coast Redwoods** and **Jedediah Smith Redwoods State Park** (which features in the original *Star Wars*). Collectively they constitute an International Biosphere Reserve and World Heritage Site, yet remain little visited compared to their southern brethren.

NORTHERN CALIFORNIA & THE REDWOOD COAST EXPERIENCES

19 SEAFOOD
to Wild Mushrooms

SEAFOOD | WINERIES | CRAFT BEERS

NorCal is the epicenter of healthy eating. Virtually every town has a farmers market, certified organic produce is standard on many restaurant menus and 'locally sourced' a given. Sample bodacious seafood on the coast while inland wineries work their magic. Don't fear though: with all those long stretches of highway, plenty of greasy spoons serve up chicken fried steak and the like.

SOLLINA IMAGES/GETTY IMAGES ©

🗺 How to

Cheap eats Northern California is rife with wonderful places to enjoy a picnic, so it's no poor meal to stop by one of the locally sourcing grocery stores and pick up provisions; most also have a deli counter where you can buy sandwiches and homemade soup.

Crab season Local crabbing season runs November to late June or early July – key for knowing if you'll get fresh or frozen morsels.

LARRY MILLER (CC BY-SA 2.0) ©

ROB CRANDALL/ALAMY STOCK PHOTO ©

NORTHERN CALIFORNIA & THE REDWOOD COAST EXPERIENCES

Far left Crab fishing, Northern California. **Left** Anderson Valley Brewing Company. **Bottom left** Cod and sweet potato fries, Patterson's Pub.

Native foodways After millennia of habitation, native foodways run deep on the North Coast, where you'll taste the influence of Ohlone, Pomo and Miwok traditions. Nature has been kind to this landscape, yielding bonanzas of wildflower honey, berries, wild grains and nuts. Along this rugged coastline, you'll find traditional shellfish collection and Native Californian–run fishing operations, alongside sustainable oyster farms and fish hatcheries. Fearless foragers have identified every edible plant from wood sorrel to Mendocino sea vegetables here – though key spots for wild morel mushrooms remain closely guarded local secrets.

Beer! The craft breweries of the North Coast don't mess around – bold hop profiles, Belgian-style ales and smooth lagers are regional specialties, and they're produced with style. Some breweries are better than others, but the following tour makes for an excellent long weekend of beer tasting in the region: **Anderson Valley Brewing Company** (Boonville); **Overtime Brewing** (Fort Bragg); **Gyppo Ale Mill** (Shelter Cove); **Redwood Curtain Brewing** (Arcata); and **Seaquake Brewing** (Crescent City).

Valley vintners Vineyards are the pride and joy of Mendocino's **Anderson Valley**. Take a scenic drive past heritage apple orchards and redwood trees, and pull into barn tasting rooms that are full of surprises: top-notch sparkling wines, complex pinot noirs and delicate dry gewürztraminer. Top hits include **Toulouse Vineyards** and **Husch Vineyards**.

Top Chef Tips

Double-Michelin-starred chef Matthew Kammerer shares his favorite local spots. Or visit him at his own exemplary restaurant at **Harbor House Inn**.

Elk Store (theelkstore.com) Amazing sandwiches across the street from one of NorCal's most beautiful beaches.

Cafe Beaujolais (cafebeaujolais.com) Beautiful outdoor gardens with wood-fired pizzas and an extensive beer list.

Patterson's Pub (pattersonspub.com) Old Irish pub with great pub fare and both indoor and outdoor seating.

Wickson (wicksonrestaurant.com) Farm-to-table, plant-forward menu in Anderson Valley.

Pennyroyal Farm (pennyroyalfarm.com) Cheese and meat boards and local wines on Hwy 128 in Boonville. Great outdoor seating.

 ■ Recommended by **Matthew Kammerer**, *Executive Chef* at *Harbor House Inn* @matthew.kamm @theharborhouseinn

20 Offbeat LIVING

HAMLETS | HIPPIES | COASTLINE

▬▬▬ Link the cool small towns from Sea Ranch to Mendocino in an easy day trip taking in local arts and crafts, superb coastal views, and surfing and kayaking. The towns are tranquil bases, with exceptional accommodations and restaurants, plus secluded beaches.

BOB KREISEL/ALAMY STOCK PHOTO ©

🗺 Trip Notes

Getting around This easy itinerary flows from Sea Ranch to Albion, just 46 miles. It's a straight shot of about an hour by car, or take to pedal power and make a day (or two) of it.

Go deeper **Unbeaten Path Tours & Yoga** (unbeatenpathtours.com) runs intriguing area tours focusing on everything from architecture to landscapes or meditation. The nature walks, which culminate in a yoga session, are particularly popular.

🐋 See Whales

From November to April, you may spy gray and humpback whales during their annual migration. **Point Arena Lighthouse** (pictured) is tops for spotting spouts and breaching pods (actually, anywhere coastal will do). Or, follow Hwy 1 north beyond charming **Point Arena**, through bucolic fields descending from the hills to **Manchester State Beach**.

Mendocino

05 Launch river and ocean kayaking from tiny **Albion**, which hugs the north side of the Albion River mouth, and check out **Albion River Bridge**, the last remaining wooden bridge on Hwy 1.

Albion River Bridge

Navarro River Redwoods State Park

04 Cruise itty-bitty, supercutey **Elk** for its famous cliff-top views of 'sea stacks,' towering rock formations jutting out of the water.

Manchester State Beach

Point Arena Lighthouse

○ Manchester

03 Meander from the small harbor at one end of **Point Arena** through arty shops, cafes and restaurants in pretty Victorian-era buildings to **Arena Cove** and join surfers mingling with fisherfolk and other locals.

Arena Cove

○ Anchor Bay

02 Explore the boutiques and sunny coastline at **Gualala** (pronounced by most locals as 'Wah-la-la,' a Native American Pomo name meaning 'where the waters flow down') and **Anchor Bay**.

○ Sea Ranch

○ Stewarts Point

01 Wonder at iconic non-denominational **Sea Ranch Chapel** (open dusk to dawn) featuring a swooping cedar roof that's accented with copper, bisected by stained glass and topped with a bronze spire.

PACIFIC OCEAN

0   20 km
0   10 miles

Hiking & Kayaking the
HINTERLAND

TREKKING | WILDERNESS | GRANDEUR

The north's coastal trails and mountain ranges weave inland to some of the country's best wilderness hiking, not to mention kayaking, rafting and other outdoor pursuits. Whether you're taking a stroll or tackling a multiday trek, this is the region for you: choose between ocean views, redwood groves and geological disneylands.

🗺 **How to**

Ask before you go Visitor centers are vital for learning current conditions. Plus, get trail maps and tide charts (some trails are inaccessible in high tides). For the Lost Coast, that's Bureau of Land Management (BLM;

blm.gov), but each park has its own.

Safety regulations On the Lost Coast, overnighters need a bear canister and backcountry permit, available from the BLM, though the latter is best acquired weeks in advance at recreation.gov.

Far left Kayaking, Smith River. **Left** Fern Canyon hiking trail. **Bottom left** James Irvine hiking trail.

Stretch your legs Every regional, state and national park you pass has trails galore. At **Redwood National & State Park** (nps.gov/redw) the trail network passes through diverse landscapes, offering hiking experiences for all fitness levels. For example, in the exceptional **Prairie Creek State Park**, the most popular is the 0.7-mile loop into **Fern Canyon**, along a creekside path framed by fern-covered cliff faces. The 6.3-mile **Rhododendron Trail** shines gloriously between mid-May and early June when flamboyant pink and red rhododendrons tower as high as 35ft overhead. For a classic loop through some of the park's most majestic redwoods, followed by a short jaunt along the Pacific Ocean and a return walk along a 19th-century gold-mining trail, take the 9-mile **James Irvine-Miner's Ridge** loop.

Also great is the hike to **Trillium Falls** – a 2.5-mile trail leading to a small waterfall, accessed from Davison Rd at Elk Meadow.

Take to the water West of Jedediah Smith Redwoods State Park, the **Smith River**, the state's last undammed waterway, originates high in the Siskiyou Mountains. Its serpentine course cuts through deep canyons beneath pristine thick forests in the park's northern reaches. Kayaking is exceptional here. In summer park rangers lead half-day trips along a 3.5-mile class I and II section of the river, which includes minor rapids interspersed with moving flat water. During rainy season (December through April), independent boaters pit their skills against more challenging rapids, rated up to class V.

Hiking the North Coast

King Range National Conservation Area Walk a remote shoreline to abandoned **Punta Gorda lighthouse** on California's **Lost Coast**. This moderate 6.4-mile out-and-back hike heads south from the end of Lighthouse Rd just south of Petrolia; the final section is impassable at high tide.

Prairie Creek Redwoods State Park Hike through continuous old-growth redwood forest, then travel an empty beach roamed by a herd of Roosevelt elk. This moderate 6.2-mile loop starts at the park's **Fern Canyon trailhead** and follows the Fern Canyon, James Irvine, Clintonia and Miner's Ridge trails to **Gold Bluffs Beach** and then heads north for 1 mile.

■ Recommended by Matt Heid, *outdoor writer and author* of 101 Hikes in Northern California @into_wilderness, intowilderness.substack.com

Creative
MECCA

ART | CULTURE | HISTORY

Beginning with the rich Native American culture and continuing to the redwood barons' shingle houses in Mendocino through to artists working today, the Northern California coast has always been a gathering place for creative people: some using the abundant natural resources and others importing their exotic ways. A tour of the region offers rich inspiration everywhere you turn.

How to

Getting around The most effective way to take in the cool corners of the region is by car.

Map it The free *Eureka Visitors Map,* available at tourist offices, details walking tours and scenic drives, focusing on architecture and history.

Kick it on a commune Local farms and communes keep a low profile, but some offer work-stay programs or artist-in-residence opportunities. Ask around.

Larry Spring was an extremely eccentric physicist, and the storefront **Larry Spring Museum** (larryspring museum.org) in Fort Bragg is filled with fascinating and weird experiments, including the Mendocino Brushless Levitating Solar Motor. I also like to be amazed by the collection of rocks laid out to

look like food (like, trompe-l'oeil-level realism). It feels good to be confounded by the interface between genius, savant and cloud cuckoo land. Also in Fort Bragg, there's **Lost Coast Found**, a vintage extravaganza.

Mendocino Arts Center (mendocinoartcenter.org) is a stalwart on the North

Coast. It's always worth dropping into to see what's on show (also a good little theater). It's worth checking out the galleries in Fort Bragg and Mendocino, particularly **North Coast Artists Gallery** (northcoastartists.org) in Fort Bragg and the **Highlight Gallery** (thehighlightgallery. com) in the gorgeous Odd

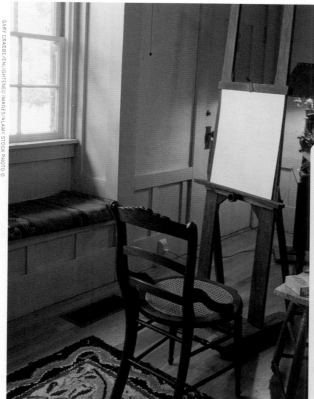

GARY CRABBE/ENLIGHTENED IMAGES/ALAMY STOCK PHOTO ©

Above Sun House, Grace Hudson Museum, Ukiah.

🏛 Inspirational Hubs

Peruse beautiful Pomo basketry and artifacts – or read about local scandals – at the **Mendocino County Museum** in Willits, also home of the **Skunk Train** (skunktrain.com).

The **Grace Hudson Museum** (gracehudsonmuseum. org) in Ukiah hosts ethnological work and Native American art, and fascinating rotating art exhibits. The lovely 1911 **Sun House** was the former Hudson home and is typical of the arts-and-crafts style of that era.

Eureka's Old Town, along 2nd and 3rd Sts from C St to M St, is a buzzing pedestrian district, and F Street Plaza and Boardwalk runs along the waterfront. Gallery openings are the first Saturday of every month.

Fellows Hall in Mendocino. Both feature North Coast crafts artists. The Highlight Gallery is worth visiting for the building alone, and the views from the upstairs landing.

Walking into an old-growth redwood stand, like **Montgomery Woods** or **Hendy Woods**, feels the same to me as walking into a Gothic cathedral. And I've got to mention the two shows of fine woodworking we have each year by students and faculty of the Krenov School (where I teach). In late January and mid-May, we use venues in Fort Bragg or Mendocino – keep an eye on our website (thekrenovschool.org).

■ **By Laura Mays,**
woodworker, educator and designer, Director of the Krenov School,
Mendocino College, Fort Bragg,
@laurabmays

Listings

BEST OF THE REST

Hot Spring Havens

Harbin Hot Springs

This beloved hippie-dippie clothing-optional resort basks on 1700 acres of meadows and forestland with eight baths of varying temperatures, plus a sauna and sundeck offering sweeping valley views. Lodging and camping, too. Bookings essential.

Orr Hot Springs

Reserve ahead for a soak in the thermal waters of this rustic clothing-optional resort. Enjoy the private tubs, a sauna, a spring-fed rock-bottomed swimming pool, steam room, massage and storybook gardens.

Vichy Hot Springs Resort

This historic spa has the only warm-water, naturally carbonated mineral baths in North America. Swimsuits are required to soak here, where Mark Twain, Jack London and Robert Louis Stevenson did the same.

Creative Expression

Mendocino Coast Botanical Gardens

The art of cultivation is on grand display along 47 seafront acres of serpentine paths. The living tableau of native flora, rhododendrons and heritage roses are only lead-ins to the amazing succulent garden.

Holly Yashi

The renowned hometown jeweler, famed for its nature-inspired niobium metalwork, has its headquarters in Arcata's up-and-coming Creamery District. Take a 30-minute tour to watch the jewelry-making magic.

Blacksmith Shop & Gallery

From wrought-iron art to sculpture and jewelry, this is the largest collection of contemporary blacksmithing in the US. The Ferndale shop and the gallery are two doors apart – check them both out.

Foodie Finds

Humboldt Bay Provisions $$

Sit at the long redwood bar at this rustic-chic establishment and watch experts shuck local oysters, topping them with sauces like habanero and peach. The locavore menu includes charcuterie platters and regional wines and ales.

Bird Cafe & Supper Club $$

Chef Aaron Peters works with farmers and ranchers to create locavore Mendocino cuisine, pairing it alongside a stellar list of Anderson Valley wines. Saturdays are reservation-only supper-club events with a prix-fixe menu.

Larrupin' Cafe $$$

Moroccan rugs create a moody atmosphere, and consistently good mesquite-grilled seafood and meats are best enjoyed on the garden patio in summer. The cafe, which has live music some nights, is in Trinidad.

Salt Fish House $$

This welcoming restaurant on Arcata's plaza promises sustainably harvested seafood, locally sourced produce and thoughtfully crafted cocktails. It delivers on all three.

Saw Shop Bistro $$

The best restaurant in Lake County serves a California-cuisine-inspired menu of wild salmon and chili-rubbed flank steak, plus a small-plates menu of harvest salads, pasture-raised beef burgers and flatbread pizzas.

Schat's Bakery & Cafe $

Founded by Dutch bakers, Schat's makes a dazzling array of chewy, dense breads, sandwiches, wraps, big salads, dee-lish hot mains, full breakfasts and homemade pastries.

Wine or Pub?

Parducci Wine Cellars

Sustainably grown, harvested and produced, 'America's Greenest Winery' offers affordable, bold, earthy reds. It's got a charming tasting room and a terrace overlooking the vineyards.

Graziano Family of Wines

The Italian Graziano family is one of the oldest grape-growing families in Mendocino County. It specializes in 'Cal-Ital' wines – including primitivo, dolcetto, barbera and sangiovese – at some fantastic prices.

Olof Cellars

If you visit one winery in Lake County, make it Olof Cellars. Wines are excellent – most are reds aged for a minimum of three years – and there're informative winemaker-led tastings in the old chicken coop.

Shanachie Pub

The kind of intimate, make-instant-friends, small-town bar you dream of stumbling across while traveling, full of intellectual puzzle games, excellent live indie music and dark, scarlet-lit corners. Located in Willits.

Memorable Stays

Thatcher Hotel $$

This grand 1890s-era hotel's got a full bar with curated cocktails, a tempting cafe, handsome library and a pool. Rooms are Nordic-esque with hardwood floors and a cooling palate.

Timber Cove Resort $$$

This dramatic and quirky '60s-modern seaside inn has been refurbished into a luxury lodge. The rustic architecture is stunning, and a duet of tinkling piano and crackling fire fills the lobby.

Gualala Point Regional Park $

Shaded by redwoods and fragrant bay laurel trees, this creekside campground connects to the windswept beach. Its quality makes it the best drive-in camping on this part of the coast.

St Orres Inn $$

Famous for its striking Russian-inspired architecture, including dramatic stained glass and copper domes, on mushroom-laden 90 acres. Hand-built cottages range from rustic to luxurious. The inn's fine restaurant is worth the splurge.

Boonville Hotel $$

Decked out in contemporary American-country style with sea-grass flooring and fine linens, this historic hotel's got beautiful gardens and an inviting sitting room with board games and books.

Alegria $$

A perfect romantic hideaway: beds have views over the coast, decks have ocean views and all rooms have wood-burning fireplaces. Outside, a gorgeous path leads to a big, amber-gray beach.

Front Porch Inn $$

Not only does this converted motor lodge have artsy rooms – all with kitchens and quirky design touches – but the bathhouse behind a living wall of ferns has a striking sauna made from local river rocks.

 Scan to find more things to do in Northern California and the Redwood Coast online

23 VOLCANIC
California

WILDERNESS | HIKING | DRAMATIC VIEWS

▬▬▬ Prepare yourself for something completely different. In this remote northeast quadrant of the state, blistered badlands of petrified fire crisscross the land – from lava tubes to volcanoes and jagged mountaintops. The wilderness – some 24,000 protected acres – is divided by wildlife-rich rivers and streams, and dotted with cobalt lakes, horse ranches and alpine peaks.

MARK DE LEEUW/GETTY IMAGES ©

🗺 How to

When to go Summer's warm weather and snow-free passes are ideal for backcountry camping.

Where to base Small character-rich towns like Weaverville, Quincy and Dunsmuir are tops for stays.

Learn Park headquarters like Lassen's **Kohm Yah-mah-nee Visitor Center** (nps.gov/lavo) are vital for hiking maps and the latest conditions.

ZACH ZHENG/SHUTTERSTOCK ©

ALISA_CH/SHUTTERSTOCK ©

Far left Bumpass Hell. **Left** Devils Kitchen. **Bottom left** Mt Shasta.

Volcanic views You'll see **Mt Shasta** from miles away. It's part of the Cascade Range and though it looks peaceful now, it's still active. Smoke was seen puffing out of the crater on the summit as recently as the 1850s.

At 10,463ft, **Lassen Peak** is the world's largest plug-dome volcano. In **Lassen Volcanic National Park** admire steaming hydrothermal sulfur pools and cauldrons on the boardwalk in **Bumpass Hell**. The park's 150 miles of hiking trails include a 17-mile section of the **Pacific Crest Trail**.

A wild landscape of charred volcanic rock and rolling hills, remote **Lava Beds National Monument**, perched on a shield volcano, is reason enough to visit the region. Immediately south of **Tule Lake National Wildlife Refuge**, it's a truly remarkable 72 sq miles of volcanic features – lava flows, craters, cinder cones, spatter cones and amazing lava tubes – plus Native American pictographs and petroglyphs.

At **McArthur-Burney Falls Memorial State Park** clear, lava-filtered water surges over the top and from springs in the waterfall's face.

Hiking Wilderness expert Matt Heid (@into_wilderness) recommends **Castle Crags State Park**. He says, 'ascend among jagged pillars of granite and savor views north to Mt Shasta. It's a strenuous 5.2 miles out and back on the Castle Dome Trail. Or in **Lassen Volcanic National Park**, visit **Devils Kitchen**, where hissing fumaroles and boiling mud pots burst forth in a little-traveled corner of the park. It's an easy 5 miles out and back from the Warner Valley Trailhead northwest of Chester.'

A Chinese Shrine

The walls at Weaverville Joss House State Historic Park basically talk – they're papered inside with 150-year-old donation ledgers from the once-thriving local Chinese community, the immigrants who built Northern California's infrastructure. It's a surprise that the oldest continuously used Chinese temple in California (and an exceptionally beautiful one), dating from 1874, is in Weaverville.

The blue-and-gold Taoist shrine contains an ornate altar, more than 3000 years old, brought here from China. The adjoining schoolhouse was the first to teach Chinese students in California. It's a rare treat to see all of the ancient features so well preserved.

CENTRAL COAST

SCENERY | OCEAN | ADVENTURE

Experience
the Central
Coast online

MARGARET.WW/TOR/SHUTTERSTOCK ©

Hit the beach and surf the waves in **Santa Cruz** (p130)
🚗 1½hrs from San Francisco

● Santa Cruz

○ Hollister

Monterey Bay

○ Moss Landing

● Salinas

Pinnacles National Park

Pacific Grove ☆

○ Monterey

Carmel-by-the-Sea

Learn about the extraordinary bay at the superb **Monterey Bay Aquarium** (p123)
🚗 2hrs from San Francisco

Discover geologic wonders amid volcanic drama at **Pinnacles National Park** (p127)
🚗 1¼hrs from Monterey

Stop often along Hwy 1 for natural delights in **Big Sur** (p120)
🚗 1hrs from Monterey

● Big Sur

King City ○

Los Padres National Forest

Lucia ○

Sample wines aplenty in the Mediterranean climate of **Paso Robles** (p127)
🚗 2hrs from Monterey

○ Gorda

Lake Navimiento

PACIFIC OCEAN

San Simeon ○

Paso Robles

Cambria ○

CENTRAL COAST
Trip Builder

○ San Luis Obispo

Pismo Beach

Get your sunscreen on at old-time beach town **Pismo Beach** (p125)
🚗 3hrs from Los Angeles

Bookended by the Bay Area and Southern California, this often-wild stretch of coast is a misty mix of redwoods, beaches and ocean vistas best seen from Hwy 1. Enticing towns and cities mix with inland surprises.

Ⓝ 0 ———— 50 km
0 ———— 25 miles

Practicalities

ARRIVING

Air Monterey Regional Airport has connecting flights from other major California airports.

Train Amtrak has stops in Salinas, Paso Robles and San Luis Obispo.

FIND YOUR WAY

Download map info onto your navigation app in advance, as there are many cell-service dead zones on the remote coast.

MONEY

Cash-free transactions are the norm (but you can use currency). Costs are at the higher end.

WHERE TO STAY

Place	Pro/Con
Monterey	Wide range of places to stay. Nearby options include Carmel and Pacific Grove. Fills up in summer.
Cambria	Hub for motels at the southern end of coastal Hwy 1.
San Luis Obispo	Large variety of accommodations on Hwy 101, close to wineries and Paso Robles.

GETTING AROUND

Car You can access the Central Coast via famous Hwys 1 and 101 from the north and the south. Both offer sublime scenery and experiences. If you're only going to rent a car in one part of California, make it the Central Coast.

EATING & DRINKING

Fresh seafood is the specialty in Monterey, Santa Cruz and other coastal towns. Don't miss much-loved local Dungeness crab (pictured bottom) in the winter. Farm-to-table meals served with local wines star across the region. Every town along Hwy 101 has beloved spots for Mexican street fare. Farmers markets are held year-round and are amazing.

Best sour beer
Libertine Brewing Company
(p135; pictured top)

Must-try burrito
El Charrito
(p135)

Bike Very serious cyclists enjoy narrow, hilly, curvy, busy and beautiful Hwy 1.

JAN-MAR	APR-JUN	JUL-SEP	OCT-DEC
Crisp, clear and sunny most days, with a (much-needed) chance of rain	Beautiful sunny days and mild nights	The coast can be foggy and surprisingly cold, inland is dry and hot	Warm in October, cooler later

24 Discovering
BIG SUR

BEACHES | DRIVING | BEAUTY

Cruising over the famous concrete arches of the Bixby Bridge on Hwy 1 is the moment you'll fall in love with the Central Coast. Craggy cliffs and pocket beaches beguile. Along the way, the towns of Santa Cruz, Monterey, Carmel and more give reason to park. Inland, Hwy 101 traverses fertile valleys with missions, wineries and hidden parks.

🗺 **How to**

Getting around Your own vehicle is the only way to go, allowing unlimited exploration, detours and adventure.

When to go Summer is busiest, but the cold fog dampens enjoyment. Spring and fall offer thinner crowds and bright, sunny days.

Don't rush Traffic, road closures and detours due to weather, forest fires and even falling rocks slow travel along Hwy 1. Plus there are all the diversions that entice you to stop for a spell. Or two.

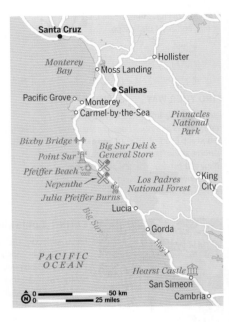

The myth of Big Sur Ask residents to draw Big Sur's boundaries on a map and each will give you a different answer. This mystical, mythical place denotes a spectacular stretch of the California coast where the blue sky touches the blue Pacific, where rocky, treacherous cliffs plunge down to ceaselessly churning breakers. Tiny pocket beaches hide in coves, some splashed by waterfalls. Amid this magnificence, Hwy 1 twists and turns around the corrugated mountainsides, linking tiny communities of idiosyncratic individualists, who've found their own independence at what feels like the edge of the world.

Driving the 100 miles between Carmel and Cambria – which encompass the concept of 'Big Sur' – takes a minimum of three hours, although expect to make it an all-day (or more) adventure as diversions are many.

JTBASKINPHOTO/GETTY IMAGES ©

🏰 Cue the Castle

Citizen Kane he was not. Over three decades starting in the 1920s, larger-than-life media baron William Randolph Hearst (1863–1951) built a flamboyant monument to wretched excess high on a hill overlooking the coast just north of Cambria. Although popularly known as Hearst Castle, its owner preferred to call it La Cuesta Encantada (The Enchanted Hill) or simply 'the ranch.'

The vast spaces often echoed with the laughter of Hollywood glitterati, thanks to Hearst's longtime companion, the movie star Marion Davies. Much of the fantastical Moorish design is thanks to the underrated Julia Morgan, California's first female architect. Book visits (by tour only) well in advance at hearstcastle.org.

Above McWay Falls, Julia Pfeiffer Burns State Park..

No shortage of stops From north to south, the attractions great and small are myriad. State parks not to miss include **Point Sur** (an 1889 lighthouse) and **Julia Pfeiffer Burns** (waterfalls and hiking). **Pfeiffer Beach** amazes with weird rocks, crashing waves and purple sand.

Among the natural beauty are businesses as unique as the shape of each Monterey pine clinging to the cliffs. **Big Sur Deli & General Store** is the place for gossip and picnic supplies. Visitor-thronged **Nepenthe** delivers sweeping views that will blow your schedule away.

Marvelous Monterey Bay

SEE AN INCREDIBLE DIVERSITY OF SEA LIFE

Monterey Bay is home to an extraordinary variety of sea life above and below the water. It's easily the richest natural habitat on the entire California coast; every year new species are discovered. Casual visitors standing on the beach or visiting a harbor will see some of the bay's animals.

GEORGE D. LEPP/GETTY IMAGES ©

All of Monterey Bay is a national marine sanctuary, which encompasses over 5300 sq miles of ocean and extends along one-quarter of the state's coast. Over 130 species of bird and 345 species of fish call these bountiful waters home. Below are four of the 34 species of mammal you can find here (plus one really fierce fish).

Gray Whales

Dramatic breaches and the puffs of water spouts mark the passage of these school-bus-size mammals. Pods of whales migrate yearly between Mexico and Alaska. Monterey Bay is an important feeding point between December and April, when you can join whale-watching tours leaving from the harbors in Santa Cruz, Moss Landing and Monterey.

Adult whales live up to 60 years, grow longer than a city bus and can weigh up to 40 tons, making quite a splash when they leap out of the water. Every year they travel from summertime feeding grounds in the arctic Bering Sea, down to southern breeding grounds off Baja California then all the way back up again, making a 6000-mile round trip.

Sea Lions & Seals

With doglike faces and oversized flippers, vocal sea lions typically haul out in large social groups. They are boisterous year-round residents of the bay and you can find them lounging in the sun on piers and rocks while barking their trademark 'arf arf arf.' Adult males exceed 600lb.

Lithe and active, harbor seals are the frisky, fitness-freak cousins of the sea lions. Topping out at 200lb, they can be found swimming in the surf looking for fish.

Above left Gray whale flukes. **Above middle** Sea lions. **Above right** Monterey Bay Aquarium.

Sea Otters

Unapologetically adorable, California's sea otters are famed for floating on their backs while using rocks to crack open sea urchins, abalone and other treats brought up from the bay's bottom and kelp forests. They are one of very few animals to use tools. Only about 4ft long, the playful mammals were nearly extinct 100 years ago, with just a few survivors of the fur-hunting era living south of Big Sur.

Strict protections have allowed a resurgence of sea otters in the bay. Look for them around piers, the surf near shore and along rocky coasts. The best place to spot them is **Elkhorn Slough** at Moss Landing, where otters enjoy the sheltered, food-rich waters.

Great White Sharks

Because of global warming, Monterey Bay has become a spawning ground for great white sharks, as warming waters have attracted the species north from Southern California. The area just offshore from Aptos is a spawning ground for the star of *Jaws* from April to October. Surfers and kayakers often have no idea that great whites are swimming right around them. In 2020 an Aptos surfer died after being bitten by a shark.

Best Spot to See Bay Wildlife

Don't miss the **Monterey Bay Aquarium**, which is one of the top sights on the coast and a world-renowned center for marine research. Tickets must be booked in advance, by several months if possible. Unmissable sights include an entire kelp forest, the cradle for life in the bay.

⭐ Two and a Half Tons of Fun

At the south end of the Central Coast, up to 18,000 elephant seals weighing as much as a remarkable 5000lb each gather at a beach right off Hwy 1 at **Point Piedras Blancas**, some 4.5 miles north of the entrance to Hearst Castle. The best months are November and December when the males return from months of nonstop feeding at sea. They are joined by females in January and February, who give birth and mate for the following year. Everybody comes and goes from March through May. At other times the odd straggler shows up.

Coastal Cities
& TOWNS

FOOD | CULTURE | WATERFRONTS

Bookended by Santa Cruz in the north and Pismo Beach in the south, with Monterey, Pacific Grove and Carmel-by-the-Sea in between, the Central Coast cities and towns take their character from the sea. Once humble fishing villages, today you'll quickly see why all five enjoy charm and vibes that lure visitors and supercharge ever-escalating real-estate values.

🗺 How to

Getting here It's all Hwy 1 baby, the magical artery linking this string of burgs along the coast. Buses will get you to all these places as well.

When to go There's no bad time along the coast. The towns and cities are year-round hubs of local – and visitor – activity.

Don't get caught without accommodations On weekends, holidays and for much of the (often foggy) summer, coast towns fill up. Reserve ahead.

From north to south, every one of these places is worth at least a one-night stop.

Santa Cruz The funkiest of California's funky beach towns makes liberal icon Berkeley seem almost conservative. But who has time for politics when the waves at world-famous **Steamers Lane** beckon, the beaches and boardwalk are sun-drenched, and the tide pools alive with critters coming out of their shells? Hike up into the redwoods and then stroll the beguiling downtown, with its cool cafes and genial taprooms.

Monterey The biggest city on the Central Coast dates back to Spanish times; don't miss the state park with its 18th-century buildings. The famous **aquarium** is the highlight of souvenir-happy Cannery Row, just down from the still-working fishing docks.

Pacific Grove Monterey's charming little neighbor has fabulous waterfront walks

ROBERT MULLAN/SHUTTERSTOCK ©

✕ Where the Cooks Dine

The south end of Monterey Bay has some of the region's best restaurants. When not cooking something great for others, you can find local chefs enjoying meals at these humble yet superb spots.

La Balena Unbelievably good, real Italian food in Carmel-by-the-Sea.

ACME Coffee Enjoy great house-roasted coffee and espresso in Seaside. Perfect on a foggy morning.

El Salvadoreño Pupuseria Amazing *pupusas* (corn tortillas filled with cheese, beans, meat or vegetables) in an unassuming strip mall a few blocks from Hwy 1 in Marina.

El Charrito For real-deal burritos, housemade everything and quick service in Salinas.

■ **Recommended by Matt Glazer,** *General Manager at Deetjen's Big Sur Inn* @glazer_big_sur

that turn the corner on the bay and offer serial sweeping views. Decades of gentrification haven't robbed it of its salty, Victorian charm.

Carmel-by-the-Sea Just Carmel to mere mortals, the 1-square-mile town oozes gentility. Once a Spanish mission, its cypress-shaded streets are lined with high-end galleries and bistros.

Pismo Beach You can sense the beach vibe from Southern California at this old-time seaside town set right on the wide – and warm – sand. A wooden pier stretches over the waves into the sunset. Surf shops abound.

Above Carmel-by-the-Sea.

26 Savoring the **LAND**

WILDERNESS | PARKS | WINERIES

Away from the Pacific Ocean, the Central Coast has beauty that lacks the seaside drama of the coast but beguiles through its own rugged charms and majestic expanses. Rolling hills – carpeted in amber grasses for much of the year – give way to steep mountains and often dense forests. In many places vineyards have added their own visual and quaffable pleasures.

JASON BUSA/SHUTTERSTOCK ©

How to

Getting around Driving is easiest, but you can also cycle, especially inland where mountain roads and trails offer views and thrills.

When to go Winter can be wet and cold (or clear and sunny), spring brings idyllic conditions, while summer inland is hot and dry. Fall has mild temps and bronzed hills thirsty for rain.

April surprise California's hills turn emerald green, enlivened by wildflowers, especially the brilliant orange California poppy.

JUPITERIMAGES/GETTY IMAGES ©

Far left Pinnacles National Park. **Left** Vineyards near Paso Robles. **Bottom left** Henry Cowell Redwoods State Park.

See the forest for the trees Twenty minutes inland from Santa Cruz, **Henry Cowell Redwoods State Park** (Felton) is the place to see soaring old-growth redwoods while famous Big Basin recovers from the devastating 2020 fire. North of San Simeon on Hwy 1, **Los Padres National Forest** is a vast, desolate and wildly beautiful land covering the coastal range and laced with superb outback hikes. In the northern reaches, the **Ventana Wilderness** has trails to hot springs.

See the grandeur through the rocks East of Soledad off Hwy 101 is one of America's least known natural spots, **Pinnacles National Park**. Soaring rock spires erupt from the classic California chaparral landscape of rolling hills dotted with wild oaks. Hikes traverse the geologic wonders and detours descend into spooky, pitch-black caves.

See the wine through the glass While the Salinas Valley is known as the nation's salad bowl for its vast produce farms, large swaths of the inland Central Coast are fast gaining fame for their wineries. Best known is **Paso Robles**, where grapes are now the number-one crop and dozens of well-regarded wineries line Hwy 46. The Mediterranean climate means you can enjoy outdoor tastings (and meals) year-round. Less known, but fast-developing, **Edna Valley** is a rural idyll close to delightful San Luis Obispo known for its family-run vineyards producing pinot noirs and chardonnays.

CENTRAL COAST EXPERIENCES

❀ Tasting Carmel

Wine tasting in **Carmel Valley Village** is a must! There are many tasting rooms within walking distance of each other, most with tried-and-true regional varietals including pinot noir and chardonnay. For lesser-known grapes, try **Joyce Wine Company**, which makes albariño and gamay rouge in addition to its pinot and chard. As you walk down the promenade, at the end you will find **I Brand & Family Wines** making vermentino and cabernet franc.

In **Carmel-by-the-Sea**, I like the tasting rooms for **Wrath Wines** and **Kori Wines**. **Lepe Cellars** is also a fantastic place to taste lesser-known varietals grown in the region, including a sangiovese rosé and petit verdot.

■ Recommended by Sabrine Rodems, *winemaker at Scratch Wines @scratchwines*

27 Walking the
SHORELINE

NATURE | OCEAN | PARKS

One of California's best walks follows the shoreline of Monterey and Pacific Grove for 4 miles. Allow at least half a day for the delights, including views across the ocean, tide pools brimming with life and waves crashing onto battered rocks.

IV-OLGA/SHUTTERSTOCK ©

🗺 Trip Notes

Getting around The Monterey Bay Aquarium starting point is in the heart of the city and easily reached. It's a 2.7-mile walk back to there from Asilomar State Beach or you can get a bus for about half the distance from downtown Pacific Grove.

When to go This walk is good year-round.

Wear sturdy shoes Exploring the unmissable tide pools along the walk requires clambering about rugged and sometimes slippery rocks.

🚲 Cycling the Peninsula

There is probably no coastal cycling route in the world that is as beautiful as the coastline of the Monterey Peninsula. I love cycling along iconic **17-Mile Drive** in Pebble Beach. Other routes include **Scenic Drive** in Carmel-by-the-Sea, the seaside paths at **Fort Ord** and cycling to **Point Lobos**.

■ **By Jennifer Blevins,** founder, Mad Dogs & Englishmen Bike Shop, Carmel-by-the-Sea @maddogsbikeshop

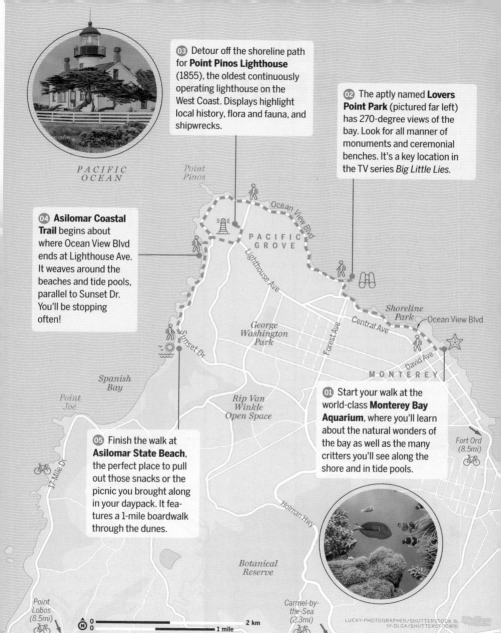

03 Detour off the shoreline path for **Point Pinos Lighthouse** (1855), the oldest continuously operating lighthouse on the West Coast. Displays highlight local history, flora and fauna, and shipwrecks.

02 The aptly named **Lovers Point Park** (pictured far left) has 270-degree views of the bay. Look for all manner of monuments and ceremonial benches. It's a key location in the TV series *Big Little Lies*.

04 **Asilomar Coastal Trail** begins about where Ocean View Blvd ends at Lighthouse Ave. It weaves around the beaches and tide pools, parallel to Sunset Dr. You'll be stopping often!

05 Finish the walk at **Asilomar State Beach**, the perfect place to pull out those snacks or the picnic you brought along in your daypack. It features a 1-mile boardwalk through the dunes.

01 Start your walk at the world-class **Monterey Bay Aquarium**, where you'll learn about the natural wonders of the bay as well as the many critters you'll see along the shore and in tide pools.

PACIFIC OCEAN

Point Pinos

Ocean View Blvd

PACIFIC GROVE

Lighthouse Ave

Shoreline Park

Central Ave

Ocean View Blvd

George Washington Park

Forest Ave

David Ave

MONTEREY

Sunset Dr

Spanish Bay

Point Joe

Rip Van Winkle Open Space

Fort Ord (8.5mi)

17-Mile Dr

Holman Hwy

Botanical Reserve

Point Lobos (8.5mi)

Carmel-by-the-Sea (2.3mi)

N 0 / 0   2 km / 1 mile

LUCKY-PHOTOGRAPHER/SHUTTERSTOCK ©, IV-OLGA/SHUTTERSTOCK ©

28 Hit the **BEACH**

SWIMMING | PLAYING | FUN

California is synonymous with beaches. The Central Coast has over 100 named beaches that vary from hidden coves perfect for quiet contemplation to long sweeps of sunny sand backed by arcades and amusements. No matter your tastes, mood or desire (surfing? lounging? walking? tide-pool exploring?), you'll find a beach to suit. And all are easily accessed via Hwy 1.

🗺️ How to

Getting around Beaches around Monterey Bay are mostly easily reachable by public transportation. Elsewhere you'll want your own wheels.

When to go Winter storms offer dramatic surf and cold winds. In summer the coast is often blanked by cold, thick fog, especially in the morning. Spring and fall are most reliable for warm, sunny days.

Go everywhere Open access to *all* California beaches is cherished by residents and enshrined in state law.

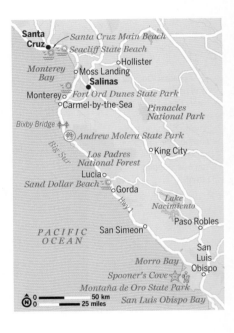

Santa Cruz Main Beach
The quintessential California beach, with volleyball courts, a pier out onto the bay, views of Steamers Lane surfing and all the carnival fun of the boardwalk with its historic **Giant Dipper** roller coaster.

Seacliff State Beach The northern start to the incredible sweep of sand that curves around the bay to Monterey. Offshore are the remains of a freighter built of concrete that served as a fishing pier.

Fort Ord Dunes State Park Right off Hwy 1, the eponymous hills of sand offer sublime escapes along the undeveloped beach. You'd never know the US army trained soldiers here from 1940 to 1976.

Andrew Molera State Park An often uncrowded Big Sur beach 8 miles south of Bixby Bridge. Pounding surf and great wildlife-watching are its main appeals. Check for condors overhead.

HARRI JÄRVELÄINEN PHOTOGRAPHY/GETTY IMAGES ©

☀ Fun at the Beach

Even with the Central Coast water temp hovering in the brisk 50s Fahrenheit (the modern wetsuit was invented here by Jack O'Neill in the 1950s), the beaches offer myriad activities.

Surfing In Santa Cruz, surfing has centered on famous Steamers Lane. Elsewhere, any place there are waves (most places!), you'll find surfers. Pismo Beach has a great spot right at the pier.

Shore diving and snorkeling Rocky shorelines and vast kelp forests make the ocean a natural for underwater exploration. Try the critter-rich coves at Point Lobos State Natural Reserve.

Seeing wildlife Conditions for bird-watching and animal-spotting on the beaches are idyllic thanks to California's strict environmental laws.

Sand Dollar Beach The parking lot is nicely removed from the longest beach in southern Big Sur. Part of **Los Padres National Forest**, high bluffs protect the beach from the blustery winds common to this wild strip of coast.

Montaña de Oro State Park Spring wildflowers gave this park its name, which means 'mountain of gold.' Trails along the bluffs are popular with cyclists and hikers. Some 15 miles west of San Luis Obispo, the park's wide-open beaches include **Spooner's Cove**, which has tide pools and a small visitor center with exhibits.

Above Surfers off Pismo Beach.

29 Body & Soul PLEASURES

SPAS | FESTIVALS | CULTURE

Self-indulgence is not a sin on the Central Coast, in fact for many it's a way of life. Spas, yoga studios and health centers are common. Many are artfully creative in their techniques and therapies. Festivals are another way to celebrate flavors of the palette and creative endeavors like art and music, providing a fun window into local culture.

🗺 How to

When to go Just a few of the festivals on the Central Coast are listed here; you can expect to find something someplace almost any weekend of the year. Spas and yoga studios are open year-round.

Costs Food and drink festivals tend to be free to browse but cost for tastings and treats. Cultural festivals usually sell tickets for performances, which can be expensive for top talent. Spa prices vary widely.

Far left Ledici performs at the Monterey Jazz Festival. **Left** Esalen Institute. **Bottom left** Artichoke Festoval, Castroville.

♨ Soaking Up the Vibe

In the final scene of *Mad Men*, Don Draper ends up finding his zen at a Big Sur retreat much like the **Esalen Institute**, the legendary new-agey holistic retreat on the cliffs above the ocean.

Its hot mineral springs are famous. Who can resist the idea of bubbling away your cares – most people are naked – while the surf crashes right below? The only catch: it is only open to the public from 1am to 3am (!).

We reserved our hard-to-get spots a couple of months in advance and stayed nearby at the Big Sur River Inn. It's worth the late-night hour.

■ Recom-mended by **John McGrath**, *marketing professor and former ad man* @mcgrath409

Savor a Spa

You are never far from a spa on the Central Coast. **Well Within Spa** (Santa Cruz) offers saunas and massage in a Japanese garden setting. **Om Studios** (Monterey) is renowned for its yoga.

Carmel is ground zero for luxe indulgence on the Monterey Peninsula. Try **Refuge**, with its silent plunge pools and massage therapies. Neighboring Pebble Beach is a playground of billionaires. The **Spa at Pebble Beach** offers sumptuous relaxation rooms and therapies. **Spa Alila** at the posh Ventana Big Sur resort specializes in Indonesian herbal therapies.

In Paso Robles, **River Oaks Hot Springs Spa** has its own source of heated mineral water and offers many treatments and soaks to visitors.

Festivals to Enjoy

Castroville's **Artichoke Festival** (June) celebrates more than just that huge spindly flower bud that grows in the fields. Look for Watsonville strawberries and regional wines as well.

An international event, the **Monterey Jazz Festival** (September) draws top talent that plays music that's a balm for devoted fans' souls. Paso Robles throws several wine festivals each year. The most important is simply called the **Wine Festival** (May, others are pegged to specific types of wine), with swaths of tastings that extend to local foods as well.

All things good that come from a large shell are celebrated at the (October). Expect plenty of chowders made fresh from clams harvested on the beach.

Listings

BEST OF THE REST

Guided Pleasures

Sanctuary Cruises

Operates whale-watching, dolphin-spotting and otter-loving cruises year-round aboard biodiesel-fueled boats out of Moss Landing (reservations are essential).

Central Coast Outdoors

Leads kayaking tours, guided hikes and cycling trips along the Central Coast and to Paso Robles and Edna Valley vineyards.

Out in Nature

Seymour Marine Discovery Center

The University of California, Santa Cruz operates this marine biology center on a stunning cliffside location. Exhibits include tidal touch pools, aquariums and the world's largest blue-whale skeleton. Watch for whales offshore.

Partington Cove

This breathtaking Big Sur spot is at the end of a steep, half-mile dirt hike across a cool bridge and down through an even cooler tunnel. The cove's water is unbelievably aqua.

Morro Rock

Chumash tribespeople are the only people legally allowed to climb this volcanic rock, now the protected nesting ground of peregrine falcons. Laze on a small beach.

History & Culture

Santa Cruz Surfing Museum

Right above the famous surf break at Steamers Lane, this tiny museum inside an old lighthouse is packed with memorabilia, including vintage redwood surfboards. Outside, see surfers catch waves.

Monterey State Historic Park

This 1847 adobe building has in-depth exhibits covering California's early Spanish, Mexican and American eras. The park encompasses several more buildings dating to the 18th and 19th centuries.

Mission San Carlos Borromeo de Carmelo

Carmel's strikingly beautiful mission is an oasis of solemnity with flowering gardens and a thick-walled basilica. The mission was established by Franciscan friar Junípero Serra in 1772.

Henry Miller Memorial Library

Novelist Henry Miller was a Big Sur denizen from 1944 to 1962. A beatnik memorial, alt-cultural venue and bookshop, this community gathering spot hosts regular events.

Mission San Juan Bautista

Founded in 1797, this mission claims the largest church among California's original 21 missions. Alfred Hitchcock shot part of *Vertigo* here, although the bell tower in the movie's climactic scenes was a special effect. The surrounding historic state park makes this an evocative stop.

National Steinbeck Center

Salinas' Nobel Prize–winning native son, John Steinbeck (1902–68), portrayed the troubled spirit of rural, working-class Americans in novels like *The Grapes of Wrath*. This fascinating museum is captivating.

Mission San Luis Obispo de Tolosa

Founded in 1772 and named for a 13th-century French saint, this lavishly preserved mission has bountiful gardens and a modest church with an unusual L-shape.

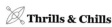 Thrills & Chills

Richard Schmidt Surf School

This award-winning surf and stand-up paddle-boarding (SUP) school in Santa Cruz can get you out and up on the frigid waters of Monterey Bay. Wetsuit and equipment included.

Kayak Connection

Kayaking and SUP are fantastic ways to see wildlife-rich Elkhorn Slough at Moss Landing. Reserve ahead for kayak or SUP rentals, guided tours and lessons.

Monterey Bay Kayaks

Rents kayaks and SUP equipment in Monterey, offers paddling lessons and leads guided tours of the bay.

Central Coast Kayaks

Paddle among sea otters and seals and through sea caves, grottoes, arches and kelp forests in the waters around Pismo Beach. All types of gear are available for rent.

Pours & Portions

Santa Cruz Farmers Market　　$

Organic produce, baked goods, arts and crafts, and food booths all give you an authentic taste of the local vibe at one of the region's best markets.

Bad Animal　　$$

A thoroughly modern menu – including contemporary interpretations of French flavors and natural and organic wines – complements this brilliant bookshop showcasing Santa Cruz' bohemian and counterculture roots.

Lupulo Craft Beer House　　$

Named after the Spanish word for hops, this is an essential downtown Santa Cruz destination for beer fans. The ever-changing tap list includes hard-to-get seasonal brews from local breweries.

Alvarado Street Brewery　　$

Innovative brews harnessing new hop strains, sour and barrel-aged beers regularly filling the taps, and superior bar food make this Monterey taproom unmissable. Great beer garden.

Cultura Comida y Bebida　　$$$

In a brick-lined courtyard, this elegant Carmel-by-the-Sea restaurant pairs art and candlelight with food inspired by Oaxacan flavors and a huge trove of mezcal.

Cayucos Sausage Company　　$

The carefully assembled grilled sausage sandwiches at this beloved spot in tiny seaside Cayucos are worth the wait.

El Charrito　　$

There's tough competition for Mexican fare in Salinas, but this spiffy storefront is a perennial fave. Tacos, burritos and tortas come with superb housemade salsas.

Les Petites Canailles　　$$$

Les Petites Canailles' excellent seasonal menus blend Central Coast ingredients with the best of Gallic and European culinary traditions. Warm and welcoming ambience in Paso Robles.

Libertine Brewing Company　　$

Wild and sour beers are the standout brews at this sprawling bar in San Luis Obispo.

Ember　　$$

Chef Brian Collins, who once cooked at Alice Waters' Chez Panisse, serves up a casual menu of local fare to legions of fans in Pismo Beach.

Tastes of the Valleys　　$$

Inside a Pismo Beach wine shop stacked floor to ceiling with hand-picked vintages from around California and beyond, you can sample more than 1000 wines poured by the glass.

 Scan to find more things to do in the Central Coast online

30 The Capital City: SACRAMENTO

HISTORY | FOOD | HEAT

█████ Long written off by Californians elsewhere as a place where their taxes are misspent, Sacramento does have plenty of politics as it's the capital of the world's fifth-largest economy. But it also has trendy districts, great museums, a fantastic food scene fed by Central Valley produce, and proximity to outdoor adventures in the Sierras.

FROZENSHUTTER/GETTY IMAGES ©

🗺 How to

Getting here Sacramento International Airport has flights from across California and major US hubs. Amtrak has frequent service to the Bay Area and long-distance trains to Chicago, Seattle and LA.

When to go Sacramento is a year-round destination, although summer is dry and very hot. The California State Fair in late July is a two-week festival of old-time fun.

Watch *Ladybird* (2017), the Oscar-nominated coming-of-age movie set in Sacramento.

SUNDRY PHOTOGRAPHY/SHUTTERSTOCK ©

KIT LEONG/GETTY IMAGES ©

Far left California State Capitol. **Left** Sutter's Fort State Historic Park. **Bottom left** California State Railroad Museum.

SIDE TRIP SACRAMENTO

In Town

The modern **California Museum** honors famous Californians. The Native American exhibit is a highlight, with the histories of more than 10 tribes – most were nearly wiped out during a genocide by settlers in the 18th and 19th centuries. Nearby, the **State Indian Museum** has excellent exhibits and handicrafts on display. Stroll within the walls of **Sutter's Fort State Historic Park**, where furnishings and a blacksmith shop are straight out of the 1850s.

The gleaming dome of **California State Capitol** is Sacramento's most recognizable structure. Paintings of governors Jerry Brown, Arnold Schwarzenegger, Ronald Reagan et al hang in the West Wing.

The historic river port of **Old Sacramento** near downtown has a large concentration of 19th-century buildings. It's touristy and the smell of fudge is everywhere. Nearby, the **California State Railroad Museum** has an incredible collection of vintage trains and exhibits showing how railroads built the state.

Nearby

The **Sacramento Delta** is a sprawling wetland of waterways and one-stoplight towns plucked out of the 1930s (don't miss **Locke**, founded by Chinese laborers). It encompasses a huge swath – from San Francisco Bay to Sacramento. If you have time, travel the iron bridges and levees of winding Hwy 160 instead of I-80.

In Coloma, the **Marshall Gold Discovery State Historic Park** is a fascinating collection of buildings in a riverside setting at the site of James Marshall's riot-inducing 1848 discovery.

⚔ Top Eats

Cafeteria 15L (15th St; cafeteria15l.com) is a Sacramento staple that serves new American comfort food in a modern setting. On the menu you'll find American classics but with a new and unexpected twist.

The ultratrendy **Beast + Bounty** (R St; eatbeastandbounty.com) restaurant is in the up-and-coming R District. It serves fresh fare (seafood, pizza, salads and pasta) inside a bright, airy venue.

Take a trip to Vietnam with a meal at **Saigon Alley Kitchen** (L St; saigonalley.com). You'll find both traditional Vietnamese cuisine and new takes on classics. The ambience and food are stylish. Sacramento has a large Vietnamese community.

■ Recommended by Gennifer Rose, *Sacramento food blogger* at genniferrose.com, @genniferrose_blog

31 Thrilling Lake
TAHOE

NATURE | BEAUTY | FUN

The shimmering blues and greens of Lake Tahoe make this high-altitude lake unforgettable. It's a region of boundless beauty and a place where fun – by day, by night, in winter, in summer – seems limitless. Skiing, hiking – even hedonism – are all here.

Above Pier, South Lake Tahoe.
Right Skiers, Kirkwood.

MICHAEL MARFELL/GETTY IMAGES ©

How to

Getting here The misleadingly named Reno-Tahoe International Airport is over 50 miles away in Reno, NV. Connecting buses take around 90 minutes for the trip to South Lake Tahoe. Buses run from the Bay Area and Sacramento.

When to go Winter sports and summer activities give the Tahoe region year-round appeal. Summer and winter weekends and holidays are busiest.

Driving around the lake This takes three hours without stops and covers 72 miles.

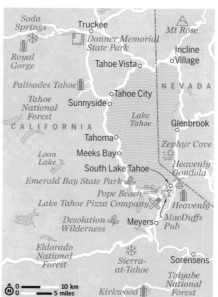

SIDE TRIP THRILLING LAKE TAHOE

Winter Resorts

Lake Tahoe has phenomenal skiing, with thousands of acres beckoning at more than a dozen resorts. Ski season generally runs November to April, although it can start as early as October and last until the last storm in May or even June.

Not only does it have the most acreage, **Heavenly** also has the longest run (5.5 miles), great tree-skiing and the biggest vertical drop around. **Kirkwood** is in a remote, high-elevation valley with great snow that it holds longer than most. Cute **Soda Springs** is a winner with kids, who can snow-tube, ride around in pint-size snowmobiles, or learn to ski and snowboard.

Previously known as Squaw Valley before a name change in 2021 to end racist and sexist associations, **Palisades Tahoe** played host

to the 1960 Olympic Winter Games and still ranks among the world's top ski resorts. The stunning setting amid granite peaks makes it a superb destination in any season.

North America's largest cross-country resort, **Royal Gorge**, has 85 miles of groomed track. **Sierra-at-Tahoe** is snowboarding central, with six raging terrain parks and a 17ft-high superpipe.

Nature

Sculpted by glaciers eons ago, the relatively compact **Desolation Wilderness** spreads south and west of Lake Tahoe and is the most popular backcountry area in the Sierra Nevada.

At the eastern end of Donner Lake, lovely **Donner Memorial State Park** occupies one of the sites where the doomed Donner Party got trapped during the fateful winter of 1846.

Sheer granite cliffs and a jagged shoreline hem in glacier-carved **Emerald Bay State Park**, a teardrop cove of virescent water.

Outdoor Fun

Heavenly Gondola Soar 2.4 miles up the mountain to 9123ft and absorb panoramic views of the entire Tahoe Basin.

 South Lake Tahoe Local Food Tips

Primos Italian Bistro offers a lovely night out indulging – but not oversplurging. Don't miss the carbonara pasta (yes, homemade) with South Lake Brewing Company's Pillow Line Pale Ale.

MacDuff's Pub is a must, with faves like shepherd's pie and fish-and-chips paired with Clockwork White ale. It warms you up inside and out, plus it's walking distance from **Sidellis**, my brewpub!

Lake Tahoe Pizza Company is a win for its salad bar alone, but the pizzas are scrumptious too, especially Barnyard Massacre or Southwestern Chicken. Bonus: the crusts are handmade. Wash them down with OB Amber beer.

 ■ **By Chris Sidell,** *brewmaster at Sidellis* @sidellislaketahoe

🗺 What's Where?

Northern Shore Quiet, less developed.

Stateline The Nevada border bisects the lake's southeast corner. Where the casinos are.

South Lake Tahoe The main (maybe over-)developed area.

Truckee Northwest of the lake, a mountain town on I-80 with an Amtrak stop.

Western Shore Idyllic parks, beaches and dense forests.

Boating and water sports In South Lake Tahoe several vendors rent powerboats, sailboats and Jet Skis, as well as kayaks, canoes and paddleboats.

Hiking Miles of summer hiking trails start from the top of the Heavenly Gondola, many with mesmerizing lake views. On the Nevada side, **Lam Watah Nature Trail** meanders for just over a mile each way across forest service land.

Beaches and swimming In South Lake Tahoe, the nicest strands are **Pope Beach**, **Kiva Beach** and **Baldwin Beach**. Elsewhere, beaches dot the shore. Always-busy **Zephyr Cove** has a sandy mile-long shoreline.

Mountain biking For experts, the classic, 6-mile-long **Mr Toad's Wild Ride**, with steep downhill sections and banked turns, is a blast.

Gambling

Stateline, NV, is home to four high-rise casino hotels that hug the California border. Watch for big-name entertainers. **Hard Rock Hotel & Casino** is rock and roll to the core. Music memorabilia is scattered across the casino and hotel. **Harrah's** is Stateline's top contender with a vibrant buzz 24/7. Snag a window table at one of the upper-floor restaurants.

Left Lake Tahoe Pizza Company.
Above top Desolation Wilderness.
Above Kiva Beach.

YOSEMITE & THE SIERRA NEVADA

MOUNTAINS | PARKS | WILDERNESS

Experience Yosemite and the Sierra Nevada online

YOSEMITE & THE SIERRA NEVADA
Trip Builder

Three national parks are just the start of the natural wonders that await in the Sierra Nevada. Surging rivers, eons-old forests, soaring peaks and countless trails await in summer, while world-class winter resorts are ready all winter.

NEVADA

Travel back in time in evocative gold-rush-era towns like **Columbia** (p158)
🚗 *2hrs from Sacramento*

Marvel at the nearly unfathomable beauty of **Yosemite National Park** (p146)
🚗 *3hrs from San Francisco*

Ski world-class slopes at the myriad runs of **Mammoth Mountain** (p156)
🚗 *5hrs from Los Angeles*

Find high alpine surprises in the arid eastern **Sierras** (p154)
🚗 *2hrs from Lake Tahoe*

Lose yourself in the wilderness in **Kings Canyon National Park** (p152)
🚗 *4hrs from San Francisco*

Gaze at towering, ancient trees in **Sequoia National Park** (p152)
🚗 *4¼hrs from San Francisco*

CALIFORNIA

Camanche Reservoir

Arnold

Murphys

Sonora

Sonora Junction

Bridgeport Reservoir

Mono Lake

Groveland

Lee Vining

El Portal

Yosemite Village

Midpines

Mariposa

Wawona

Fish Camp

Mammoth Lakes

Oakhurst

Eastman Lake

Sierra Nevada

Hensley Lake

Kings River

Fresno

Independence

Death Valley National Park

Mt Whitney

San Joaquin Valley

Three Rivers

Visalia

Sequoia National Park

MICHAEL VI/SHUTTERSTOCK ©
SEBASTIEN BUREL/SHUTTERSTOCK ©

N
0 ___ 50 km
0 ___ 25 miles

Practicalities

ARRIVING

Airports within a reasonable drive of Yosemite and the Sierras include those in Reno, NV, Sacramento and Fresno. Public transportation is limited; YARTS buses to Yosemite link with Amtrak and Greyhound.

FIND YOUR WAY

Download mapping info for navigation apps in advance, as there are many remote areas without cell service.

MONEY

Prices in the region tend to be moderate, although ski resorts can get costly quickly.

WHERE TO STAY

Town	Pro/Con
Sonora	Decent size, good selection, in the heart of Gold Country.
El Portal	Closest town to Yosemite; similar to nearby Fish Camp, Mariposa and Oakhurst.
Visalia	Low on charm, but large and close to Kings Canyon and Sequoia National Parks.

EATING & DRINKING

Hearty, basic fare is found throughout the Sierras. In the parks, the food service can veer toward the uninspired and institutional. At the base of the Sierras, towns and cities in the Central Valley have some of California's best Mexican food.

Best fresh bread
Erick Schat's Bakkery (p161; pictured top)

Must-try huckleberry ice cream
Legends Books, Antiques & Old Fashioned Soda Fountain (p161)

GETTING AROUND

Bus Other than Yosemite service, public transportation throughout the Sierras is sporadic at best.

Car The Sierras are best toured in your own vehicle, which gives you the freedom to explore. Note that many high alpine passes are closed for the winter, often for six months or more. This includes portions of Hwys 4, 108 and 120.

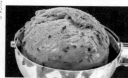

JAN–MAR
Many roads are closed, except for those serving ski resorts

APR–JUN
Waterfalls gush from the spring melt and high passes reopen

JUL–SEP
Summer is the time to be outdoors everywhere

OCT–DEC
Businesses and roads close with the first snows

32

Discovering
YOSEMITE

ACTIVITIES | NATURE | BEAUTY

▬▬▬ Granite magnificence, ribbons of waterfalls, emerald-green valleys, sky-filling vistas, giant sequoias reaching for the heavens – and these are just some of the treasures in America's premier national park. The sites would be fantastic movie special effects if they weren't so jaw-droppingly real.

Above Merced River.
Right View of Half Dome from Glacier Point.

🗺️ How to

Getting around The park service runs an extensive shuttle-bus service across the park, although it can be oversubscribed in summer. Bikes and hiking are good options in the valleys.

When to go In summer everything is open and packed; in winter Yosemite all but hibernates. Late spring and early fall can combine good weather with smaller crowds.

Road closures Check at quickmap.dot.ca.gov

Don't feed the bears.

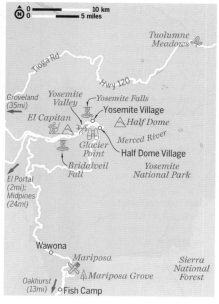

Don't Miss

Yosemite Valley The park's crown jewel is 7 miles long, bisected by the rippling Merced River and hemmed in by some of the most majestic chunks of granite anywhere on earth. Ribbons of water, including some of the highest waterfalls in the US, fall dramatically – **Bridalveil Fall** tumbles 620ft. The counterpoint to this sublime natural scene is bustling Yosemite Village, which does boast the **Yosemite Museum**, where you'll find exhibits on the Miwok and Paiute people who once lived here.

Glacier Point Right near the parking lot are views over the entire eastern Yosemite Valley, from **Yosemite Falls** to **Half Dome**. Half Dome looms practically at eye level.

Wawona About 27 miles south of Yosemite Valley, the park's historical center is home to the recently restored **Mariposa Grove** of over 500 giant sequoias.

Further Afield

Tioga Road The only road to traverse the park, Tioga Rd (Hwy 120) travels through 56 miles of superb high country at elevations ranging from 6200ft at Crane Flat to 9945ft at Tioga Pass. Beautiful views, and giant sequoias in **Tuolumne and Merced groves** await after many a bend in the road. Heavy snowfall keeps it closed from about November until May.

Summer Fun

Hiking Hikers of all abilities have over 800 miles of trails to choose from. Easy hikes include **Mirror Lake** (2 miles round trip) in the valley, the **McGurk Meadow** (1.6 miles round trip) trail on Glacier Point Rd, and the trails meandering beneath the sequoias of Wawona's **Mariposa Grove**. More advanced, the **Panorama Trail** (8.5 miles one way) descends to the valley with nonstop views, including Half Dome and Illilouette Fall.

🦌 Escaping the Crowds

From late spring to early fall, driving either of two mountain passes is a sure way to find epic vistas and avoid crowds. **Tioga Rd** (Hwy 120) takes you to the less traveled but much-adored **Tuolumne Meadows** in Yosemite. To the north, **Sonora Pass** (Hwy 108) crosses gorgeous valleys of quaking aspen trees.

To really escape the crowds, head to **Stanislaus National Forest** and the **Emigrant Wilderness**, which are brimming with alpine lakes against a backdrop of granite peaks. I have found myself on many occasions in solitude in this part of the Sierras, save for the sounds of birds and rushing water.

■ **By Maddie Maney,** *naturalist and photographer from Tuolumne County @maddie_maney*

(i) Reserving Yosemite

Reserve well in advance at recreation.gov.

Cars Vehicle access is by reservation only from late May to September. Visitors arriving by bus don't need a reservation.

Camping Securing a campsite for summer is like winning the lottery.

Adventure Permits are needed for wilderness access and climbing Half Dome.

Rock climbing Yosemite is one of the world's most revered places to climb. The obvious star among the many granite attractions is imposing **El Capitan**.

Cycling Mountain biking isn't allowed but you can ride the 12 miles of trails, which provide a quick escape from congestion in summer.

Swimming A summer dip in the bracing waters of **Merced River** is a tradition for many.

Yosemite's Gateway Cities

Fish Camp This tiny village has campgrounds, motels and popularly priced eateries near Yosemite's south entrance.

Oakhurst The antithesis of Yosemite's beauty. But the strip malls are the last chance to gather reasonably priced supplies before the park. Scads of modest motels and campgrounds.

Midpines and El Portal Located in the scenic Merced River Canyon, they have unpretentious but appealing places to stay.

Mariposa Interesting and charming Mariposa has oodles of chain motels and independents and a selection of decent restaurants.

Groveland A restored gold-rush-era town with many worthy places to stay. It's 22 miles from the Big Oak Flat entrance to Yosemite.

Left Emigrant Wilderness, Stanislaus National Forest. **Above top** Rock climber, El Capitan. **Above** Diving into the Merced River.

33 SUMMER
Adventures

BEAUTY | WILDERNESS | EXCITEMENT

An enormous number of people lose themselves in the magnificence of the Sierra Nevada every summer on hikes and backpacking trips that range from hour-long jaunts to multiweek treks. Trails fan out across the peaks and valleys, many transiting impossibly beautiful spots seemingly undiscovered by others. Or you can plunge through the wilderness on a pulse-pounding white-water-rafting adventure.

How to

Reserve ahead Many hikes require wilderness reservations. Routes may be covered by the National Park Service, US Forest Service, California State Parks and other agencies, most of which offer hiking info.

White-water costs Raft trips start at about $75 and climb to $200 and more, depending on the trip's length and difficulty.

Stay alert Forest fires can upend plans before and during your time in the wilderness.

Map showing: Pacific Crest Trailhead, Sonora Junction, NEVADA, Stanislaus River, Hoover Wilderness, Bridgeport, Mono Lake, Cherry Creek, Yosemite National Park, Lee Vining, Tuolumne River, Groveland, Yosemite Village, Inyo National Forest, Merced Canyon, Merced River, Wawona, Mammoth Lakes, Mariposa, Fish Camp, Eastman Lake, Ahwahnee Hills Regional Park, Hensley Lake, John Muir Trail, CALIFORNIA, Kings Canyon National Park, Fresno, Mt Whitney, Sequoia National Park. Scale: 0–50 km / 0–25 miles.

Backpacking and hiking The Sierra Nevada is laced with hiking trails, from the legendary **Pacific Crest Trail**, which traverses the peaks on its route from the Mexico border to British Columbia, to myriad unnamed trails that begin at roadside pullouts under Douglas firs. There are over 850 miles of maintained trails in Sequoia and Kings Canyon National Parks alone.

The 211-mile **John Muir Trail** links Yosemite Valley and Mt Whitney (14,505ft) via Sierra Nevada's high country. For many, this excursion is the hike of a lifetime.

Excellent hikes can be found in the **Ansel Adams**, **John Muir**, **Golden Trout** and **Hoover Wilderness** areas. **Inyo National Forest** is another prime spot. Get information at the Lone Pine, Bishop, Mammoth Lakes and Mono Basin ranger stations.

White-water rafting The Sierra Nevada's snowpack melts off the mountains in spring, producing enormous torrents of water that feed

RICHARD BIZICK/SHUTTERSTOCK ©

🥾 Lesser-Known Hikes

For solitude, the trick is to find lesser-known trails, like **Chilnualna Falls Trail** in Wawona. South of Yosemite, US Forest Service roads, like the **Sierra Vista Scenic Byway**, lead to alpine meadows and lakes. A drive to **Globe Rock** with a stop at Jones Store (fabulous burgers and pies) tops my summer fun list. Nearby, the trailhead to **Fresno Dome** is a real find. This moderate hike has epic views of the Sierra range. Wildflowers fill late winter and springtime hikes at **Hensley Lake**, **Eastman Lake** and **Ahwahnee Hills Regional Park** in Madera County. I love exploring the region.

■ **By Brooke Smith,** *Sierra Nevada hiking expert @babelbrooke*

numerous white-water rivers. Runs are at their peak from April to July, with some extending into September.

Starting near Yosemite National Park, the **Merced Canyon** run is Sierra Nevada's best one-day intermediate trip. Experienced paddlers prefer ferocious runs on the **Tuolumne River** ('the T'),

with over 40 rapids in 18 miles. In summer **Cherry Creek** is a legendary class V, experts-only run.

The **North Fork of the Stanislaus River** provides rafting trips for all, from novices to the more adventure-minded through Calaveras Big Trees State Park.

Above Waterfall on the John Muir Trail.

34 Driving Kings Canyon & SEQUOIA

GRANDEUR | PARKS | WILDERNESS

With a canyon deeper than the Grand Canyon, and trees older and larger than almost all others on earth, the twin national parks of Kings Canyon and Sequoia astound in equal measure. Less visited than Yosemite, they also provide ample opportunity to find solace in nature.

MARGARET.WIKTOR/SHUTTERSTOCK ©

🗺 Trip Notes

Getting here Kings Canyon Scenic Byway (Hwy 180) runs east from Fresno to the Big Stump Entrance of Kings Canyon. Hwy 198 runs from Visalia to Sequoia's Ash Mountain Entrance. In between is one of California's most beautiful drives.

Getting around Beat summer traffic: take the shuttle bus that runs from Visalia to the Giant Forest in Sequoia.

Check the roads Park websites list seasonal closures, which can last from November into May.

⛺ Sleeping in the Parks

Campgrounds usually have space, even in summer. You'll find them throughout the parks and just outside the borders. Find lodges in Grant Grove, Cedar Grove and along the Generals Hwy. Most are open seasonally. **Three Rivers**, outside Sequoia, is a pretty town with many places to stay.

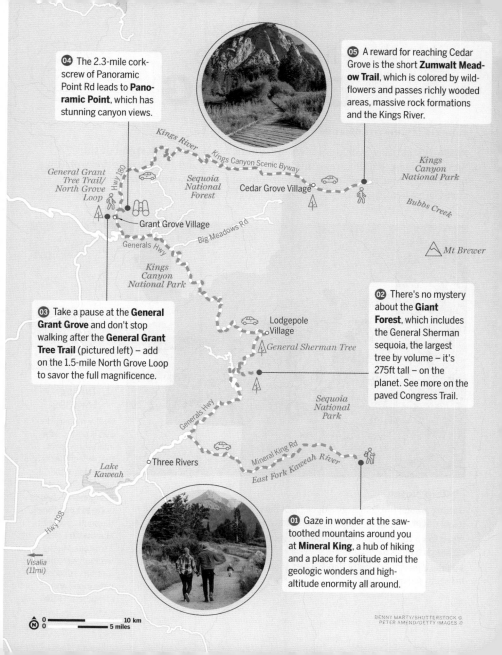

04 The 2.3-mile corkscrew of Panoramic Point Rd leads to **Panoramic Point**, which has stunning canyon views.

05 A reward for reaching Cedar Grove is the short **Zumwalt Meadow Trail**, which is colored by wildflowers and passes richly wooded areas, massive rock formations and the Kings River.

Kings River

Kings Canyon Scenic Byway

General Grant Tree Trail/ North Grove Loop

Hwy 180

Sequoia National Forest

Cedar Grove Village

Kings Canyon National Park

Bubbs Creek

Grant Grove Village

Big Meadows Rd

Generals Hwy

△ *Mt Brewer*

Kings Canyon National Park

03 Take a pause at the **General Grant Grove** and don't stop walking after the **General Grant Tree Trail** (pictured left) – add on the 1.5-mile North Grove Loop to savor the full magnificence.

Lodgepole Village

General Sherman Tree

02 There's no mystery about the **Giant Forest**, which includes the General Sherman sequoia, the largest tree by volume – it's 275ft tall – on the planet. See more on the paved Congress Trail.

Sequoia National Park

Generals Hwy

Lake Kaweah

Three Rivers

Mineral King Rd

East Fork Kaweah River

Hwy 198

Visalia (11mi)

01 Gaze in wonder at the sawtoothed mountains around you at **Mineral King**, a hub of hiking and a place for solitude amid the geologic wonders and high-altitude enormity all around.

0   10 km
0   5 miles

35 High Alpine **DRIVING**

SURPRISES | HISTORY | ADVENTURE

It's another world on Hwy 395 along the high alpine spine of the Sierra Nevada. Fertile areas mix with near desert and there's an otherworldly feel, from a lost ghost town to odd geologic wonders, from dark history to surprising beauty.

JOSON/GETTY IMAGES ©

🗺 Trip Notes

Getting around Hwy 395 is open throughout the year. However, Bodie and, to a lesser extent, other destinations in this itinerary are subject to winter closures.

When to go The eastern Sierra Nevada can get very hot in summer. Spring and fall are ideal times to visit.

Add the desert Death Valley National Park is only 20 miles from Lone Pine at the south end of this trip.

🚗 Driving Hwy 395

Gently winding Hwy 395 is dotted with interesting towns that reflect the flinty character of the high country. From **Bridgeport** in the north to **Lone Pine** in the south, and with **Mammoth Lakes** a true oasis in the middle, you're never far from a decent indie motel and characterful cafe.

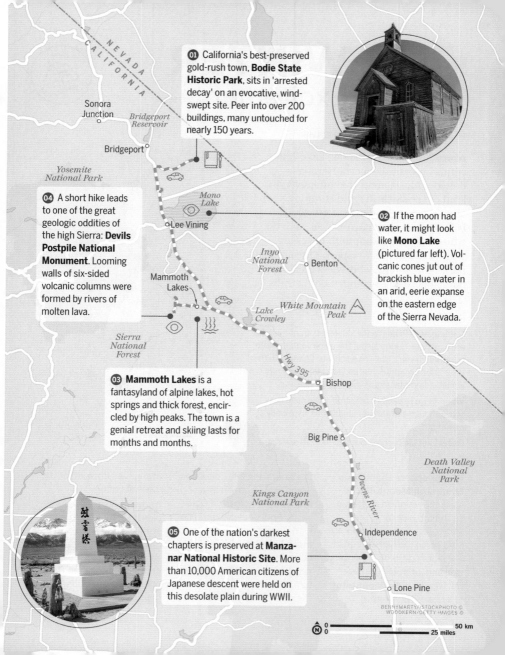

01 California's best-preserved gold-rush town, **Bodie State Historic Park**, sits in 'arrested decay' on an evocative, windswept site. Peer into over 200 buildings, many untouched for nearly 150 years.

04 A short hike leads to one of the great geologic oddities of the high Sierra: **Devils Postpile National Monument**. Looming walls of six-sided volcanic columns were formed by rivers of molten lava.

02 If the moon had water, it might look like **Mono Lake** (pictured far left). Volcanic cones jut out of brackish blue water in an arid, eerie expanse on the eastern edge of the Sierra Nevada.

03 **Mammoth Lakes** is a fantasyland of alpine lakes, hot springs and thick forest, encircled by high peaks. The town is a genial retreat and skiing lasts for months and months.

05 One of the nation's darkest chapters is preserved at **Manzanar National Historic Site**. More than 10,000 American citizens of Japanese descent were held on this desolate plain during WWII.

NEVADA
CALIFORNIA

Sonora Junction
Bridgeport Reservoir
Bridgeport
Yosemite National Park
Mono Lake
Lee Vining
Inyo National Forest
Benton
Mammoth Lakes
Lake Crowley
White Mountain Peak
Sierra National Forest
Hwy 395
Bishop
Big Pine
Death Valley National Park
Kings Canyon National Park
Owens River
Independence
Lone Pine

0 — 50 km
0 — 25 miles

36 WINTER
Excitement

THRILLS | SPORTS | MOUNTAINS

South of the famous Lake Tahoe winter resorts, the Sierra Nevada is dotted with ski areas that offer every kind of snowy thrill amid stunning alpine scenery, and often for prices below tonier alternatives. That said, the winter sports at Mammoth Lakes are world class in every respect. The national parks, forests and wilderness areas all offer superb cross-country skiing trails.

🗺 How to

Getting here Roads to the ski resorts from the west are kept open during all but the worst winter weather, although you'll likely need chains. Check with the resorts for any winter bus service. Mammoth has limited commuter flights and bus service.

When to go November to March is the main season, although extra snow extends this, especially at Mammoth.

Costs Lift tickets cost from $90 to $210 and more.

Winter sports champions Mammoth Mountain has stats that confirm its status as the top pick for winter sports lovers in California. Lifts serve the highest run in the state (11,053ft) and every skill and interest is catered for. Nearby **June Mountain** is a relaxed alternative for beginners and intermediates. Some years both enjoy a ski season that lasts from October to April or even later. The high alpine town of **Mammoth Lakes** has lodging, eating and nighttime fun for every taste. One caveat is you have to access the area from the east via Hwy 395, so it is a long haul from either the Bay Area or LA.

In the parks California's oldest ski resort is the **Badger Pass Ski Area**, some 22 miles from the valley floor in Yosemite. It's known for its gentle slopes. **Kings Canyon** offers extensive cross-country trails all winter long.

🏔 Sierra Snow Sports

Winter sports in the Sierras offer much: alpine scenery, slopes dusted with fresh powder and runs ranging from easy to black-diamond terror.

Skiers and snowboarders are well catered for, with most resorts having a variety of runs, including steep chutes, halfpipes, tree skiing, all manner of bowls, and wide, groomed runs suitable for every skill level.

There are usually areas devoted to freestyle as well as trails into the typically gorgeous forests for snowshoeing and cross-country skiing. Families, and those not ready to strap on skis, can frolic on hills for sledding and tubing. Some even offer toboggan and luge runs.

Delightful discoveries

Between Tahoe and Yosemite, there are two ski resorts often overlooked, except by savvy skiers who appreciate less crowded slopes and lower prices. On Hwy 4, which parallels the surging Stanislaus River, **Skyline Bear Valley Resort** has 56 runs for all skill levels and is beloved for its family-friendly policies. The next major road south, Hwy 108, reaches **Dodge Ridge Ski Resort**, which has 67 runs, many for advanced skills. It's family-run and unpretentious in every respect.

Above Skier, Mammoth Mountain.

37 GOLD-RUSH
Towns & Villages

HISTORY | WINE | GOLD

Every road into the Sierra Nevada starts in the foothills, the amber-hued rolling lands where the modern state of California got its start in the lawless goldfields of the 1840s. Today towns here offer a genteel look back into the state's controversial heritage. Restored buildings set an evocative mood where you can enjoy modern pleasures and outdoor recreation.

How to

Getting here Hwy 49 runs south through the foothills from the northern Sierras all the way to Oakhurst. Every road into the mountains north of here crosses this scenic highway.

When to go Gold Country and foothills towns are year-round destinations. Look for July 4 celebrations, wine festivals pegged to fall harvests and other special events.

Try your luck Many towns and parks offer hands-on gold panning. Good luck!

Sutter Creek A perfect Gold Country town with raised arcade sidewalks and high-balconied buildings with false fronts that are excellent examples of California's 19th-century architecture.

Volcano This old village is home to **Indian Grinding Rock State Historic Park**.

The park honors the Miwok, who were enslaved and decimated in the gold-rush era.

Angels Camp Memphis has Elvis and this town has Mark Twain. His *The Celebrated Jumping Frog of Calaveras County* was set here. Twain impersonators prowl Main St; the **Jumping Frog Jubilee** is

held the third weekend in May.

Murphys A highlight of the south end of Gold Country, refined Main St has wine-tasting rooms, boutiques, galleries and good strolling.

Columbia Home to **Columbia State Historic Park**, which blurs the lines between present and past with a

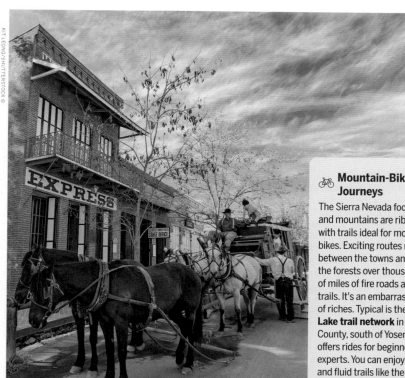

KIT LEONG/SHUTTERSTOCK ©

🚲 Mountain-Bike Journeys

The Sierra Nevada foothills and mountains are ribboned with trails ideal for mountain bikes. Exciting routes run between the towns and in the forests over thousands of miles of fire roads and trails. It's an embarrassment of riches. Typical is the **Bass Lake trail network** in Madera County, south of Yosemite. It offers rides for beginners and experts. You can enjoy fast and fluid trails like the **007 First Trail** or very technical double-black-diamond trails such as **Willow Creek**. Riders interested in longer epic rides will enjoy **Blind Squirrel**, which goes to the top of a massive granite dome.

■ **Recommended by Mike Broderick,** *owner of Pedal Forward Bikes & Adventure in Oakhurst* @pedalforwardbikes

carefully preserved gold-rush town at the center of a modern community. As much as $150 million in gold was found here.

Sonora and Jamestown Racial unrest with the arrival of white miners in 1848 drove the Mexican settlers out and their European usurpers got rich on the Big Bonanza Mine, which yielded 12 tons of gold in two years. Today the highlight of these neighboring preserved towns is **Railtown 1897 State Historic Park**, which re-creates 19th-century choo-choos in a setting popular with Hollywood productions. Yosemite is 45 miles east.

Above Columbia State Historic Park.

Listings

BEST OF THE REST

 Out in the Wild

Calaveras Big Trees State Park

Giant sequoias are distributed in two large groves, one easily seen on the North Grove Trail, a 1.5-mile self-guided loop, near the park entrance. It's near Arnold on Hwy 4.

Redwood Canyon

More than 15,000 giant sequoias cluster here, making it one of the world's largest groves of these trees. It's in an almost-forgotten corner of Kings Canyon National Park.

Convict Lake

One of the Mammoth Lakes area's prettiest lakes has emerald water embraced by massive peaks. A hike along the gentle trail skirting the shore, through aspen and cottonwood trees, is lovely.

Stanislaus National Forest

This vast swath of the Sierra Nevada comprises almost 900,000 acres north and west of Yosemite. It's a wonderland of hiking and wilderness adventure. Highways 4 and 108 traverse the forest.

Ancient Bristlecone Pine Forest

Northeast of Big Pine and Hwy 395, these gnarled, otherworldly-looking trees thrive above 10,000ft on the slopes of the inhospitable White Mountains. The oldest tree is more than 4700 years old.

Mt Whitney

Summiting this 14,505ft-tall peak is an obsession for many. The main Mt Whitney Trail (the easiest and busiest one) climbs about 6000ft over 11 miles. It's a superstrenuous, really, really long walk.

Panum Crater

Rising above the southern shore of Mono Lake, this crater is the youngest (about 650 years old), smallest and most accessible of the string of craters scattered south toward Mammoth Mountain.

History & Culture

California State Mining & Mineral Museum

Rock hounds in Mariposa thrill to the 13lb 'Fricot Nugget' – the largest gold specimen from the gold-rush era – and other gems and machinery here. Don't miss the glow-in-the-dark minerals.

Laws Railroad Museum & Historic Site

This railroad and Old West museum in Bishop re-creates the village of Laws, an important stop for the train that ran across the Owens Valley for nearly 80 years.

Eastern California Museum

This museum in Independence contains a huge collection of Paiute and Shoshone baskets, as well as historic photographs of primitively equipped local rock climbers scaling Sierra peaks, including Mt Whitney.

Museum of Western Film History

More than 400 movies, not to mention numerous commercials, have been shot in the Lone Pine area. See items from *Django Unchained*, *Tremors*, *Star Trek* and other films shot locally.

Hot Spring Soaks

Travertine Hot Spring

A bit southeast of Bridgeport, head here to watch a panoramic Sierra sunset from three small but entirely natural hot pools set amid impressive rock formations.

Buckeye Hot Spring

Near Twin Lakes, hot water trickles down into several pools by Buckeye Creek, which is handy for taking a dip. One pool is partially in a small cave. Clothing optional.

Inn at Benton Hot Springs

This small, historic resort in a 150-year-old former silver-mining town nestled in the White Mountains offers dips to day-trippers. It's reached by scenic and undulating roads from the Bishop area.

 Thrills & Chills

June Lake Loop

Under the shadow of massive Carson Peak (10,909ft), this stunning 16-mile drive (Hwy 158) meanders through a horseshoe canyon, past the relaxed resort town of June Lake and four sparkling lakes.

Mammoth Mountain Bike Park

Come summer, Mammoth Mountain winter resort morphs into the massive Mammoth Mountain Bike Park, with more than 80 miles of well-kept single-track trails.

 Guided Pleasures

McGee Creek Pack Station

Veteran owners offer multiday backcountry packing trips and hour-long horseback rides on nearby trails. A great way to explore the Mammoth Lakes area.

Yosemite Mountaineering School

This school in Curry Village offers two-day Learn to Backpack trips for novices, and all-inclusive three- and four-day guided backpacking trips. It also rents gear.

 Pours & Portions

Legends Books, Antiques & Old Fashioned Soda Fountain $

Sip sarsaparilla and share a scoop of huckleberry ice cream at a 26ft-long mahogany bar that's been here in Sonora since 1850. Browse antiques and books downstairs.

Iron Door Grill & Saloon $$

Claiming to be the oldest bar in the state (established in 1852), this Groveland legend is an atmospheric place, with a giant bar, mounted animal heads and classic bar chow.

Evergreen Lodge $$

Enjoy big and delicious breakfasts plus good burgers and other casual fare at one of Yosemite's better choices. The homey wooden tavern has a fine wine and beer list.

Ahwahnee Dining Room $$$

This restaurant at the Ahwahnee lodge in Yosemite Valley has a formal ambience and features sumptuous decor, a soaring beamed ceiling and palatial chandeliers. There's a dress code at dinner, but it's casual at other times. Book ahead, especially for Sunday brunch. Great bar.

Narrow Gauge Inn $$$

Excellent food and knockout views make this Oakhurst favorite one of the best options in the Yosemite region. The menu changes each season. The old-fashioned lodge-like atmosphere is casual. Lovely views.

Erick Schat's Bakkery $

A deservedly hyped tourist hub in Bishop with racks of fresh bread and other goodies, Schat's has been making baked goods since 1938. The crispy cookies and bear claws are addictive.

 Scan to find more things to do in Yosemite and the Sierra Nevada online

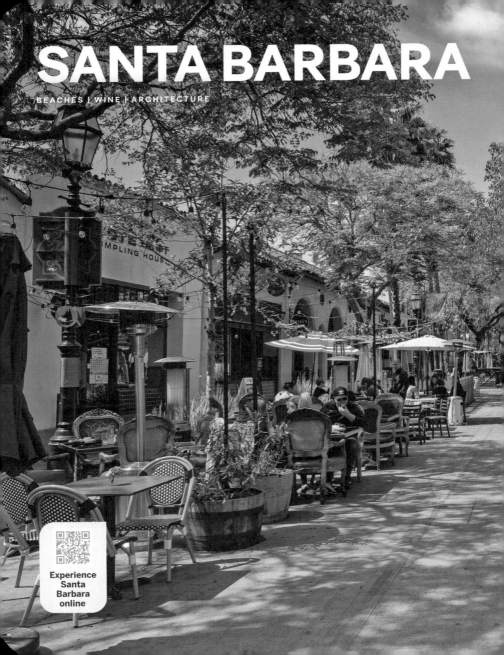

SANTA BARBARA

BEACHES | WINE | ARCHITECTURE

Experience Santa Barbara online

Los Alamos

San Rafael Wilderness

Taste small-production wines in bucolic **Santa Barbara Wine Country** (p172)
🚗 *1hr from Santa Barbara*

Picnic at the foot of pretty **Old Mission Santa Barbara** (p171)
🚗 *1½hrs from Los Angeles*

Los Olivos

Buellton

Santa Ynez

Solvang

Lake Cachuma

Walk around and taste at **Funk Zone** wineries and breweries (p166)
🚗 *1½hrs from Los Angeles*

Goleta

Santa Barbara

Bike or stand-up paddleboard along beachfront **Cabrillo Blvd** (p167)
🚗 *1½hrs from Los Angeles*

Santa Barbara Channel

Prince Island

Channel Islands National Park

San Miguel Passage

San Miguel Island

Cruz Channel

Santa Rosa Island

Santa Cruz Island

Look for whale spouts and island foxes at **Santa Cruz Island** (p169)
🚗 🚢 *2hrs from Santa Barbara*

SANTA BARBARA
Trip Builder

The American Riviera is more than just a pretty face – she has her earthy side and cultural depth, too. Beaches, coastal mountains and Channel Islands invite active recreation, while Wine Country and rich agriculture culminate in sublime sips and bites.

PACIFIC OCEAN

N
0 ___ 20 km
0 ___ 10 miles

Practicalities

ARRIVING

Los Angeles International Airport (LAX) is about 96 miles south of Santa Barbara and regional Santa Barbara Airport is 10 miles west of downtown.

FIND YOUR WAY

Downtown Santa Barbara is laid out in a grid system. Be aware of the many one-way streets.

MONEY

Accommodation in Santa Barbara can be pricey, especially on weekends and holidays. Goleta and Carpinteria are often cheaper.

WHERE TO STAY

Place	Pro/Con
Santa Barbara	Convenient base. Can be expensive, especially on weekends and holidays.
Los Alamos	Directly off Hwy 101. Tiny, and a bit isolated.
Solvang	Central to Wine Country. Can feel touristy and crowded.
Ventura	Launching point for Channel Islands National Park. Far from Wine Country.

EATING & DRINKING

With all the county's agricultural richness, Pacific Ocean bounty and plenty of homegrown wine, many of Santa Barbara's restaurants emphasize freshness, sustainability and local sourcing. You could also spend your entire stay sampling amazing tacos.

Best one-stop food stop
Santa Barbara Public Market (p176; dish pictured top)

Must-try uni (sea urchin)
Santa Barbara Fish Market (p176; pictured bottom)

GETTING AROUND

Car You'll need a car to access almost everywhere in the greater Santa Barbara region.

Bicycle and walking The best ways to explore on your smaller-scale adventures.

Boat Departing from Ventura Harbor, boats shuttle passengers from the mainland to several Channel Islands.

MAR-MAY
Variable weather; fewer crowds and more wildflowers

JUN-AUG
Busiest season, with Solstice and Old Spanish Days festivals

SEP-NOV
Clear weather and fewer crowds; harvest bustle in Wine Country

DEC-FEB
Surf's up, tourism's down – cooler and slower-paced

38 Funk Zone &
BEACH

BEACH | BIKING | WINE

▬▬▬ Balance out your day with a little sweat session along palm-lined Cabrillo Blvd before dipping into Santa Barbara's urban wine trail. Choose your own adventure, from stand-up paddleboarding the harbor to biking the beachfront path or walking the beach. Stop for a seafood lunch before roaming in and out of the breweries, tasting rooms and eateries of the Funk Zone.

JENNIFER WRIGHT/ALAMY STOCK PHOTO ©

🖾 How to

Getting around Spend a day walking, biking and paddling around this easily navigable slice of beachfront SB.

When to go Summer in coastal Santa Barbara can be crowded, and foggy until mid-afternoon.

The Mediterranean climate means temperate weather year-round. Fall warms up and has fewer crowds.

Day drinking Wine-tasting in the Funk Zone is a daytime sport; most tasting rooms close in the early evening.

L PAUL MANN/SHUTTERSTOCK ©

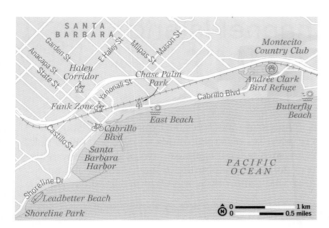

Top left Cabrillo Blvd. **Bottom left** Andrée Clark Bird Refuge.

Cruise Cabrillo Boulevard Enjoy 4.5 miles of Santa Barbara's coastline from local favorite **Butterfly Beach** to **Shoreline Park** on the Mesa, cruising on a bike (or multiperson surrey) or on foot along **Cabrillo Blvd**. Toward the eastern end, play a pickup game of beach volleyball at **East Beach** or look for shorebirds and turtles at the **Andrée Clark Bird Refuge**. Chill out on the grass or shred the small skate park of **Chase Palm Park**, then head west up the short uphill to Shoreline Park for a yoga session and watch the surfers below at **Leadbetter Beach**.

Get on the water See a wide-angle view of the city and foothills from the water, paddling the harbor on a kayak or stand-up paddleboard, looking for seals and pelicans hauled out on the buoys, and the occasional dolphin, ray or shark below. Or take a surf lesson at **Leadbetter Beach**, where the slow-rolling waves are great for beginners.

Funk it up Across Cabrillo Blvd, Anacapa St is your entry point to the heart of Santa Barbara's urban wine offering, the **Funk Zone**. Here you'll find locally produced wine and beer, some of Santa Barbara's best dining, vintage and antique spots, plus art galleries, murals and surf shops all distilled in just a few square blocks. After your active morning, pace yourself but enjoy drinking it up.

Beyond the Zone

For a more chill wine-tasting experience, it's worth roaming beyond the Funk Zone to seek some respite from its buzzy but sometimes overstimulating energy.

The industrial **Haley Corridor** has a smattering of excellent tasting rooms and breweries, and the inviting Spanish Colonial Revival passageways of **El Paseo** lead to several well-regarded restaurants and tasting rooms.

Back on the beach side of Cabrillo Blvd, **Stearns Wharf** has a tasting room, as well as plenty of seafood joints and the hands-on **Santa Barbara Museum of Natural History Sea Center** (sbnature.org), where you can check out intertidal-zone and marine sea life up close.

39 Channel Island **JAUNT**

WILDLIFE | HIKING | KAYAKING

The Channel Islands define Santa Barbara's horizon, but surprisingly there are many locals who've never ventured out to this seemingly faraway but accessible national park. The boat ride itself is almost always a wildlife-watching experience, with superpods of dolphins (numbering in the hundreds) not an unusual sight. This is magical, wild California in a rewarding island day trip.

CAVAN IMAGES/ALAMY STOCK PHOTO ©

🗺 **How to**

Getting here Island Packers (islandpackers. com) ferries passengers to the islands from Ventura Harbor, 30 miles south of Santa Barbara.

When to go Summer is busy season. Spring has fewer crowds and more wildflowers. Fall brings warmer weather and water temperatures. Winter has the fewest visitors and magnificent whale-watching opportunities.

What to wear Swell and chop on the channel can occur any day, and island weather is fickle. Layers are essential, especially a waterproof shell.

ILDIKO HORVATH/SHUTTERSTOCK ©

Far left Kayaker off Channel Islands.
Left Common dolphins. **Bottom left**
California brown pelican.

Island Wildlife

With one-third of the world's cetacean species found in the **Santa Barbara Channel**, your chances of spotting marine mammals are high. Frequent sightings include pods of common and Risso's dolphins, while majestic gray whiles migrate through from late November to late April.

Once you've landed, keep an eye out for petite (house-cat-sized!) island foxes. With no natural predators, they can often be seen trotting along established trails during the day, unfussed by your presence. Also look for seals and sea lions, bald eagles and soaring lines of pelicans.

Adventures Onshore & Off

Kayak through the intriguing sea caves and offshore arches of Santa Cruz Island, or go snorkeling to find anemones, sea stars and bright-orange garibaldi (California's state marine fish). **Santa Barbara Adventure Company** (sbadventureco.com) organizes gear rentals and guided kayaking trips. Hiking trails pass through coastal grasslands and along high bluffs, with dramatic views of neighboring islands.

Post-Trip Happy Hour

On your way back to Santa Barbara, detour into beachside Carpinteria to the industrial strip housing a trio of tiny fermentation operations – the **Apiary** (drinkapiary.com), **brewLAB** (brewlabcraft.com) and **Rincon Mountain Winery** (rinconmtn.com). Find small-batch beer, mead, cider, kombucha and wine made with locally sourced raw ingredients.

 Day Trip Tip

Taking a kayak tour is one of the most memorable things to do at Santa Cruz Island. It's a really spectacular way to see the outer edge of the island, which most people don't get to see. This also gives you just enough time to squeeze in a hike, like the **Cavern Point Loop**. It's short, about a 2-mile hike that's rated as a moderate trail and is pretty accessible for most people. It's usually possible to take a guided hike with either a volunteer naturalist or park ranger, to learn a little more about the uniqueness of this delicate island ecosystem.

 ■ **Recommended by Juliana Perez,** *ranger at Channel Islands National Park @channelislandsnps*

40 DOWNTOWN
Architecture

ARCHITECTURE | WALKING | FOOD

While away an afternoon studying Santa Barbara's history and sampling contemporary eateries. Explore the original adobe Presidio built by Spanish colonizers, check out modern, offbeat architectural concoctions and admire the queen of the California missions. End at sunset hour with a picnic among locals.

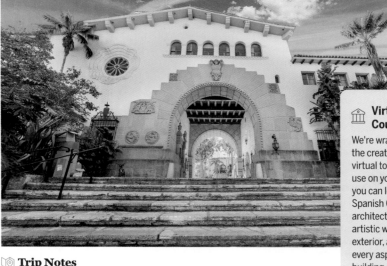

GABRIELLE MALTINTI/ SHUTTERSTOCK ©

Virtual Courthouse

We're wrapping up the creation of a virtual tour you can use on your phone – you can learn about Spanish Colonial architecture, the artistic work on the exterior, asymmetry, every aspect of the building. It'll give you details about everything you're viewing.

■ By Rodney Baker, *Chair of Courthouse Conservation Projects*

🗺 Trip Notes

Slow your stroll Downtown Santa Barbara is awash in beautiful architecture, street art and sidewalk pianos; take your time and gawk, nibble and sip along the way.

Caffeinate Hit up local roasters **Dune** or **Handlebar** to rev up your walk.

Picnic treats Pop into **Cheese Shop** (cheeseshopsb.com) or **Public Market** (sbpublicmarket.com) to pick up snacks for the Mission lawn or a stop at Alice Keck Park Memorial Garden.

05 Peek into the serene museum and cemetery of the beautiful **Old Mission Santa Barbara**. Across the street lies the Mission rose garden and its inviting lawn.

Sheffield Reservoir

Mission Park

Alice Keck Park Memorial Garden

04 The **Santa Barbara County Courthouse** (pictured far left) is a Spanish Colonial Revival–style stunner, with sunken gardens, a fountain, a clock tower, and gorgeous tile and mural interiors.

03 Check out the Spanish Colonial Revival–style **Lobero Theatre** (pictured above), and the **Carrillo Recreation Center**, redesigned by Julia Morgan after the magnitude-6.3 earthquake in 1925.

Alameda Park

Public Market

Handlebar Coffee

Cheese Shop

Dune

02 Wander through bougainvillea-splashed arcade **El Paseo** before continuing to **El Presidio de Santa Bárbara**, with 1782-era adobe and artifacts from the city's Spanish-colonial era and other surprising roots.

01 Paneled in paintings, the **Vera Cruz House** (private residence) looks like an architectural version of colorful Mexican oilcloth – an anomaly that's still very SB.

Laguna St · Mission St · Garden St · E Arrellaga St · State St · Anacapa St · E Anapamu St · Garden St · E Cañon Perdido St · E De La Guerra St · Santa Barbara St · E Cota St · E Haley St · W Carrillo St

0   1 km
0   0.5 miles

N

41 Vineyard to **BOTTLE**

WINERIES | FARMS | DRIVES

Playing the background (or starring?) role in the 2004 film *Sideways* and more recently named Wine Region of the Year in 2021 by *Wine Enthusiast,* Santa Barbara's laid-back Wine Country offers more than just viticultural pleasure.

📖 How to

Getting around If driving yourself, limit estate dates to one or two a day; alternatively, take a wine tour with a private driver.

Focus your tour Choose one area to explore at leisure rather than trying to cover too much of the entire sprawling region.

Town and country Consider exploring a walkable town one day and taking a meandering country drive the next.

The Big Picture

Santa Barbara Wine Country is comprised of seven American Viticultural Areas (AVAs), which is a good term to know when orienting yourself. The **Santa Barbara Vintners Association** (sbcountywines.com) has broken down some of these regions on its website, with maps and winery listings to make trip-planning easier.

Small-Town Tasting

Walking around a small Wine Country town is the best way to maximize your visits to multiple tasting rooms without having to drive. Pick from several superwalkable little towns, all of which have their own relaxed appeal.

Directly off of Hwy 101, the seven-block strip of tiny **Los Alamos** is lined with tasting rooms, revamped retro motels and excellent

🍽 Farm-to-Table Feasts

Besides grapes, this agricultural region grows a veritable rainbow of produce, creatively prepared at **Industrial Eats** (industrialeats.com), Buellton, and in low-key transcendent French form at Michelin-starred **Bell's** (bellsrestaurant.com), Los Alamos.

Above left Cyclists, Wine Country. **Above right** Lamb shawarma pizza, Industrial Eats, Buellton. **Left** Tasting room, Los Olivos (p174).

places to eat wood-fired flatbreads, tacos or French food.

The **Lompoc Wine Ghetto** occupies a complex of nondescript industrial spaces that belie the superb quality of the 20-plus small-production wineries housed within. Around here you may see more production spaces and process.

Come for the wine and stay for the *aeble-skivers* (round fritters). Tasting rooms in the Danish-heritage town of **Solvang** are scattered amid Danish bakeries, locally owned shops, ersatz windmills and a couple of tiny museums.

Unpretentiously elegant and laid-back, **Los Olivos** offers the best bang for your buck for highest concentration of stellar tasting rooms within a couple of blocks, in a charming country setting.

Wine Country Drives

Unless you already have wineries in mind, the area can seem a little overwhelming for all the

🍺 Cold Spring Tavern Detour

If you're driving yourself to or from Santa Barbara, consider taking **San Marcos Pass** (Hwy 154), with a pit stop at **Cold Spring Tavern** (coldspringtavern.com), a local mountain hideaway. Even when it's not featuring live music, the ivy-bedecked elven-huntsman tavern welcomes visitors with its cozy vibe, homey food and shaded outdoor space for sipping and socializing.

Originally a stagecoach stop founded in 1886, this spot is perfect on a Saturday or Sunday for the modern-day pleasure that is barbecued Central Coast tri-tip. Soak up some Santa Ynez mountain atmosphere and a local beer.

Left Cold Spring Tavern. **Below** Ballard Canyon, Santa Ynez Valley.

choice. But sticking with one AVA or wine trail narrows your options in a manageable way, and wherever you go, the entire region is shot through with gorgeous roads winding around vineyard-lined hills and valleys. Sub-AVAs within the Santa Ynez Valley, like **Ballard Canyon** or **Happy Canyon**, are also great places to focus your tasting adventures.

Foxen Canyon Rd and **Santa Rosa Rd** are hard to beat for knockout scenery, peppered with topnotch wineries offering sips in estate tasting rooms. You can also traverse the region from Santa Ynez to Lompoc along **Rte 246**, taking you through town and country with estate wineries along the way.

Play some slots at the Chumash casino, feed an ostrich and sample that pea soup you've read so much about. Exploring the valley backroads also yields opportunities to commune with miniature donkeys, pick apples and stroll through fragrant lavender fields.

Leave the Planning to a Pro

Wine tours are a fantastic option if you have no clue where to start. They run the gamut from straightforward guided drives to specialty tours like cycling from estate to estate or horseback riding to your tasting. Tour companies can customize a trip to your agenda or plan the entire itinerary for you.

FAR LEFT: FRANCISCO BLANCO/SHUTTERSTOCK ®, LEFT: CHUCK PLACE/ALAMY STOCK PHOTO ©

Listings

BEST OF THE REST

Local Flavor

La Super-Rica Taquería $

Some believe it's overhyped and under-whelming, but the handmade tortillas and small plates that shine do compensate. Whatever your order, add a rajas taco, which complements everything.

Santa Barbara Fish Market $$

This little market at the harbor is the place to pick up poke, seaweed salad, freshly shucked Santa Barbara uni and oysters for a picnic or harborside lunch.

Brophy Bros $$

Belly up to the inside bar or the outdoor bal-cony and take in harbor views and oysters on the half shell. This casual local favorite packs them in.

Santa Barbara Public Market $$

This food hall satisfies disparate cravings for ceviche, sushi, Thai noodles, falafel or artisanal ice cream, rounded out with wine and beer, naturally.

Bibi Ji $$

Organic produce and superfresh seafood go into the inventive modern Indian menu at this cozy State St spot. Food is paired spectacu-larly with carefully curated sustainable wines.

Barbareño $$$

The creative California cuisine here places an emphasis on fresh and local herbs, seasonal produce and locally harvested seafood and meat. Barbareño is an intimate neighborhood refuge away from State St traffic.

Beach, Please

Arroyo Burro Beach

Also known as Hendry's Beach, this is Santa Barbara's off-leash dog beach and a lovely one for beach walks. Find it at the bottom of the Mesa's western slope.

Summerland Beach

This beautiful, curved cove backed by sand-stone cliffs lies east of Santa Barbara. The top of the bluff is Lookout Park, with a small playground and picnic area.

El Capitán State Beach

Popular with campers, this farther-flung, wilder coastline about 20 miles west (north on Hwy 101) of Santa Barbara has plenty of shoreline to walk or chill out on the sand.

Outdoor Pursuits

Hiking and Biking the Front Country

Explore the foothills of the Santa Ynez Moun-tains by foot or mountain bike on a multi-tude of front-country trails. Get current trail information at Montecito Trails Foundation (montecitotrailsfoundation.info).

DBSOCAL/SHUTTERSTOCK ©

Arroyo Burro Beach.

Surfing

The greater Santa Barbara coastline has an array of breaks, some of which are perfectly suited for novice surfers. Several local surf schools offer private and group lessons.

Horseback riding

Take a trail ride or go horseback riding on the beach; Los Padres Outfitters (lospadresoutfitters.com) offers a tour that starts on a trail and ends up on the beach.

 Wine Tastings

Foxen $$

Among the impressive wineries along Foxen Canyon Rd in Santa Maria Valley, Foxen is one producing its wine via solar power. It has a main tasting room plus 'shack' down the road.

Demetria $$

One of the most stunning settings along Foxen Canyon Rd, this organically and biodynamically farmed vineyard could pass for a Tuscan estate. Tastings by appointment only.

Valley Project $$

This light-filled tasting room has chalk art above the bar illustrating the weather and geographical influences on Santa Barbara County grapes. A superb starting point for tasting in the Funk Zone.

 Breweries

Third Window Brewing $

Third Window brews interesting schwarzbiers, hazy IPAs and Belgian blondes, and churns out wagyu smashed burgers and rotating ranch-to-table specials from its tiny but mighty kitchen.

Topa Topa $

People-watch over Topa Topa's excellent beer in its mixed-use, sprawling space in the Funk Zone, with a wine-tasting room, taproom and bottle shop, and takeout eatery.

Santa Barbara Museum of Natural History.

Captain Fatty's $

In an out-of-the-way industrial park in Goleta, Captain Fatty's brews sours, lagers, pilsners and IPAs befitting the climate, with wood-fired pizza and food trucks complementing the beer.

🏛 **Cultural Stimulation**

Santa Barbara Museum of Natural History

Where else would you find a blue-whale skeleton named Chad? There's also a replica pygmy mammoth skeleton found on Santa Rosa Island, an excellent Chumash exhibit, a planetarium and outdoor spaces.

MOXI

With interactive, hands-on exhibits encouraging play and experimentation, the MOXI may be a children's museum but will intrigue and stimulate brains of all ages.

Arlington Theater

Beneath its stately tower and arcade entrance, attending a film screening or artistic performance is especially memorable in this theater's magical interior, posing as a courtyard under the night sky.

Scan to find more things to do in Santa Barbara online

LOS ANGELES

CITY LIFE | BEACHES | VIEWS

**Experience
Los Angeles
online**

HIDDEN
HILLS

Topanga Canyon Blvd

Ventura Fwy

WOODLAND
HILLS

TARZANA

Ventura Fwy

*Supulveda Basin
Recreation Area*

SAN
FERNANDO
VALLEY

ENCINO

CALABASAS

*Encino
Reservoir*

*Topanga
State Park*

BEL AIR

Take in the gorgeous
views (and stunning
art collection) at the
world-famous **Getty
Center** (p184)
🕐 *4hrs*

San Diego Fwy

WESTWOOD

*Santa Monica
Mountains National
Recreation Area*

Santa Monica Mountains

Sunset Blvd

BRENTWOOD

Santa Monica Blvd

Pacific Coast Hwy

PACIFIC
PALISADES

Palisades Beach Rd

*Santa Monica
Bay*

SANTA
MONICA

Stroll the **Venice
Beach boardwalk**
(p202) for un-
matched people-
watching
🕐 *2hrs–all day*

MAR
VISTA

VENICE

Culver Blvd

LOS ANGELES
Trip Builder

▬▬▬ Bordered by sandy beaches, winding canyons
and the Santa Monica and San Gabriel Mountains,
Los Angeles is a sprawling cityscape of distinct
neighborhoods, endless entertainment options and
year-round outdoor recreation.

MARINA
DEL REY

PLAYA
DEL REY

N Highland Ave

*Catalina Island
(35mi)*

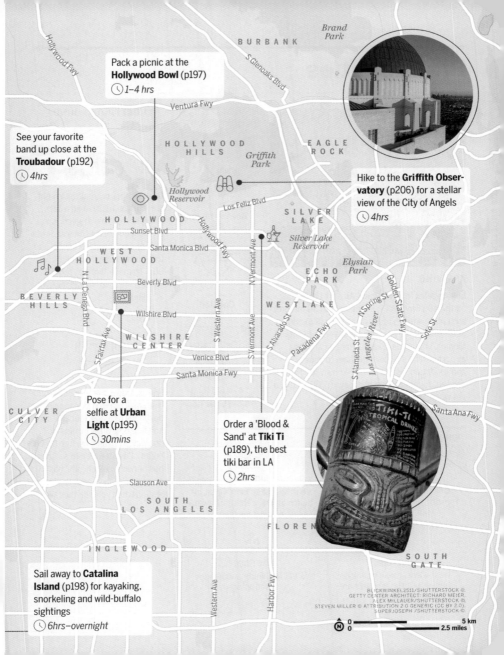

Pack a picnic at the **Hollywood Bowl** (p197)
🕐 1–4 hrs

See your favorite band up close at the **Troubadour** (p192)
🕐 4hrs

Hike to the **Griffith Observatory** (p206) for a stellar view of the City of Angels
🕐 4hrs

Pose for a selfie at **Urban Light** (p195)
🕐 30mins

Order a 'Blood & Sand' at **Tiki Ti** (p189), the best tiki bar in LA
🕐 2hrs

Sail away to **Catalina Island** (p198) for kayaking, snorkeling and wild-buffalo sightings
🕐 6hrs–overnight

BRAND PARK
BURBANK
S Glenoaks Blvd
Ventura Fwy
HOLLYWOOD HILLS
Griffith Park
EAGLE ROCK
Hollywood Reservoir
Los Feliz Blvd
SILVER LAKE
HOLLYWOOD
Sunset Blvd
Santa Monica Blvd
Silver Lake Reservoir
ECHO PARK
Elysian Park
WEST HOLLYWOOD
Beverly Blvd
N La Cienega Blvd
BEVERLY HILLS
Wilshire Blvd
WESTLAKE
S Vermont Ave
S Alvarado St
Pasadena Fwy
N Spring St
Golden State Fwy
Soto St
S Fairfax Ave
WILSHIRE CENTER
S Western Ave
Venice Blvd
Santa Monica Fwy
S Alameda St
Los Angeles River
Santa Ana Fwy
CULVER CITY
Slauson Ave
SOUTH LOS ANGELES
FLOREN
INGLEWOOD
Western Ave
Harbor Fwy
SOUTH GATE

🧭 N
0 5 km
0 2.5 miles

Practicalities

TROPICALPIXSINGAPORE/GETTY IMAGES ©

ARRIVING

Los Angeles International Airport (LAX) Just off the 405 Fwy, LAX is located about 30 minutes west of Downtown (depending on traffic) and near some of the best beaches (Venice, Santa Monica, Manhattan Beach). Rent a car at the airport or take a pricey rideshare to your accommodation. Use the lesser-known 105 Fwy to connect to other major highways (5, 605, 110) to get where you need to go a lot quicker.

HOW MUCH FOR A

Bowl of ramen $16

Cocktail $15

Parking spot $2–$5 per hour

GETTING AROUND

Driving Uber is great for a night out, but you really need a car to explore LA. Los Angeles is a combination of 88 cities and over 400 distinct neighborhoods, and they're not all well-connected. Stick to major highways (5, 10, 110, 101, 405) for distances over 30 minutes.

Trains, trams and buses LA public transit can work for specific destinations. Load your TAP card and hop on a bus or train ($1.75 one way, transfers are free for two hours). Pay attention to switching bus networks (each 'city' has its own line) and check the last station when you ride the rails.

WHEN TO GO

JAN-MAR
Cold snaps with occasional freezing temperatures at night, but fewer crowds

APR-JUN
Peak tourist season. Great for beach lovers, although beware of overcast days

JUL-SEP
Heat waves make walking a hassle, but the beaches are sublime

OCT-DEC
Great for hiking and holiday shopping

EATING & DRINKING

The ethnic food scene in LA is delicious, diverse, authentic and packed with mainstays steeped in history. From iconic doughnut shops to unbelievable Ethiopian and Sri Lankan cuisine, and LA's greasiest smash burgers and hot dogs, there's a lot to choose from. But the best food in LA is Mexican. Find your own favorite taco truck or sit-down spot and enjoy a dizzying array of tacos, tortas, tamales or more authentic birria or delicious – but Americanized – burritos (pictured top).

Best shredded beef tacos
Salazar, Atwater Village

Must-try cocktails
Tiki Ti (p189; pictured bottom)

CONNECT & FIND YOUR WAY

Wi-fi Nearly every bar and cafe has free wi-fi. Pay attention to cell service, especially on canyon hikes. You can lose reception up in the hills pretty easily.

Navigation Google Maps can be a little unreliable in LA traffic. Most people use Waze for real-time traffic info and rerouting options.

LA PUBLIC TRANSIT

Get a $2 TAP card and map out where you can take one of the two subway lines (B, D) or four light-rail lines (A, C, L, E).

WHERE TO STAY

Los Angeles is made up of over 88 cities and 400 distinct neighborhoods. So there's a lot to choose from to customize your visit.

Neighborhood	Pro/Con
Atwater Village	A quieter, budget-friendly alternative to Silver Lake steps from Griffith Park. Far from the beaches.
Silver Lake	Hipster mecca with walkable dining, cafe and shopping options. Crowded and expensive.
Venice Beach	LA's funkiest beach with epic people-watching, but limited parking on crowded weekends.
Hollywood (West Side)	Great hikes and easy access to Hollywood Blvd. Congested streets and limited freeway access.
Old Town Pasadena	Perfect during the holidays, but a little far from the beaches and city sights.

MONEY

Everything in LA is expensive, but the parking is the worst. You can usually find free street parking – or a cheap metered spot – if you look for five minutes.

42 Getty Center **VIEWS**

ART | ARCHITECTURE | GARDENS

▬▬▬ Perched in the Santa Monica Mountains, this LA icon by architect Richard Meier houses centuries of European art, modern exhibitions and panoramic views that stretch from Downtown to the Pacific. The otherworldly grounds, gardens and architecture are so impressive they've literally served as the setting for Heaven in NBC's *The Good Place*. This is LA at its best. And it's free to visit.

ANTON_IVANOV/SHUTTERSTOCK ©

⌕ **How to**

Getting here The 761 Metro bus stops at the entrance. Parking is $20 ($15 after 3pm). The free tram from the parking structure to the museum runs every five to 10 minutes.

When to go Arrive after 3pm to avoid the crowds and catch the sunset from the South Promontory Cactus Garden.

Admission The museum is open 10am to 5:30pm Tuesdays to Sundays. Entry is free but you need a reservation to visit (tickets.getty.edu).

BARBARA KALBFLEISCH/SHUTTERSTOCK ©

LWWH/SHUTTERSTOCK ©

How to See the Getty

You can actually see most of the art in the Pavilion Galleries in a few hours. So take your time! Park in front of an illuminated manuscript, 10ft portrait or bronze bust and take it in as you meander to the real masterpiece – the panoramic view from the South Promontory Cactus Garden. Make sure to explore the upper floors and Changing Exhibitions housed in the Research Institute and Library.

It's all about the details The details are the best part of the Getty. Some of the marble stones in the buildings and court-yards even have fossils in them! Try to find 'Musical Group on a Balcony' serenading you from the ceiling.

Make a day of it The Getty is less of a museum and more of a campus that encourages you to relax, wander and take it all in at your own pace. Pose for pictures with the wraparound views and modern architecture, or relax on a bench in manicured gardens and expansive marble-lined courtyards. Give yourself enough time to get lost in the landscape.

Pack a picnic The restaurant on the Plaza level is open for upscale dining (with spectacular views!) from 11:30am to 2:30pm Tuesday to Saturday, and 11am to 3pm Sunday (res-ervations recommended). Or you can grab lighter fare at the cafe downstairs or one of the coffee carts. But the best way to experience the Getty is with your own picnic on the lawn over-looking the Central Garden. Pack some snacks and a blanket (you can get beer and wine from the cafe) for the ultimate LA afternoon.

Far left Getty Center exterior. **Left** Getty Center garden. **Bottom left** Picknickers on Getty Center lawn.

Take a Nap

The lawn near the sculpture garden is soft, dry and perfectly tilted for a quick nap. No, really. You can (and should) kick off your shoes and take a nap in the grass overlooking the Central Garden. There are plenty of shade trees next to the murmuring artificial river, or you can work on your tan on the sunny side of the lawn if that's your thing.

It's not unusual to see LA locals enjoying the afternoon with a sketchbook and a glass of wine on the grass. If you really want to escape, pop in some headphones and drift away on your blanket. No one will bother you.

Secrets in the Sprawl

HOW TO FIND HIDDEN GEMS AND FALL FOR LA

LA is a tough city to love. But it isn't just one city – it's hundreds of civic centers and unique neighborhoods stitched together. LA is a package deal. And that makes it an absolute bargain. Because the good stuff is hidden in the sprawl.

Your Favorite Neighborhood

You've heard of Hollywood and Beverly Hills. But what about places like Atwater Village, Belmont Shore, Little Ethiopia and Eagle Rock? Those are just a handful of the 400-plus neighborhoods that make up LA. And each one has its secret spots.

Find that literal hole-in-the-wall, walk-up food counter that's so good it sells out of food by 1pm. Poke your head into the cinder-block building with the neon sign with the missing letters. It's not out of business. The drinks are just so good that they don't need a sign to pack the place on a Tuesday night. Pull over to grab a quick bite at the rundown corner doughnut shop for the best glazed twists you've ever had (LA doughnuts are on another level). Or go diving for out-of-print classics in the carefully curated science-fiction section of the independent bookstore. Sit on the park bench with the perfect view of the skyline. LA is a bespoke buffet of options for every appetite. You just have to find your favorites.

Up in the Canyons

Over 650 miles of freeways hide the winding canyons, hilltop hikes, palisade views and sandy beaches that make this city great. Get lost in them. Lean into the winding roads in Coldwater Canyon. Get off the 101 and carve your way through the canyons to Malibu. Explore the sideways paths and brush-lined stairways for the best views and serendipitous glimpses of the 'real' LA.

Above left Atwater Village. **Above middle** Canyons in Los Angeles County. **Above right** South Los Angeles freeways.

Los Angeles is a city in the hills wedged between the rolling peaks and palisades of the Santa Monica Mountains National Recreation Area on the coast and the rugged Angeles and San Bernardino National Forests that wall-in the city streets on the north side of town with snowcapped peaks that stretch all the way to Joshua Tree. Explore the canyons and culverts to see parts of the city that even locals forget exist.

I Love LA

LA takes effort. It takes time. You can't just hop in a cab or a train and flit from place to place. You have to sit in traffic. You have to park (far away). The sidewalks are hot and the sun is strong – even in January. Winding streets merge with freeway numbers that swap ones and zeroes so fast – 10, 110, 1, 101 – it feels like driving on an actual information superhighway. But it's worth it. Because there really is no place like LA. And if you have the patience to follow brake lights and winding pavement up into the canyons, down to the beaches and past the glitz and glamor of the typical attractions, you can discover the city's secrets beneath the sprawl. And they might just make you fall in love with LA.

> LA is a bespoke buffet of options for every appetite. You just have to find your favorites.

🚗 How to Drive in LA

Driving in LA is all about managing expectations. You will hit bumper-to-bumper traffic at 1 o'clock in the afternoon. On a Saturday. Parking is always going to be a hassle. And if you spend enough time here, you'll measure even 'close' destinations in minutes, not miles.

You have to know when to use the freeways – and when to avoid them. And either way, you'll spend more time than you want behind the wheel. But if you embrace the chaos, crank up a great playlist and leave plenty of time to change lanes, you'll be just fine. And watch out: no one uses their blinkers here.

43 Hipster **CENTRAL**

EAT | DRINK | SHOP

▬▬▬ If you like iced lattes, ramen, farmers markets, boozy milkshakes and vintage clothing, 'Sunset Junction' in Silver Lake is the place to be. Located between Santa Monica Blvd and N Alvarado St, just north of Echo Park, this stretch of shops and restaurants on Sunset Blvd is the hipster epicenter of Los Angeles.

🔖 How to

Getting here Take the 2 or 4 bus line to Sunset Blvd or walk 10 minutes from the Vermont/Santa Monica Red Line Metro stop.

When to go Arrive early for brunch at Millie's, microgreens at the Silver Lake Farmers Market (Tuesday and Saturday) and weekend vintage-clothing shopping near N Alvarado St.

Top tip Order the 'Blood and Sand' at Tiki Ti for a drink that will 'bull' you over.

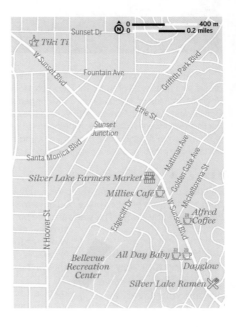

Community vibes Sunset Junction almost looks like a movie set of LA with the palm-tree-lined streets, chic crowded coffee shops, and people walking comically small dogs. You can even clearly see the Hollywood Sign if you're walking north. And yes, Sunset Junction is surprisingly walkable; one of the few neighborhoods in LA where it's fun to take a stroll. That's part of why Sunset Junction also feels like a neighborhood. People sign petitions. The **Silver Lake Farmers Market** is there every Tuesday and Saturday and there's a working community garden near the elementary school. Sunset Junction is also one of the best places in LA to grab a bite.

Hipster havens Millie's Cafe is the most popular brunch on Sunset (get there early if you want a sidewalk seat). Grab a vanilla iced latte

ELAINE SILVER/LONELY PLANET ©

⚓ Tiki Ti

Tiki Ti is one of the smallest – but best – bars in California. Founded by LA bartending legend Ray Buhen, this itty bitty tiki bar has been slinging classic tropical cocktails to die-hard fans since 1961, and it shows. Pufferfish lamps line the ceiling. Signed and faded dollar bills paper the walls. Mismatched porcelain mugs cover every shelf (unfortunately, the really fun mugs are reserved just for the regulars). Seating is limited (there are only 12 bar stools and a few tables), but this place is the real deal and well worth the wait on a busy weekend. For the authentic experience, try 'Ray's Mistake,' 'Uga Booga' or 'Blood and Sand' if you want your drink to come with some...audience participation.

Above Tiki Ti.

at **Alfred Coffee** across from the Micheltorena Stairs, or a gourmet artisanal brew at Dayglow down the street. **Silverlake Ramen** is the place for ramen in LA (try the Blaze if you like spice). But if that's not your speed (or it's too crowded) the ADB Biscuit Sandwich (with strawberry jam!) and Big Chicken Biscuit at nearby **All Day Baby** is a stellar way to start the day (breakfast from 9am to 3pm). If you're craving something sweet to beat the heat, **Creamo**'s pun-tastic menu features decadent milkshakes and sundaes and an over-the-top example of LA's unofficial food – a doughnut ice-cream sandwich.

LA
ICONS

01 The Broad
This 2015 architectural marvel (designed by Diller Scofidio + Renfro) is fast becoming the 'it' art gallery in LA.

02 Doughnut shops
There's a reason Randy's Doughnuts giant homage to breakfast food is so popular here. We love doughnuts.

03 Union Station chairs
The plush art deco chairs at Union Station beg to be sat in.

04 Sliced fruit
Keep $5 on you at all times for fresh pineapple, watermelon or mango to beat the heat.

05 Circus Liquor Clown
Like most of tinseltown, marketing is what matters.

06 Watts Tower
These 17 sculptures have been an inspiration for over 70 years.

07 Hollywood Bowl
This one-of-a-kind concert venue is the heart of Hollywood.

08 LA River
This stone canal carving through the city is lined with art deco bridges that look like forgotten Hollywood sets.

09 Santa Monica Palisades
The view from (and of!) these crumbling sandstone heights are pure SoCal.

10 Urban Lights
LA's newest public art icon. And an annoyingly perfect place for a selfie.

11 Freeway signs
You can't get anywhere without side-by-side freeway signs, even if you don't understand why they all look the same.

12 Dodger Dogs
Watching a game at Dodger Stadium with a 'Dodger Dog' hot dog is about as good as it gets.

13 Lifeguard towers
When the lifeguard towers fly the yellow flag with a black circle, it means surfers out, and swimmers in!

44 A Night at the TROUBADOUR

MUSIC | HISTORY | NIGHTLIFE

LA is packed with famous music venues, but the sheer number of legendary performers that have played the Troubadour set it apart. Not much has changed since the doors opened in 1957, and it's still the best place in LA to see intimate standing-room-only shows with acts that can sell out stadiums.

SHAWN FORNO ©

📷 How to

Getting here Take the 4 or 16 bus to Sunset Boulevard in West Hollywood. Metered street parking runs till midnight.

When to go The calendar (troubadour.com/calendar) typically books about 3 months in advance, and tickets sell out fast. If you see a show you love, book it ASAP!

Admission Tickets start around $25, but can go for over $100. However, the venue is so small that there are no bad 'seats.'

BARRY KING/ALAMY STOCK PHOTO ©

Far left and bottom left Troubadour exterior. **Left** Carole King and James Taylor at the Troubadour.

Rock & Roll History

Front row The unassuming exterior and vintage sign might throw you (it still proudly features the name of founder, Doug Weston), but once you set foot in the Troubadour you know that you're in an LA institution steeped in decades of music (and comedy) history. The sound system is epic, the vibe is 'intimate' (the venue only 'seats' 500 people) and the talent is always top tier. Discover your new favorite band or see your heroes play without having to stand on your tiptoes or watch them on a jumbotron.

Singer-songwriters Bob Dylan, The Eagles and hundreds of other legendary performers have graced this tiny stage. This is the club where Joni Mitchel, James Taylor, Neil Young, Billy Joel, The Pointer Sisters, Gordon Lightfoot and Elton John made their LA debuts.

Stand-up comedy And the Troubadour is about more than just great music. Lenny Bruce was arrested on this stage just months after it opened. Richard Pryor recorded his debut live album. Steve Martin even wooed crowds with his banjo. If the Troubadour is sold out, **Largo at the Coronet** is just a mile down the road (five-minute drive). It also has a great mix of stand-up and live music which means that you never know who's going to open for big names like Ben Folds and Fiona Apple. Grab a cocktail at the chic **Roger Room** speakeasy next door to really get you in the mood for a great show.

♫ LA's Best Music Venue

The Troubadour is hands down my favorite venue in LA. The history in the walls is just something you can feel when you walk in. Not much has changed about the venue since it opened in the late '50s and it ends up feeling like the perfect blend of rock-and-roll club meets warm, cozy folk vibes. The venue played a really central role in some of the early careers of singer-songwriters like James Taylor and Carole King, so it always leaves me feeling inspired every time I see a show there or play onstage. For an extra dose of classic Hollywood institutions, I love having dinner at DanTana's next door for an amazing bowl of pasta before or after a show.

■ **Recommended by Kate Voegele,** *singer/songwriter/ actress from TV show* One Tree Hill *@katevoegele*

45 Arts & Natural HISTORY

ART | CULTURE | TAR PITS

People say that LA doesn't have a lot of 'history.' Tell that to the woolly mammoths in the La Brea Tar Pits. Stroll LA's 'Museum Mile' on Wilshire to experience some of the best art, culture and history in the city at the Los Angeles County Museum of Art (LACMA), The Academy Museum of Motion Pictures and the now-iconic, Instagram-friendly art piece, *Urban Lights*.

📸 Trip Notes

Getting here Take the 16, 20 or 217 bus to Wilshire or Fairfax.

When to go The lawn at Hancock Park is perfect for a picnic lunch. Grab to-go food from Rosalind's in nearby Little Ethiopia (S Fairfax, five minutes away) for a great midday break.

Follow the footprints You don't have to go into the museum to experience the tar pits. Follow the footpath for a self-guided tour.

official state fossil!) collected from the nearby tar pits. The museum is closed Tuesdays, but the tar pits outside in Hancock Park are always open. Follow the footpath towards LACMA.

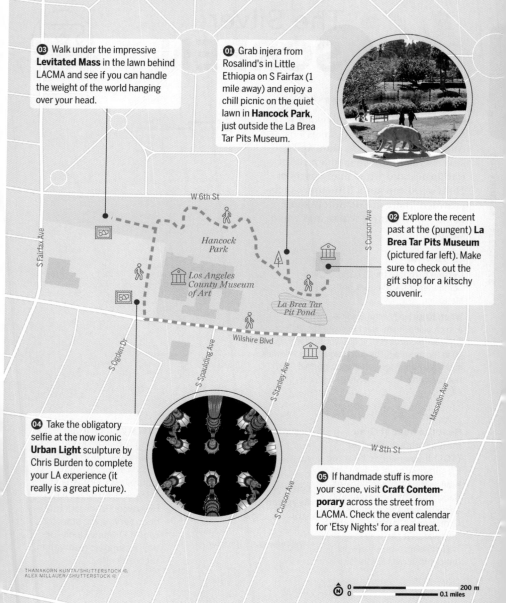

03 Walk under the impressive **Levitated Mass** in the lawn behind LACMA and see if you can handle the weight of the world hanging over your head.

01 Grab injera from Rosalind's in Little Ethiopia on S Fairfax (1 mile away) and enjoy a chill picnic on the quiet lawn in **Hancock Park**, just outside the La Brea Tar Pits Museum.

02 Explore the recent past at the (pungent) **La Brea Tar Pits Museum** (pictured far left). Make sure to check out the gift shop for a kitschy souvenir.

04 Take the obligatory selfie at the now iconic **Urban Light** sculpture by Chris Burden to complete your LA experience (it really is a great picture).

05 If handmade stuff is more your scene, visit **Craft Contemporary** across the street from LACMA. Check the event calendar for 'Etsy Nights' for a real treat.

W 6th St

S Fairfax Ave

S Curson Ave

Hancock Park

Los Angeles County Museum of Art

La Brea Tar Pit Pond

Wilshire Blvd

S Ogden Dr

S Spaulding Ave

S Stanley Ave

Masselin Ave

W 8th St

S Curson Ave

THANAKORN KUNTA/SHUTTERSTOCK ©
ALEX MILLAUER/SHUTTERSTOCK ©

N

0 — 200 m
0 — 0.1 miles

46 The Silver **SCREEN**

CINEMA | PARKS | LANDMARKS

▬▬▬ Like it or not, Hollywood is a defining part of what makes Los Angeles great. Studios, stars and the silver screen have shaped Southern California, and while many parts of Hollywood can get a little touristy and crowded, there are definitely some gems – if you know where and when to go.

🎟 How to

Getting here Take the 217, 222, Cityline Commuter or DASH buses, or the B (Red) Metro line.

When to go Hollywood Blvd can get hot. And crowded. If you want to scour the Walk of Fame for pictures with your favorite star's square, go in the morning. The sun kicks off the sidewalk in the afternoon for hotter-than-normal temperatures.

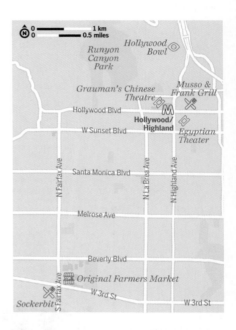

Beat the heat at Grauman's Chinese Theater (TCL) If you need to beat the LA summer heat, don't just hide in the shade looking at handprints in the cement. Grab tickets to a movie at Grauman's Chinese Theater and watch it the way it was meant to be seen – in air-conditioned splendor.

Grauman's Chinese Theater is not only a modern functioning movie theater, but one of the biggest IMAX screens in the world. The **Egyptian Theater** down the street is also great, especially if you crave that classic Hollywood art deco vibe.

Literary lunch If you're a Charles Bukowski fan, you should visit the leather-lined booths at his favorite stomping ground, the Musso & Frank Grill (p211). A rare Hollywood landmark that's been serving the stars for over 100 years. Open Tuesday to Sunday; reservation recommended.

FIIPHOTO/SHUTTERSTOCK ©

Picnic at the Hollywood Bowl

The iconic art deco bandshell at the Hollywood Bowl is one of the most picturesque and distinguished amphitheaters in the world. But most people don't know that it's also a city-run public park during the day.

Visit during the day and explore like a VIP with a backstage pass (the only rule is that you can't actually get on the stage). You might even catch a free rehearsal of the popular summer concerts. Bring a picnic and a bottle of wine to enjoy an insider look at one of LA's most iconic destinations.

Climb the nearby secret La Presa Stairways (East or West) for wraparound views of the Hollywood Hills and an up-close look at LA's best deco architecture complete with a residents-only elevator from the 1930s.

The Original Farmers Market Head down Hollywood Blvd to Fairfax to visit another LA classic – the Original Farmers Market in nearby Beverly Grove. This open-air farmers market has been around since 1934, and it's still serving up fresh produce, delicious deli-style sandwiches and tons of sweets, nuts and tasty souvenirs. Open Sunday to Thursday, 10am to 8pm, Friday and Saturday to 9pm.

Swedish treats If you really have a sweet tooth, you have to visit nearby **Sockerbit** (W 3rd St). It has the best selection of Swedish licorice and sour candies in the US. You can load up a bag for less than $10.

Above Grauman's Chinese Theater.

47 Catalina
DAY TRIP

ISLAND | ADVENTURE | KAYAKING

Santa Catalina Island is the ultimate day trip to escape the city streets of LA. Just a short ferry ride away, this quaint island with 4000 full-time residents has mellow vibes with no traffic (cars aren't allowed on the island). Pack a day bag with gear for some of the best hiking, snorkeling, diving, fishing and kayaking in California.

ⓘ How to

Getting here The Catalina Express from Long Beach ($76 round trip) is the best way to get to Avalon, Catalina's main town. The trip takes about an hour, with multiple sailings every day starting at 6am.

When to go Catalina is best in the spring or fall as 'June Gloom' can often shroud the island in a thick marine layer until the afternoon. Avalon gets crowded during the Catalina Jazz Festival (two weekends in October). Major cruise ships also regularly visit the island a few times a week, so check the schedule to avoid the crowds.

Try Your Luck at the Casino

No day trip to Catalina is complete without a visit to the **Catalina Casino**. Opened in 1929, this art deco masterpiece has become the symbol of Catalina to locals and tourists alike. But despite the name, the Catalina Casino has never actually featured any gambling. Instead, the Casino has served as an elegant event space and decadent destination for Californians seeking a tranquil escape from the traffic and noise of the city for a few hours. The dance floor on the top floor is still the world's largest circular ballroom (without supporting pillars). In its heyday, the Catalina Casino hosted the hottest Big Bands of the '30s and '40s with thousands of dancers sharing the expansive dance floor.

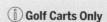 **Golf Carts Only**

Catalina is the perfect break from hectic LA traffic as cars aren't allowed on the island. It's golf carts only. You can rent carts by the hour (one hour is more than enough). Take a lap from the Casino to Lover's Cove, or just relax on the beach near the Avalon pier.

Above left Avalon. **Left** Catalina Casino.
Above right Golf cart, Santa Catalina Island.

Today, the Casino is only open for weddings and private events – like the annual New Year's Eve Celebration, Catalina Conservancy Ball and Catalina Island JazzTrax Festivals. It also offers two guided tours (regular or 'Behind the Scenes'). You can book a tour guide in advance or try your luck on the day. And if a tour isn't your thing, walk down the stairs to take a dip at Casino Point, one of the best snorkeling and kayaking spots on the island.

Island Safari

The story goes that a small herd of bison (aka 'buffalo') were shipped to Catalina for a film shoot in the 1920s. And the film crew just never rounded them up. Today the **Catalina Island Conservatory** maintains a herd of about 150 American bison, and yes, you can take a tour out to see them ($85). If you want one of the most unique safari tours, hitch a ride on the 4WD Hummer and get ready for a very different look at Southern California.

Underwater Paradise

Catalina Island is all about getting on (and into) the water. Snorkel – or dive if you're scuba certified – in the crystal-clear waters off **Casino Point Dive Park** to explore towering kelp forests and abundant marine wildlife like giant sea bass, bat rays, leopard sharks and the unmistakably orange garibaldi, California's state fish. Visibility can often be as good as 100ft!

If you're not up for a dip (it can be chilly), rent a kayak and explore the top of the kelp forest all the way up to Frog Rock. You might spot a harbor seal or pod of dolphins! You can also book a glass-bottom-boat tour or a semisubmersible 'undersea sub expedition' to explore the underwater world without a bathing suit.

ERIC LOWENBACH/GETTY IMAGES ©

Far left Diver and garibaldi.
Left American bison. **Below** Avalon.

You can also go diving for lobsters (at night!) if you're feeling particularly adventurous. Just make sure you have the right gear – including mesh gloves, fins, snorkel, mask, flashlight and a weight belt – because while west coast lobsters don't have claws, their spines are still sharp! Peak season: October to March. Closed April to September.

Bargains & Fresh Air

If hunting for bargains is more your speed, stroll down **Crescent Ave** starting from the beachfront plaza to window-shop the charming souvenir and clothing stores. You can also just close your eyes, listen to the seagulls and breath in the fresh harbor air at one of the cafes or restaurants located in 'downtown' Avalon for a refreshing change of pace from the grind of LA gridlock.

FAR LEFT: KEVINPANIZZA/GETTY IMAGES ©.
LEFT: ELVIRA LASKOWSKI/GETTY IMAGES ©

48 SoCal's Boho **BEACH**

BEACHES | SKATING | BOARDWALK

▬▬▬ Venice Beach isn't quite as wild as it used to be, but the artist-lined bohemian boardwalk, concrete bowl at the famous Venice Beach Skatepark, and iconic Muscle Beach 'Weight Pit' still boast some excellent people-watching. If you like your beaches with a dash of weirdness, Venice Beach is for you.

🗺️ How to

Getting here Catch the 1 or 33 bus to N Venice Blvd and Pacific Ave (four minutes' walk from the closest bus stop to the sand).

When to go Year round. You can soak up rays on the beach in February. Weekends can get crowded, but it's still not as popular as other nearby beaches.

Head to the bowl
The always-packed basketball courts and Muscle Beach 'Pit' get all the attention. But the Venice Beach Skatepark is where the locals hang.

SoCal's Hidden Surf Beach

LA's surf scene isn't just Malibu. There's a decent little beginner shore break between the Venice Beach Pier and the breakwater if you want to rent a board and try your hand at catching some waves. It can close out pretty frequently, but it's still a good time, and one of the more accessible waves around. If you get there at low tide, you can see dogs chasing Frisbees and the ocean spray crash over the jetty, so it's still a win if the surf is flat.

Beach Reads & Burgers

Take a break from all the 'gnar' at **Small World Books** and the always popular **Sidewalk Cafe** just across the street from the Venice Beach Skatepark. Both the bookstore and adjacent cafe have been staples of the beach boardwalk for decades thanks to the outdoor

☀️ Muscle Beach Venice

The center of bronze bodies and raw power made famous by bodybuilding legends like Arnold Schwarzenegger. The 'Weight Pen' (or 'Pit') at Venice Beach is where hard-bodies have been going to get swole since the 1960s. Reopened in 2022, with new equipment for die-hard lifters and onlookers to enjoy.

Above left Venice Beach Skatepark (p204). **Left** Sidewalk Cafe. **Above right** Bodybuilders, Muscle Beach.

patio dining, and the carefully curated selection of philosophy, poetry and mystery sections with your next great beach read. Enjoy brunch or lunch on the patio outside to watch all kinds of people strolling, skating or biking by. The smash burgers at little burger joint **The WinDow** ($4) are a cheap, delicious alternative to sit-down dining, and a great way to fuel up for a boardwalk stroll, but listen closely for your order because the speakers are terrible.

The 'Other' Venice Canals

This surprisingly tranquil pocket of Venice is home to paddling ducks, sleepy sidewalks and some of the most interesting architecture in LA. Stroll the sidewalks next to the canals and marvel at the mix of modernist architecture and abandoned kayaks moored at the miniature docks. Located just a few minutes' walk from the beach, each front yard is a private oasis and a reminder that pockets of LA are still quiet places to watch the world go by.

◎ Skate or Die!

The **Venice Beach Skatepark** might just be the most 'Californian' place you'll ever see. Kids, teens, adults and Venice veterans all throw down with smooth lines, sick grinds and everything in-between. Seriously, it's a clinic. You can sit here and watch the show for hours. Grab a spot at the rail and make sure you've got your camera ready because this is one of the most photogenic places in SoCal.

If roller skating is more your speed, the nearby **Roller Skate Dance Plaza** (it's a slab of concrete) is just steps away. Watch people groove away the day to the ever-present music most days.

EWY MEDIA/SHUTTERSTOCK ©

Far left Roller Skate Dance Plaza.
Left Venice canal. **Below** Ye Olde
Kings Head Shoppe & Restaurant.

British Invasion

The iconic **Santa Monica Pier** is located just 2 miles north of Venice Beach (you can see the Santa Monica Ferris Wheel in the distance) and is accessible via bike or scooter. The Santa Monica Pier is a California icon, but it's also crowded, pricey, loud and parking can be an expensive hassle. If you make the trip north, you have to stop by **Ye Olde Kings Head Shoppe & Restaurant** (aka the 'British Store'). This authentic British pub, shop and restaurant has been leading the British invasion in Santa Monica since 1974. Stocked with British snacks, sweets, pastries and foods, the 'Shoppe' is a Santa Monica staple. Pick up a traditional bakewell tart and if you have the time, grab a bite or a shandy at the attached restaurant or bar for outdoor dining. The sticky toffee pudding is ridiculous. It even serves afternoon tea (Wednesday to Saturday, 11:30am to 4pm).

FAR LEFT: SALTY VIEW/SHUTTERSTOCK ©
LEFT: FREDERIC J. BROWN/AFP VIA GETTY IMAGES ©

49 Hike to the **STARS**

VIEWS | PARKS | HIKING

▬▬ An absolute must for any active visitor. Griffith Park is LA's version of Central Park (except it's about five times bigger!). The park's hiking trails cover over 4000 acres of rugged terrain smack in the middle of the city. Once you step foot onto any of the paths leading up to the Griffith Park Observatory or Mt Hollywood, you'll feel instantly transported out of the city sprawl.

MAGRAPHY/SHUTTERSTOCK ©

🗺 How to

Getting here There are dozens of trails that lead to the observatory, as well as the DASH Observatory shuttle (50¢). One of the most popular (and direct) ways to get here is the Boy Scout Trail (aka 'The East Observatory Trail').

When to go Griffith Park is open year-round for hiking, but the observatory is only open Fridays (noon to 10pm) and weekends (10am to 10pm).

Solar System Lawn Model Trace the bronze arcs of each planet's orbit in this 'map' embedded in the sidewalk and plaza outside the observatory.

TREKANDSHOOT/SHUTTERSTOCK ©

IAN G DAGNALL/ALAMY STOCK PHOTO ©

Far left Griffith Park hiking trail. **Left** Griffith Park Observatory. **Bottom left** Walkway to Griffith Park Observatory.

Iconic LA Don't let the name fool you. The Griffith Park Observatory isn't just for science nerds (but it does help). The observatory is always free, and the upper balconies feature quite possibly the best views in LA. Adventurous souls can make a day of it with a short 1.4-mile hike up to the art deco dome on one of the trails that zigzag Griffith Park. Once inside the observatory, you can relive your favorite moments from *La La Land* at the swinging Foucault Pendulum in the central rotunda, buzz by the Tesla Coil demo or float into the stars at the Planetarium. Ticketed shows range from $3 to $7, but they're super worth it.

Hollywood stargazing Go in the evening to take advantage of the free telescopes. Staff members can even help you make sense of what you see as you stargaze. If you're really lucky, you'll catch the monthly 'Star Party' – a free event hosted by the Los Angeles Astronomical Society, the Planetary Society and the Los Angeles Sidewalk Astronomers. Check their sites for more details and info to geek out with other astronomy ethusiasts.

Picturesque picnic If you don't have time to wait until the sun goes down, pack a picnic and lounge on the lawn before taking in the wraparound views of downtown and the Hollywood Sign from the lawn at the entrance. It's easily one of the best ways to see just how beautiful LA can be.

🔭 How to See the Hollywood Sign

There are three unofficial 'best' views of the Hollywood Sign. Lake Hollywood Park on the west side of Griffith Park is one of the easiest ways to see a great view of the sign. But if you want to get even closer, walk up Mulholland to the Deronda Gate then hike about 1 mile up to the top of Mt Lee. This will put you directly behind the Hollywood Sign for the ultimate behind-the-scenes look at a Hollywood icon.

Lastly, the view from the Griffith Observatory is probably the most popular and rewarding view, since you'll have access to a lot more than just a view of the sign.

Listings

BEST OF THE REST

Unique Eats

Courage Bagels

This walk-up window spot in Silver Lake (Virgil Village) specializes in crispy Montreal-style bagels. Bagels are sold by the half, but they still run out, so get there early!

Steep

Some of the best ramen, bespoke tea (hot and iced) and Japanese style 'tapas' in Chinatown. Ask about the seasonal teas to try something you've never had before, and stick around for Steep 'After Dark' when it takes over the whole courtyard.

Phoenix Bakery

A Chinatown classic that's been serving the same time-tested sweets for decades. Find some room at the counter and order as many almond cookies or steamed buns as you dare.

Domenico's Pizza

One of the oldest (and most delicious) pizzerias in California, Belmont Shore's Domenico's has been serving its famous 'upside down pies' (the sauce goes on top!) and the housemade garlic dressing since 1954. It just opened its second location in Mission Viejo.

In-N-Out

This isn't 'fast food' – it's a California staple. Get the double double animal style, with fries and a chocolate shake. You're welcome. Pick up a pair of socks or shoes for the ultimate California souvenir.

Suds & Speakeasies

Frogtown Brewery

An unassuming brewery in Atwater Village, near the LA River, with a wide range of delicious beers on tap and a (very!) dog-friendly beer garden for enjoying some suds in the sun after a long day of sightseeing.

Brennan's

This local watering hole in Marina Del Rey is famous for its turtle races every first and third Thursday of the month. Get there early for great seats, and bet on your favorite steed!

Galco's Soda Pop Stop

Teetotalers can stop by Galco's for their pick of over 500 brands and flavors of that good bubbly stuff from past eras, alternate realities and international destinations.

Farmers Markets & Fleas

Hollywood Night Market

Food, vendors, crafts and live music with a killer view of the Hollywood Hills from atop Yamashiro (Thursdays 5pm to 10pm). Hit the Pagoda Bar for a sunset cocktail.

In-N-Out.

Silver Lake Farmers Market

Skip the sprawling brunch lines and fuel up with local produce, fresh fruit and more at this small, but diverse collection of local goods (Tuesday and Saturday).

Rose Bowl Thrift Market

One of the best (and biggest) thrift markets in California at the Pasadena Rose Bowl on the second Sunday of each month. The entry fee is $20, but it's worth the price of admission.

Cannonball & Tilly

A curated collection of vintage fashions spanning a century of trends (1890s to 1990s). The store is tiny, but packed from floor to ceiling with top-quality examples of the best from each fashion era.

Zuma Beach, Malibu.

 **Beach Bums**

Point Dume

Absolutely stunning views form the short hike to the point. Parking is extremely limited (you might have to wait 30 minutes for a spot!), but it's worth it.

Santa Monica

You can cruise 'The Strand' bike path from Will Rogers Beach all the way to Redondo if you dare. Although most people use this path to bike from Santa Monica to Venice Beach.

Malibu

'Zuma Beach' is classic Southern California. Find a spot to stop along the Pacific Coast Hwy (PCH) and embrace the good vibes, chill atmosphere and top-tier public beach in one of the wealthiest neighborhoods in California.

Huntington Beach

Technically located in Orange County, this surfing mecca has a lively and walkable promenade near the pier. Grab a fish taco and watch pro surfers put on a clinic! Rent a board

if you're feeling adventurous. It's a great place to learn how to surf.

El Matador

Rugged cliffs and isolated coves hug PCH on the way north to Santa Barbara. Find a hidden section of the sand for a rare secluded LA beach experience, or stop for a picnic on your way up the coast to Santa Barbara.

Newport Beach

Some of the chillest vibes and great shore breaks are located behind the bungalows and rentals near 52nd St, just off PCH. Visit the Wedge in Balboa to watch surfers drop into one of the most dangerous waves in the US.

Rosie's Dog Beach

Got a four-legged friend that loves the ocean? Take 'em to Rosie's, the only off-leash dog beach in California. Located in Belmont Shore, Long Beach, this laidback stretch of beach is a great place to people- (and pup-)watch.

 Take a Hike

Runyon Canyon

Hollywood's most popular walking/hiking trail. Keep your eyes peeled for LA's 'beautiful people'. Located just off Hollywood Blvd, it's a great way to catch glimpses of the city and even the Hollywood Sign.

LOS ANGELES REVIEWS

Mt Baldy

An incredibly challenging hike (the peak is over 10,000ft with year-round snow), this is an all-day trek for adventure seekers. Don't forget your sunglasses!

Bronson Caves

if you're hiking to the Hollywood Sign, make sure you check out the original site of Adam West's 'Batcave.'

Escondido Falls

It doesn't rain in LA very often, but when it does, head here to see a gorgeous waterfall in the most unlikely place.

Arroyo Seco Greenway Bike Path

If biking is more your thing, explore the San Gabriel Mountains north of Pasadena on this beginner-friendly mountain-bike trail. It's even shaded on several sections which can be great during a hot summer ride.

☼ Destination Kitsch

Museum of Jurassic Technology

One of the most unique museums in California with a wide and unusual range of exhibits. This confusingly named destination has little to nothing to do with dinosaurs.

The LA River

People make fun of the LA 'River,' but the bike paths and trails nearby have quickly become a secret summer spot for active locals. Many bridges still have the original light fixtures from the 1930s. Start at the 1st Bridge to snap a few photos from a setting you might recognize from iconic chase scenes in *Terminator 2* and *Grease.*

Echo Park Lake

Rent a swan paddleboat ($11 per hour) for one of the quirkiest ways to experience this painfully hip neighborhood that's quickly becoming a family-friendly LA staple.

Time Travel Mart

A great place to get the perfect souvenir that also supports a great cause, this cathedral to kitsch in Echo Park sells canned 'mammoth meat' and robot toupees. Proceeds support 826LA – a nonprofit for creative writing students.

Hollywood Forever Cemetery

Hundreds of Hollywood celebs have chosen this as their final resting place in this 'who's who' of the afterlife. Search the headstones to pay your respects to your favorites or catch an outdoor movie (usually a classic) at the Cinespia screenings in summer. Get there early because tickets go fast!

Magic Castle

The Magic Castle has been the go-to club for magicians and performers for decades. Unfortunately, it's members only, but if you email a performing magician, they might 'magically' put you on the guest list. And if you stay at the Magic Castle hotel, you magically get a free pass.

Angel's Flight Funicular

Touted as 'the shortest train in the world,' this 121-year-old funicular will save you the grueling 315ft journey up Bunker Hill.

JOSHUA RESNICK/SHUTTERSTOCK ©

Runyon Canyon (p209).

Page-Turners

The Last Bookstore

People actually line up to get into this temple to literature in the heart of Downtown LA. Browse the discounted classics up front, search for rare vinyl or recline on the comfy leather couches. No one will bother you. But the best part is the science fiction section upstairs. It's unbelievable.

Small World Books

This tiny gem in Venice Beach is great if you're looking for fiction, poetry, philosophy or something unique. Pick up your next beach read!

Skylight Books

Open every day from 10am to 10pm, here you can browse the extensive graphic-arts and visual-arts collections in this Los Feliz icon for inspiration until the streetlights come on.

As Seen On...

Bradbury Building

You'll probably recognize the lacework balconies and caged elevator cars from *Blade Runner*, but this LA icon has been the setting for numerous shows, movies and commercials over the years, including the final scene of *500 Days of Summer*.

Formosa Cafe

This Golden Age film icon has been the watering hole of choice for stars from Humphrey Bogart to Sinatra. Pull up a seat and relive your favorite moment from *LA Confidential*, *Swingers*, *The Majestic* and *Euphoria*.

The Last Bookstore.

Musso & Frank Grill

Virtually unchanged since it opened in 1919, Musso & Frank's is more than a restaurant. Order a whiskey where Bukowski spent his royalties, or pull up a barstool where Hemingway, Fitzgerald, Charlie Chaplin and Marilyn Monroe whet their whistles.

Capitol Records Building

This music-industry icon is more than just a unique part of the LA skyline. It's a secret message hidden in plain site. The blinking light at the top of the tower has been spelling out the word 'Hollywood' in Morse code since it opened in 1956.

 Scan to find more things to do in Los Angeles online

50 Beachfront Time MACHINE

BEACH | NOSTALGIA | SWEETS

Take a day trip to the ridiculously charming Balboa Island for a glimpse of old Orange County. Stroll the boardwalk, load up on saltwater taffy, play arcade games and beat the heat with frozen bananas and ice-cream sandwiches. This quaint pocket has managed to preserve what makes summer great – the beach.

How to

Getting here The best way to get to Balboa Island is on the ferry (adult $1.25, two minutes, 6:30am to midnight Monday to Sunday); catch it from Palm St on the peninsula. Alternatively, park on the 'mainland' at the back bay and make your way over the bridge on Marina Ave on foot or cruiser bike (parking on the island is limited for nonresidents).

When to go Especially magical around the holidays, including Christmas with its boat parade, and Halloween, when homeowners go all out with decorations.

SIDE TRIP BEACHFRONT TIME MACHINE

Frozen in Time

Multimillion-dollar homes line the streets and sidewalks on Balboa Island, but aside from real-estate valuations, the area is frozen in time. The ferry has been ferrying summer visitors from the same tiny wharf since 1919.

The **Balboa Fun Zone Ferris Wheel** on the peninsula side has classic and updated carnival games to keep the spirit of summer fun on the boardwalk intact.

Buy a hefty bag of saltwater taffy at the aptly named **Balboa Candy** store nearby (it has dozens of constantly changing flavors to choose from), and let the afternoon slide by to the sound of seagulls, waves and bike bells as you stroll the promenade.

⚓ Come Sail Away

Newport Harbor is one of the largest recreational harbors in the US. It's home to calm waters, easygoing vibes and plenty of navigable crafts. Why not rent an electric Duffy boat (starting at $225; seats eight to 12) to cruise the waterways in style? These cool little boats were invented in Newport!

Above left Boardwalk, Balboa Island. **Left** Balboa Candy. **Above right** Balboa Fun Zone Ferris Wheel.

Eats & Sweet Treats

Kitschy shops and cafes line Marina Ave for some top-tier window-shopping. If you're hungry, head to **Wilma's Patio** for a home-cooked meal with huge portions. And if you're still craving something sweet after your salt-water taffy, choose from two frozen-banana stands located just steps from each other – **Dad's Donut & Bakery Shop** or **Sugar 'n Spice**. They both make a mean frozen banana, although most locals have a favorite.

If frozen fruit isn't your idea of dessert, the hand-dipped 'Balboa Bars' are fantastic.

Surf the Wedge

The more adventurous can crank it up a notch at 'the Wedge.' Located at the very tip of the peninsula, this point features some of the largest (and most dangerous) shore-break waves in the world. Watch the pros jockey for position at this crowded wave during a big swell, for California surfing at its most extreme.

🗺️ Nearby & Notable

While in the area, it's also worth checking out a few more OC options, all within a short drive of Balboa Island.

Huntington Beach Pier
Rent a soft-top longboard from any of the surf shops and catch some waves in 'Surf City USA' at the chill beach break on the pier's south side.

Main Street, Seal Beach
Visit this charming beach enclave north of Huntington Beach for even more small-town beach vibes and locally owned shops.

Sawdust Fine Arts Festival (Laguna Beach) This funky world-class arts festival takes over Laguna Beach every summer with thousands making the trip down south to see the spectacle.

1000 Steps Beach (Laguna Beach) This secluded cliffside white-sand beach isn't actually down 1000 steps (but it feels like it!).

JON BILOUS/SHUTTERSTOCK ©

Far left Huntington Beach Pier.
Left Balboa Pier. **Below** Surfer,
Newport Beach.

FAR LEFT: HIROYUKI MATSUMOTO/GETTY IMAGES ©, LEFT: ANTHONY FONTANEZ/SHUTTERSTOCK ©

If catching 20ft-plus waves isn't your idea of fun, you could drive (or cycle) to nearby 52nd St in **Newport Beach** for calmer, but still-world-class waves that are popular with bodyboarders and surfers alike. Also check out the beaches and parks around **Balboa Beach**, full of less intense ways to spend your day.

Pier to Pier

You might prefer to skip the surf altogether and stroll on a pier instead – in which case, you have two options. **Balboa Pier** is a short walk from the Balboa Island ferry, and popular with local fisherfolk. It's a surprisingly quiet place to watch the sun set (with some saltwater taffy from nearby Balboa Candy), a great way to unwind after a day of sightseeing.

If a beer and a fish taco is more your speed, head to **Newport Pier** (a five-minute drive north) for a more lively experience with beach cruisers, skateboarders, and crowds enjoying the sandy boardwalk, local shops, restaurants and beach bars.

51 Explore Balboa PARK

PARK | ART | MUSEUMS

This sprawling San Diego playground is nearly twice the size of New York's Central Park. With over 1200 acres of lawns, fields and courts, 65 miles of trails, 16 museums, dozens of shops, stalls and restaurants, and attractions like the world-famous San Diego Zoo, Balboa Park is a destination truly worth exploring.

SHOLMES370/SHUTTERSTOCK ©

 How to

Getting around You can't walk the entire park, so plan according-ly. Park in the paid lot near the Balboa Carousel (or for free on Florida Dr) and head through the shops and museums on the way to the iconic California Tower.

When to go Open year-round. Especially great during summer, fall and around the holidays.

Top tip North Park and Altadena are home to tons of great breweries like Thorn St Brewery, pizza spots, and niche cuisine like New Zealand–themed Dunedin. Benny's Mexican Food on 30th St has massive California-style burritos.

PAULEISSG/GETTY IMAGES ©

SIDE TRIP EXPLORE BALBOA PARK

Park Highlights

Balboa Park is home to 16 prestigious (and very specific) museums. Visit the world-class anthropology museum, the **Museum of Us**, for an in-depth look at the light and dark side of human nature, including cannibalism.

The (free) **Timken Museum of Art**, home to European old masters – including the only Rembrandt in San Diego – is a sophisticated mid-century architectural gem located in the heart of the park.

Enjoy a more natural exhibit outside the **Natural History Museum**. The Moreton Bay fig tree is a shocking reminder of how time marches on, so you better enjoy yourself. Take a few minutes to appreciate how this behemoth grew from a potted plant over 100 years ago.

EQROY/SHUTTERSTOCK ©

Disc it Up

Kickstart your morning with an early round of Frisbee golf (or 'disc golf' if you insist) at the **Morley Field Disc Golf Course**, one of the most comprehensive 18-hole courses in California. Be sure to bring your A-game, and get a tee time (yes, really!) as spots fill up quickly, especially on weekends.

Above left California Tower (p218). **Left** Timken Museum of Art. **Above right** Morley Field Disc Golf Course.

If you visit in the summer you can catch a performance of the Bard at the **Old Globe Theater** or hunt for handmade souvenirs from dozens of local artists in the **Spanish Village Art Center**.

If you want to take it all in, climb 125 stairs to the top of the eight-story **California Tower**, Balboa Park's iconic structure (adults $20). Tours are tiny (only six people at a time) and last 40 minutes, so you can take in the wrap-around views at your own pace.

Grab the Brass Ring

Many parks have a carousel, but this 1910 Herschell-Spillman menagerie carousel is one of the few remaining wooden carousels that still lets riders try to grab the 'brass ring' to win a free ride. It's the perfect spot for kids and carousel fans – the whimsical creatures, authentic pipe music and high-stakes brass-ring game are worth the price of admission ($3 per ride). Open Saturday, Sunday and school holidays from 11am to 5:30pm.

🐢 Ping-Pong Rally On

Keep the alternative sports going into the night with Ping-Pong at the **Triple Crown Pub**, easily the most competitive yet down-to-earth Ping-Pong scene in California (maybe the world). Get your butt kicked by the local pros or show your stuff. Local players swap stories, tips and (shockingly) encouragement. If you play here regularly, you will get better. Most players bring their own paddle, but you can borrow one at the bar. You can also play darts.

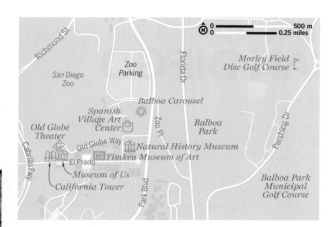

Left Spanish Village Art Center.
Below Spreckels Organ.

The World's Largest Outdoor Organ

Balboa Park is so sprawling that some of the most unique experiences can get lost in the crowd. But if you dig a little, you can find one-of-a-kind gems in the lesser explored corners of the park – like the **Spreckels Organ**.

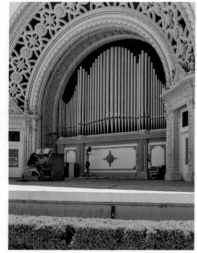

Donated by brothers John and Adolph Spreckels in 1914, the Spreckels Organ Pavilion houses the largest outdoor organ in the world with more than 5000 pipes ranging from pencil-sized to 32-footers. And this massive instrument isn't just for decoration. Since 1917, Balboa Park has kept an organist on the payroll to perform free one-hour concerts every week (Sundays at 2pm). The best part? The concerts happen rain or shine, so if you hit an uncharacteristically wet San Diego day, you can still have one of the most memorable concert experiences of your life – just bring an umbrella (the seats at the bandstand are open air).

If you're lucky enough to visit during the summer (late June through to the end of August), you can enjoy a bonus concert every Monday night at 7:30pm to celebrate the International Summer Organ Festival.

52 Surf's Up
SAN DIEGO

BEACH | SURFING | CHILL

You can fight the crowds and learn to surf at Ocean Beach or Pacific Beach, but Tourmaline Beach in La Jolla has some of the best (slow!) waves for longboarders and beginners, long sandy beaches, and one of the chillest local vibes in San Diego.

JOSEPH S GIACALONE/ALAMY STOCK PHOTO ©

🗺 How to

Getting here Located just a mile north of crowded Pacific Beach, you don't have to worry about parking here. The parking lot is free and there's always room.

When to go Best in the summer or fall, depend-ing on the swell. Some weekends can get a little crowded, but it's never too bad.

Top tip It's an easy walk down the sand to the grassy cliffs of Law Street Beach or all the way down to the pier at Pacific Beach.

VIVIAN CHEN/ALAMY STOCK PHOTO ©

STEPHEN SIMPSON/GETTY IMAGES ©

Surfin' USA

Honestly, there's nothing more quintessentially Californian than learning to surf while you're in San Diego. And **Tourmaline Beach** is the place to do it. Rent a foam-topped longboard (at least 8ft if it's your first time), make sure to wear a 3/2mm wetsuit (even in the summer!) and get out there. There's not much of a current here, so you should be good to stay right at the beach break to practice your paddle and pop up.

You'll be sure to catch a few waves even on a small day, and if you luck into a monster day, you might be able to tell everyone back home that you're going pro.

Surf Alternatives

If surfing isn't your thing (or you're tired from all those waves!), bring a beach chair and a blanket – Tourmaline Beach is still one of the chillest beaches in San Diego, and a great place to spend a sunny afternoon.

You can also explore the rocky beachfront and quiet tide pools of **Bird Rock** to the north. Wear water shoes or hiking sandals to protect your feet and enjoy a closer look at the California coast.

Signature San Diego Fare

After the surf, drive (the walk up from the parking lot is a little steep!) to some of the best local Mexican food in town on Turquoise St. Head to **Oscar's** for great fish tacos (a signature San Diego dish) or some of the best ceviche you've ever had to finish off your salty day by the sea.

Far left Surfer, Tourmaline Beach. **Left** Bird Rock. **Bottom left** Fish tacos from Oscar's.

 Hang 10

Learning to surf can be tough when there are too many people in too small a space. Tourmaline Beach solves that problem by combining the best of La Jolla (great waves) with the best of Pacific Beach (an accessible beach) without the massive crowds. Local surfers can get territorial over the waves near Black's Beach to the north, but the vibe at Tourmaline is always mellow for new surfers. Enjoy the sand, surf and free showers (nice!). Find a peak that's yours and learn to carve those curls like a local!

PALM SPRINGS & THE DESERTS

SUNSHINE | DESERT | DREAMSCAPE

Experience Palm Springs and the deserts online

PALM SPRINGS & THE DESERTS
Trip Builder

Nothing clears the mind like starry desert nights – but sunrise reveals desert dreamscapes of green palms, turquoise pools, golden dunes and lavender mountains. All things seem possible: junk becomes art, polo fields become festival grounds and restless travelers find solace.

Watch spring wildflowers revive **Death Valley National Park** (p227)
🚗 4½hrs from LA

Find inspiration in old junk at **Noah Purifoy's Outdoor Museum** (p234)
🚗 1hr from Palm Springs

Picnic among puffy trees at **Joshua Tree National Park** (p227)
🚗 1hr from Palm Springs

See modern-art masterpieces at **Palm Springs Art Museum** (p235)
🚗 2hrs from LA

Rock out at megafest **Coachella** (p232)
🎪 1½hrs from Palm Springs

Hear wind caves sing at **Anza-Borrego Desert State Park** (p231)
🚗 1hr from Palm Springs

Primm

NEVADA

CALIFORNIA

Mojave National Preserve

Fenner

Mojave

Palmdale

Amboy

Angeles National Forest

San Bernardino National Forest

Twentynine Palms

● San Bernardino Yucca Valley

Colorado River Aqueduct

○○ Palm Springs

● Indio

Salton Sea

PALM SPRINGS ART MUSEUM

Escondido ●

Julian ○

0 ——— 50 km
0 ——— 30 miles

● La Jolla

Practicalities

ARRIVING

Palm Springs International Airport is a regional airport served year-round by 11 airlines, including United and American.

FIND YOUR WAY

Download maps before you head to desert destinations and parks, where signals are spotty.

MONEY

Credit and digital payments are widely accepted, as in the rest of California. Cash is primarily used for tipping.

WHERE TO STAY

Place	Pro/Con
Greater Palm Springs	Fab mid-century motels with pools and high-style house rentals. Priced accordingly.
Joshua Tree	Choose starlit camping or geodesic dome home rentals. Avoid weather-beaten motels.
Route 66	Classic kitsch motels from LA to Vegas. Park lodges require advance booking.

GETTING AROUND

Bicycle Palm Springs is flat and easy to bike – many hotels loan bicycles, or you can rent one at Bike Palm Springs. Not all desert trails allow mountain bikes; check park rules.

Car Necessary to access far-flung desert destinations. Pick up rentals at the airport. Hwy 111 is slow going in traffic – take I-10 instead.

EATING & DRINKING

Bring a full water bottle everywhere. For park visits, bring 1 to 2 gallons per person per day. Reserve ahead for date-worthy dining in Palm Springs – the best selection by far for pickdy eaters, serving farm-fresh ingredients in stylish settings.

Best coffee in the great outdoors
Joshua Tree Coffee
(pictured top)

Must-try cocktail
Joshua Treason at Blackbook (p239; pictured bottom)

DEC-FEB
Weekenders and snowbirds flock here for extended holidays in winter sunshine

MAR-MAY
Wildflowers bloom and outdoor festivals attract hikers and hipsters

JUNE-SEP
Pools are the place to be in peak heat – but smaller crowds mean bigger deals

OCT-NOV
Warm but not crowded, with more room on trails and in restaurants

53 DUNES
& Megablooms

SAND | WILDFLOWERS | HIKING

▬▬▬ Southern California's deserts seem vast, rocky and relentlessly beige when you're just driving through – but stop and look around, and you'll find soft, honey-colored dunes and fields of pink, yellow and purple wildflowers in spring. Time your visit to hear dune sands sing under the full moon or watch desert canyons erupt into bloom – you'll never feel so alive.

LMK PHOTOGRAPHY/GETTY IMAGES ©

🗺 How to

When to go March to April is peak wildflower season, but September to October rainstorms trigger second blooms. From June to September, dunes can melt sandals – hike before 10am or by moonlight.

Supplies Come prepared with a full gas tank, 1 to 2 gallons of water per day per person, closed-toe walking shoes, sunblock, warm layers and trail snacks.

Off-roading All-terrain vehicles threaten fragile desert ecosystems and endanger wildlife, and are not allowed in parklands.

JNJPHOTOS/SHUTTERSTOCK ©

Far left Mesquite Dunes. **Left** Kelso Depot Visitor Center. **Bottom left** Anza-Borrego Desert State Park.

PALM SPRINGS & THE DESERTS EXPERIENCES

Death Valley dunes Between salt flats and craggy mountains, a ribbon of sand unfurls. **Death Valley National Park** holds US records for temperatures topping 134°F (57°C) – but with the right timing, this 5300-sq-mile park is a brilliant adventure. East of Stovepipe Wells Village, **Mesquite Dunes** rise 100ft and blush rose-gold at sunrise and sunset. Sandboarding is only permitted here and hard-to-reach **Saline Dunes** – go before 10am, when the sand radiates heat.

Shifting sands sing at majestic **Eureka Dunes**, rising 680ft above the valley. From Death Valley's Big Pine outpost, follow narrow paved roads 28 miles to reach this 3-mile stretch of dunes, where wildflower enthusiasts seek the endangered white Eureka Dunes Evening Primrose (night-blooming April to June).

Mojave's Kelso Dunes Mojave National Preserve is a 1.6-million-acre rocky moonscape – NASA's Mars Rover was tested here – dotted with abandoned mines, Joshua trees and mysterious military test sites. But 7 miles south of **Kelso Depot Visitor Center**, rippling sands sing and boom under-foot at 700ft tall **Kelso Dunes.** Follow the gravel road (no 4WD needed) 3 miles west of Kelbaker Rd to reach the trailhead. Count on two to three hours for the strenuous round-trip hike through cresting sands. The trail's unshaded, so wear sun-screen for early-morning treks November to April or hike by moonlight June to October. Bring layers – temperatures can dip under 50°F after sunset.

🌿 Best Wildflower Sightings

Desert gardens Wild-flowers sweep across Coyote Canyon lands donated to **Anza-Borrego Desert State Park**, where steep **Alcoholic Pass** reveals positively stagger-ing views. Call the park's **Wildflower Hotline** for updates: 760-767-4684.

Death Valley floor Grape-soda lupine, red desert paintbrush and yellow desert marigolds start blooming late February. For current bloom conditions, call the park hotline: 760-786-2331.

Joshua Tree Mormon settlers renamed *Yucca brevifolia* after the biblical prophet who pointed the way to the promised land, and in spring each mysti-cal tree sends up one huge cream-colored flower. Call the park's hotline for info: 760-367-5500.

Modern Design
LANDMARKS

DESIGN | ARCHITECTURE | MID-CENTURY MODERNISM

Palm Springs does mid-century modernism differently. Architects did their best work here not just for the rich, but for ordinary people starting over after WWII. Here, homes are open to the outdoors and to new ideas, built through forward-thinking collaborations among Native landowners, Black entrepreneurs and European refugee designers.

⌖ Trip Notes

Walking and biking tours Palm Springs Historical Society offers eye-opening morning biking tours ($55) and themed walking tours ($25, 1½ to 2½ hours) – book ahead for popular Hollywood Homes and Women Built This Town tours.

Mod motels Stay in a smart, recently restored modernist landmark: William Cody's redwood-and-stone 1947 Del Marcos, Herbert Burns' sunwashed 1951 Holiday House, or Albert Frey's playful 1960 Monkey Tree, legendary hideaway of JFK and Marilyn Monroe.

⊙ The Struggle for the City

The Agua Caliente Band of Cahuilla Indians owns half of Palm Springs. An 1876 US treaty limited development until 1954, when Agua Caliente's all-women council led by Vyola Ortner successfully sued the government to allow development. City leaders retaliated, razing houses on Agua Caliente land – many housing Native, Latinx and Black residents. Forward-thinking Agua Caliente Council granted 99-year leases to Black urban planner Lawrence Crossley, whose vision for diverse modern cities flourishes in Lawrence Crossley Neighborhood.

STEVE CUKROV/SHUTTERSTOCK ©

PALM SPRINGS & THE DESERTS EXPERIENCES

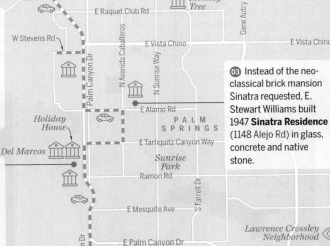

Tramway Gas Station

01 The cantilevered triangular roof of **Tramway Gas Station** (Albert Frey c 1965; pictured far left) is raised like a friendly hand, inviting drivers along Rte 111 into the **Palm Springs Visitors Center**.

Monkey Tree

N Indian Canyon Dr

E Raquet Club Rd

W Stevens Rd

E Vista Chino

E Vista Chino

Gene Autry Tr

02 William Krisel designed most of **Las Palmas'** 290 modernist homes c 1950s–1960s, except Charles Du Bois' 15 'Swiss Miss' A-frame homes – not actually Alpine, but inspired by pitched-roof Polynesian MGM movie sets.

Palm Canyon Dr

N Avenida Caballeros

N Sunrise Way

E Alamo Rd

P A L M   S P R I N G S

03 Instead of the neoclassical brick mansion Sinatra requested, E. Stewart Williams built 1947 **Sinatra Residence** (1148 Alejo Rd) in glass, concrete and native stone.

Holiday House

Mt San Jacinto Wilderness State Park

Del Marcos

E Tarquitz Canyon Way

Sunrise Park

Ramon Rd

S Farrell Dr

04 The floating glass box housing **Palm Springs Architecture & Design Center** (300 S Palm Canyon Dr) was a bank c 1961 – now E. Stewart Williams' Brazilian-inspired pavilion showcases design.

E Mesquite Ave

S Indian Canyon Dr

E Palm Canyon Dr

Lawrence Crossley Neighborhood

E Palm Canyon Dr

Toledo Ave

Murray Canyon Dr

San Bernardino National Forest

05 **Indian Canyons resort**'s custom homes feature Palm Springs' most Instagrammed doors – including Walt Disney's Minnie Mouse–red door (2688 S Camino Real).

N 0 — 2 km
   0 — 1 miles

55 MYSTICAL
Moonscapes

ROCK FORMATIONS | CRATERS | CAVES

Nature's own rock sculpture garden wasn't installed in Southern California deserts overnight by some obsessive alien artist who discovered psychedelic mushrooms (though it looks that way). The combined forces of erosion, earthquakes and ancient volcanoes took 100 million years to create this otherworldly desertscape. Escape here to reset your internal clock.

ROBERT MIRAMONTES/SHUTTERSTOCK ©

🏞 How to

When to go November to March are best for afternoon hikes with peak color and dramatic shadows – bring layers for temperature drops. May to September desert temperatures can reach 130°F, so hike before 10am.

Supplies The nearest park concessions are often miles away. Fuel up and bring 1 to 2 gallons of water per person per day, walking shoes, sunblock, warm layers and trail snacks.

Camping Reserve camping spots in advance to watch moonrises over rock formations and witness meteor showers.

REY RODRIGUEZ/SHUTTERSTOCK ©

GUNTER MARX PHOTOGRAPHY/GETTY IMAGES ©

Far left Wonderland of Rocks.
Left Badwater Basin salt flats.
Bottom left Ubehebe Crater.

Rock out at Joshua Tree Massive hanging granite boulders frame the landscape like Spanish exclamation marks at Joshua Tree's aptly named **Wonderland of Rocks**. Rock formations along the 0.6-mile **Indian Cove Trail** or 1-mile **Hidden Valley Trail** look ready to collapse – they'll probably hang there for another century, but the thrill of survival feels real. **Skull Rock** looms ominously near **Jumbo Rocks Campground** – take the 1.7-mile loop trail past rock arches for the obligatory skull-eye-socket photo-op. To try your pick of 10,000 rock-climbing routes, gear up with Joshua Tree Outfitters and get trained with Uprising Adventure Guides (4/6/8hr-course from $125/140/165).

Death Valley's sci-fi scenery Marvel at white **Badwater Basin** salt flats and 600ft **Ubehebe Crater** – formed 2000 years ago by a magma-fueled explosion – and take the 3-mile round-trip hike through **Golden Canyon** to iron-oxidized **Red Cathedral** cliffs. If this surreal scenery gives you déja-vu, maybe you recognize *Star Wars* scenes filmed here.

Anza-Borrego's hidden glories Wind-sculpted sandstone whispers encouragement along **Wind Caves Trail**, a steep 2-mile path lined with caves and badlands vistas. **Pictograph and Smugglers' Canyon Trail** is an easier 3-mile hike, past a boulder etched with ancient Kumeyaay pictographs and sunbleached canyon walls opening onto **Vallecito Valley**. Rent a 4WD to reach trailheads or reserve guided California Overland Desert Excursions (from $145). Check conditions with Anza-Borrego Desert State Park Visitor Center.

✂ Best Scenic Drives

Artists Drive Late afternoons paint the mountain scenery along Death Valley's 9-mile, one-way drive. The showstopper at mile five is Artists Palette, where metallic strata glow iridescent pink, green and purple in the late-afternoon light.

Geology Tour Road Follow Joshua Tree's 14-mile backcountry drive west of Jumbo Rocks to see 16 geological wonders, insightfully explained in informational markers.

Cima Rd South off I-15 you can't miss strikingly symmetrical, 1500ft Cima Dome, with volcanic cinder cones and basalt outcroppings rising above a Mojave Desert preserve where almost a million Joshua trees burned in 2020 – stop to admire the volunteer-run habitat restoration in progress.

56 Like a Desert DIVA

FREEDOM | STARDOM | WOMEN'S HISTORY

■■■ Ever since Nellie Coffman used her divorce settlement in 1909 to build Palm Springs' first resort, divas who dare to be different have headed here to live and love without compromise. Now Palm Springs regulars known by one name – Marilyn, Cher, Beyoncé, Lucy, Dinah, Kim, Liz, Miley – are graciously sharing their playground with you. Whatever you do this weekend, make it iconic.

🞕 How to

Star sightings Hollywood comes to the desert for Palm Springs International Film Festival in January. Stars and directors make cameo appearances year-round for revivals and cult classics at the 1967 movie palace housing the Palm Springs Cultural Center.

Presidential visits Get inspired to run for office at Sunnylands, where ambassadors Leonore and Walter Annenberg hosted heads of state for 50 years at retreats in their stately modernist home (tours $49; book ahead) and songbird-filled gardens (visits free).

Map:
Pappy & Harriet's Pioneertown Palace
Yucca Valley
Joshua Tree
Morongo Valley
Joshua Tree National Park
Desert Hot Springs
Coachella Valley
Palm Springs Walk of Fame
Trina Turk
Wil Styles
Palm Springs
Purple Room
Thousand Palms
Four Twenty Bank
Cathedral City
Palm Desert
Little Bar
N 0 / 0   10 km / 5 miles

Swing like Dinah The honorary female member of Sinatra's Rat Pack, Dinah Shore beat the boys at their own games – out-singing them at the **Purple Room**, hosting hit TV shows, and swinging golf clubs like a pro. The women's golf tournament Dinah founded inspired Palm Springs' spin-off lesbian

megafestival **The Dinah**, featuring headliners like Lady Gaga, Eve and Katy Perry.

Dinah's own parties were legendary, leaving Hollywood studios scrambling to hush her flings with men decades her junior. When she commissioned architect Donald Wexler to build her low-key, high-style pool-party pad in

1964, it caused an uproar – and set global modernist trends. Today Dinah's **432 Hermosa Road** estate is owned by Leonardo di Caprio, who hosts swinging Modernism Week cocktail receptions under Dinah's portraits.

Break out like Beyoncé As Beyoncé proved at **Coachella**, every star shines brighter in

ELENA RAY/ALAMY STOCK PHOTO ©

Best Diva Fashion Statements

Trina Turk Make a splash in high-drama caftans made of vintage silk and mod-print swimsuits, available in juicy colors for all genders.

Wil Styles Update vintage looks with Wil Stiles' signature leather-daisy-appliqued coats or glittery fun-fur stoles – fabulous for any gender, anytime.

Lustrewear Score mint-condition vintage rompers and maxi dresses from Melaina Tracy's curated collection at Palm Springs pop-ups or Instagram drops for local pickup.

Frippery Mid-century dream boutique lined with one-of-a-kind finds from Pucci to Alice of California, plus house-label O'pell caftans made with vintage fabric.

the desert. Between Coachella and country-cousin festival **Stagecoach**, artists test new tracks at Tack Room bar at Coachella's **Empire Polo Club**. To perform yourself, hit Monday open mikes at **Pappy & Harriet's Pioneer Palace**, the star-making Western-movie-set saloon – or for an easygoing audience,

Thursday open mikes at **Four Twenty Bank** cannabis lounge. Music moguls unwind at Palm Desert's **Little Bar**, covered with ticket stubs by its Coachella-impresario owner. If you'd rather dance, bust moves on city sidewalks with **MOGO Silent Disco**, and claim an imaginary star on the **Palm Springs Walk of Fame**.

Above Trina Turk.

57 Desert DREAMERS

INSPIRATION | SCULPTURE INSTALLATIONS | PERFORMANCES

▬▬▬ Rub your eyes, and you'll realize this isn't a desert mirage. Artists have taken to SoCal deserts to realize dreams too sprawling and strange for any museum: junk-art carnivals, backyard robots, a ghost-town opera house, a trailer-load of crocheted creatures and a channel to the universe.

🖏 How to

Get crafty Find inspiration at Joshua Tree's World Famous Crochet Museum and biennial Desert Guilds Quilt Show (held in March of even-numbered years), and mingle with local artisans at downtown Palm Springs Villagefest (Thursdays, sunset to 10pm).

Integratron Sound Bath Meditate to the hum of 20 quartz-crystal bowls inside a domed structure hand-built by aerospace engineer George Van Tassel to channel universal magnetic frequencies ($50, one hour; book two months ahead).

Noah Purifoy's Outdoor Museum When police brutality ignited 1965's Watts Riots, Watts Towers Art Center cofounder Noah Purifoy turned debris into assemblage artworks that traveled internationally, changing how the world saw Black art, struggle and community. The Black LA Movement founder filled his 10-acre, free desert museum with provocative art installations – from a colorful carousel lined with delightfully destroyed computers to a political theater made of scorched newspapers and shattered glass.

Robolights Enter a pop-art wonderland of pink techno-dinosaurs, yellow TV-headed robots, psychedelic Santas, and 200-plus robot-creatures upcycled from junk in artist Kenny Irwin's backyard over 30 years. His holiday light shows attracted 60,000

Map labels:
10 km / 5 miles
Noah Purifoy's Outdoor Museum
World Famous Crochet Museum
Joshua Tree
Yucca Valley
Amargosa Opera House (220mi)
Morongo Valley
Joshua Tree National Park
Desert Hot Springs
Palm Springs Art Museum
Coachella Valley
Robolights
Palm Springs
Thousand Palms
Frey House II

Side tab:
PALM SPRINGS & THE DESERTS EXPERIENCES

Desert Visionaries

Restless creative spirits fill the **Palm Springs Art Museum**'s stellar collection, from Noah Purifoy assemblages to Angela Ellsworth's Seer Bonnet – a Mormon pioneer bonnet made of 31,863 pearl-tipped corsage pins. Highlights range from transcendental-ist painter Agnes Pelton's luminous 1940s desert-mirage dreamscapes to contemporary photographer Wendy Red Star's satirical self-portraits in fake Western landscapes. Don't miss SoCal modernist painters Helen Lundeburg and her husband Lorser Feitelson, whose distilled desertscapes vibrate seismic energy. Book ahead for tours of **Frey House II**, architect Albert Frey's 800-sq-foot home built into San Jacinto Mountain, with panoramic views.

visitors annually, generating traffic complaints – so he's building a holiday-themed Robolights outside town. Text 760-774-0318 to book and confirm free visits.

Amargosa Opera House A car broke down in Death Valley...luckily, the story doesn't end there. After dancer Marta Becket fixed her car in Death Valley Junction, she revived its social hall, providing music and dance for appreciative crowds – Marta painted cheering fans on auditorium walls. After 50-plus years, her opera continues to inspire desert pit stops.

Above Amargosa Opera House.

58 LGBTIQ+
Palm Springs

PRIDE | GAY LIFE | LGBTIQ+ VENUES

Fewer than 50,000 people call Palm Springs home, but around half identify as LGBTIQ+ – and on Friday nights, it seems like everyone's out and about here. The city that elected America's first all-LGBTIQ+ city council in 2019 takes care of business and keeps a busy social calendar, with lesbian pool parties, drag brunches, biker scenes, rainbow rodeos and more gay good times.

KAMIL ZELEZIK/SHUTTERSTOCK ©

🗺 How to

Show local pride Local makers at Palm Springs Queertique outfit all gay occasions with sailor towels, peacock kimonos, Cher bear tees, Gaypin' enamel badges and Grace Jones blankets.

LGBTIQ+ bar crawl See how far you can get on Arenas Rd between S Indian Canyon Dr and S Calle Encilia.

White Party Palm Springs' gay spring break is three days of nonstop DJs, divas in all-white costumes and extrasplashy pool parties.

BARRY KING/ALAMY STOCK PHOTO ©

Top left Pride, Palm Springs.
Bottom left Purple Room.

Out in the sunshine Rev your convertible and crank up DJ Ross Matthews on local KGAY radio – you've arrived in Palm Springs, officially. For a century, this freewheeling desert getaway was the furthest Hollywood studios would let their stars go – and what the world didn't know about Rock Hudson, Liberace and other gay stars was an open secret in Palm Springs.

Today flags fly gaily over weeklong November **Pride**, March **TransPride Fair**, and year-round LGBTIQ+ pool parties – especially September's lesbian megaparty **The Dinah**, and February's **International Bear Convergence**, where burly, furry men make a splash. **PS Hot Rodeo** bull-riding and country-dancing fundraisers benefit LGBT Community Center of the Desert, Desert AIDS Project and other trailblazing nonprofits.

Gay cabaret When Palm Springs was a WWII Air Force base and USO entertainment hub, 'don't ask, don't tell' policies were enforced. Today Palm Springs' **LGBTQ Veterans Memorial** honors long-unacknowledged contributions, and historic lounges like the **Purple Room** showcase gay cabaret. For showtimes, check online at Gay Desert Guide.

All-star drag Drag stars dazzle at **AsiaSF Palm Springs**, where trans queens hold court Friday to Sunday, and at Trixie Mattel's drag-themed pink **Trixie Motel**, featured on Discovery Channel's motel-makeover series. Top drag brunches are **Chill Bar**'s Amazing Sundays with *RuPaul's Drag Race* Mayhem Miller and **Roly China Fusion**'s Drag Dim Sum, where ingredients and talent are local and fresh, honey.

🏳️‍🌈 PS Hot Spots

Chill Bar Everyone's chill here thanks to daily drink specials, retro Latin nights, body-positive Thicc Thursdays, bingo-go-go Saturday afternoons and throw-down weekend house parties.

Toucan Tiki Monday Latin nights, live cabaret acts, and drag shows five nights a week are good times had by all – especially when strong tropical drinks kick in (cover $10 to $25).

Eagle 501 Bar Strap on your leathers for $2 off drinks at Thursday's Gear, and come out of hibernation for alternative retro-rock and $4 Tito's cocktails at Bear Trap Fridays.

Oscar's Stop by for live music outdoors, stay for showroom cabaret, and go all out for Saturday's Mimosa Men and Sunday's 'Bitchiest Brunch.'

Listings

BEST OF THE REST

Decadent Brunches

Norma's $$$

At Jonathan Adler's psychedelic-chic Parker Palm Springs, brunch like a rock star on truffled artichoke eggs Benedict or brioche French toast smothered in berries. Brunch runs $35, plus fresh-peach Bellinis.

Elmer's $

Other meals are optional in Palm Springs, but brunch is a religion – and Elmer's offers all-day, affordable, soul-satisfying options like 'crabacado' omelets, crispy stuffed hash browns and lemony German pancakes.

Wilma & Frieda's $$

Sibling co-owners Kelly and Kreg spoil you with home-style brunches of churro waffles and short rib eggs Benedict, and encourage you to eat your greens with farm-fresh strawberry spinach salads.

Eight4Nine $$

Join stars plotting comebacks and fundraisers over chilaquiles with duck-fried egg, bacon bloody Marys and generous mimosas – all graciously served indoors or on the vast shaded/heated patio.

Away-From-It-All Hot Springs

El Morocco Inn & Spa

Recover from Palm Springs parties in this Desert Hot Springs mineral-water pool – a day pass is $60 per four hours or free with its signature Marrakesh melting massage ($140).

Agua Caliente County Park

Soak off trail dust from Anza-Borrego Desert State Park hikes September to May in geo-thermally heated, indoor and outdoor mineral-water pools for day use ($6) or camping/cabin stays ($30 to $60).

Delight's Hot Springs Resort

For a restorative dip after exploring Death Valley, get day passes ($20 Monday to Friday, $25 Saturday and Sunday) or night passes ($30) for soaks with sunsets and stars; prefab cabins available ($100 per night).

Palm Springs' Hidden Oases

Indian Canyons

In this Agua Caliente oasis, clifftop views reward 2- to 15-mile Palm Canyon hikes, a seasonal waterfall graces 4.7-mile Murray Canyon trail, and native palms line 1.2-mile Andreas Canyon loop trail.

Tahquitz Canyon

The 2-mile loop trail passes ancient petroglyphs, early Cahuilla settlements, and a 60ft waterfall in a canyon oasis known as the stomping ground of earthquake-causing Cahuilla shaman Tahquitz.

Moorten Botanical Gardens

Escape urban Palm Springs into this garden oasis covering a dozen desert habitats with 3000 plants, from Mojave Desert native cacti to South African aloe – and adopt a succulent at the nursery.

Outdoor Dining

Palm Desert Food & Wine $$$

Three days of tastings in Palm Desert feature chefs you'll recognize from James Beard Awards and TV shows and Coachella Valley-grown ingredients. Proceeds support Find Food Bank.

Tac/Quila $$

Margarita tastings with ceviche, mango-shrimp *aguachile,* and outstanding *al pastor* and grilled shrimp tacos are tasty excuses to linger on the shaded, sociable side patio in the heart of downtown Palm Springs.

Farm $$$

Freshness is an obsession for French farmers and their spiritual cousins at Palm Springs' Farm – no freezers or microwave in this kitchen – where cocktails and prix-fixe patio dinners ($62) change with the seasons.

Birba $$

Live *la dolce vita* in Palm Springs with Italian-accented cocktails, wood-fired pizza and roast chicken with local dates by the fire pit.

 **Signature Cocktails**

Bootlegger Tiki

You could get shipwrecked at Don the Beachcomber's 1953 desert outpost on the pirate-classic Demerara Dry Float: dark rum, tart passionfruit, enough citrus to cure scurvy, plus a shot of overproof rum.

Blackbook

Drinks sound like dares at Blackbook – go on, get the Cocked & Loaded (Fighting Cock bourbon, coffee liquor, bitters), Joshua Treason (gin, Lillet, lemon, honey), or Just F*ckin' Try It (don't ask).

Tonga Hut

These powerful tiki drinks have made starlets and sailors forget they're in the desert since 1958 – get hibiscus-spiked Mojave punch or the Pi Yi, a hollowed-out pineapple brimming with rum.

Moorten Botanical Gardens.

Star Treatment

Rancho Mirage Library and Observatory

Glimpse galaxies 500 million light years away at stargazing parties and observatory tours (9am and 3pm, Thursday to Saturday). Programs and parking are free and accessible to all.

Sky Watcher Star Tours

Take a quick trip through the cosmos on two-hour stargazing tours inside International Dark Sky–honored Joshua Tree National Park, led by informative guides with high-powered telescopes ($149 adult, $119 child).

Sky's the Limit Observatory

The Twentynine Palms nonprofit observatory behind September's Night Sky Festival also offers a meditation garden and a 20-billion-to-one scale model of the solar system.

 Scan to find more things to do in Palm Springs and the deserts online

Practicalities

ARRIVING

242

GETTING AROUND

244

SAFE TRAVEL

246

MONEY

247

ACCOMMODATIONS

248

RESPONSIBLE TRAVEL

250

ESSENTIALS

252

Right Hiker near San Diego.

EASY STEPS FROM THE AIRPORT TO THE CITY CENTER

Los Angeles International Airport (LAX) is the most heavily trafficked and a major US gateway for international arrivals in California. Most international flights arrive at the Tom Bradley International Terminal. While all nine terminals' departures levels feature shopping, dining, money-changing, wi-fi and rest areas, the Tom Bradley International Terminal is the largest and most extensive.

AT THE AIRPORT

ZSTOCK/SHUTTERSTOCK ©

SIM cards
Though it's possible to buy SIM cards at airport newsstands or currency exchanges, these can be pricey. Your best bet is to purchase a SIM card at a brick-and-mortar store for one of the major mobile carriers, AT&T and T-Mobile.

Currency exchange
Wait until leaving LAX to exchange currency. Within the airport, all of the currency-exchange kiosks are operated by the same agency (International Currency Exchange), offering unfavorable exchange rates. If you need cash immediately, exchange a small amount or withdraw from an ATM.

Wi-fi LAX offers free, unlimited wi-fi – the only catch is that each 45-minute session requires watching a short video first.

ATMs There are Bank of America ATMs in all terminals at LAX; find Citibank and Chase Bank ATMs near the airport.

Charging stations You'll find several Samsung charging stations, each with 120V outlets, in every terminal of LAX.

CUSTOMS REGULATIONS

Non-US citizens and permanent residents over the age of 21 may import 1L of alcohol, 200 cigarettes, $100 in gifts and $10,000 in cash or cash equivalents.For the most up-to-date information, visit US Customs and Border Protection (cbp.gov).

GETTING TO THE CITY CENTER

LAX-it Catch taxis or use your ride app from this waiting area (pronounced 'LA Exit'). To get there, take one of the bright-green shuttles that stop at every terminal. Note that taxis are often significantly cheaper than ride-app rides from LAX.

FlyAway bus An easy, inexpensive option if you're heading to the Union Station area or Van Nuys (in the San Fernando Valley). FlyAway buses depart from the blue, clearly marked columns in front of each terminal on the lower (arrivals) level.

Metro C (Green) Line shuttle The LA Metro runs a free shuttle bus from LAX to the nearest C-Line station. Hop on the metro for coastal cities like Redondo Beach, or to connect to other lines. Purchase a TAP card online before boarding the shuttle.

HOW MUCH FOR A...

Taxi
$47
30min

Metro Green to Blue line $2
60min

FlyAway bus
$10
30min

Plan your journey
The free Transit app (transitapp.com) helps map out your route and provides real-time vehicle location, transportation options and traffic information.

TAP LA app
Download the free TAP LA app (taptogo.net) and use it immediately for LA Metro or bus fare.

LA Metro Los Angeles was built on car culture and has never developed an efficient public-transportation infrastructure. However, the LA Metro can be useful to get from one general area to another outrageously cheaply ($7 for a one-day pass), avoiding LA's infamous traffic. Pay with exact change, the TAP app or TAP card.

OTHER POINTS OF ENTRY

Serving **northern California**, San Francisco International Airport (SFO) is the other main hub welcoming international flight arrivals. You may also fly into Oakland International Airport (OAK) across the San Francisco Bay, or into San Jose International Airport (SJC) in the heart of Silicon Valley.

Scattered throughout the state are **six other international airports**, listed roughly from north to south: Sacramento International Airport (SMF), Fresno Yosemite International Airport (FAT), Ontario International Airport (ONT), John Wayne Airport (SNA) in Orange County and San Diego International Airport (SAN). There are also around 20 smaller regional airports statewide.

If traveling by train, **Amtrak** (amtrak.com) runs several routes to California from Chicago and New Orleans via Dallas, Denver and Albuquerque – California destinations are Los Angeles and Emeryville (Bay Area), which then link to intrastate rail routes.

By bus, **Greyhound** (greyhound.com) travels throughout Canada, Mexico and the US. Various routes serve California destinations. Greyhound's website gives details on border-crossing requirements.

TRANSPORT TIPS TO HELP YOU GET AROUND

California feels custom-made for road-tripping, whether in a rental car or recreational vehicle (RV). The state also has some of the highest gas prices in the nation, which are still lower than in many countries. You could also consider taking the train between cities along the Amtrak line, or flying between California destinations to save time and gas money.

TRAFFIC Traffic in California's metro areas – especially the San Francisco Bay Area and Greater LA – can get unimaginably jammed. If your map app says it will take an hour to drive five miles, believe it. Always budget plenty of time to get anywhere.

ROAD CONDITIONS California's highways and roads are generally in good shape, but tectonics, traffic and weather vary wildly within the state's coastline, desert and mountain regions. Check current road conditions by highway number or map area at CalTrans (dot. ca.gov/travel).

CAR RENTAL & INSURANCE

What better way to experience California than with your own wheels? A slew of car-rental companies offer competitive rates, but be sure to explore your insurance options beforehand so you know what level of protection you need (or don't).

THE 'TRIPLE-A'

The Automobile Association of America (AAA, known as 'Triple-A') provides roadside assistance and other services to members. You may receive reciprocal benefits if your home country's automobile association is an affiliate; for details, see exchange.aaa. com/international-travel/international-clubs.

CAR RENTAL COSTS

rental from $75 per day

Gas approx $5 per gallon

City parking free to very high

DRIVING ESSENTIALS

 Drive on the right; the steering wheel is on the left.

 Legal driving age is 16, but minimum age for renting a car is 21.

 Speed limit on most highways is 65 unless otherwise posted.

 High-occupancy vehicle (HOV) lanes can only be accessed at dotted lines; violating occupancy rules brings big fines.

 Blood-alcohol concentration (BAC) limit is 0.08% for over-21s, 0.01% for 20 and under.

ELECTRIC VEHICLES In California, where demand is higher and charging infrastructure more established, a few major car-rental companies offer electric vehicles (EVs), including Teslas. You're most likely to find them in LA and San Francisco, with hybrids often available elsewhere. Another option is **Turo** (turo.com), a peer-to-peer car-share platform. Map out charging stations ahead of long drives for smooth sailing.

BUS Classic Greyhound (greyhound.com) buses still trundle through the country and are a cheap and guaranteed-memorable (if slower) way to get around California. Flixbus (flixbus.com) also connects a respectable number of California cities, with newer buses and more reliable service. San Francisco's MUNI (sfmta.com) goes everywhere; and while possible to bus around LA, it's infinitely better to drive or ride-app.

PLANE The frequency of shorter-hop flights between California cities makes flying an appealing option if you're short on time – and depending on ever-fluctuating gas prices, it's often cheaper to fly than to drive between LA and San Francisco, for example.

TRAIN Amtrak's Coast Starlight train (amtrak.com) runs through beautiful scenery and is a wonderful, if slower way to travel. Light-rail and metro networks are excellent for getting around locally, particularly in the San Francisco Bay Area and greater San Jose.

KNOW YOUR CARBON FOOTPRINT A domestic flight between San Francisco and Los Angeles would emit about 140kg of carbon dioxide per passenger. A bus would emit 80kg for the same distance, per passenger. A train would emit 40kg.

Native's carbon calculator (native.eco/for-individuals/calculators/#Travel) allows you to purchase carbon offsets to benefit the environment.

ROAD DISTANCE CHART (MILES) Note: Distances are approximate

	Los Angeles	Napa Valley	Palm Springs	Sacramento	San Diego	San Francisco	San Luis Obispo	Santa Barbara	South Lake Tahoe
Napa Valley	415								
Palm Springs	110	520							
Sacramento	385	70	490						
San Diego	125	540	140	510					
San Francisco	380	70	490	90	500				
San Luis Obispo	200	280	300	290	320	230			
Santa Barbara	100	380	200	385	220	330	105		
South Lake Tahoe	445	160	475	105	505	190	380	475	
Yosemite	310	200	410	165	430	190	230	340	200

CALIFORNIA GETTING AROUND

SAFE TRAVEL

Traffic accidents pose the most likely threat. Take the usual precautions of staying aware of your surroundings and properly preparing for outdoor adventures: learn about your destination's environment, watch the weather, carry enough water and dress for changing conditions.

 OPPORTUNISTIC THEFT Much more common than violent crime. If you must leave anything in your vehicle, keep it concealed.

 HATE CRIMES Though infrequent, crimes targeting people who are nonwhite, nonheterosexual or somehow 'other' are an unfortunate reality.

 TRAFFIC ACCIDENTS Leave plenty of space between you and other drivers; drive defensively.

WEATHER California weather can change surprisingly quickly (looking at you, San Francisco); always dress in layers. In desert and mountain climates, drink plenty of water to avoid dehydration.

OCEAN SAFETY Learn about local hazards, which can include stingrays (shuffle as you enter the water) and riptides (swim parallel to the shore to escape the current rather than swimming against it).

 EARTHQUAKES & TSUNAMIS Though California still awaits the 'Big One,' small tremors are not uncommon. During an earthquake, stay clear of buildings outside; indoors, take shelter under heavy furniture. Near the coast, head for higher ground.

 TRAVEL INSURANCE Medical costs in the US can reach exorbitant heights. It's likely your adventures will go swimmingly, but in the event anything goes awry, it's highly advisable to purchase coverage ahead of your travels.

QUICK TIPS TO HELP YOU MANAGE YOUR MONEY

CREDIT CARDS & APPS Credit cards are accepted almost everywhere and often preferred over cash, although sometimes not at food trucks, farmers markets or pop-ups. In places where credit cards aren't accepted, vendors are often set up to take payment via electronic apps such as Venmo or Apple Pay. If you plan on strolling an outdoor market or street fair, bring cash as a backup.

ATMS
24/7 ATMs are ubiquitous: at banks, grocery stores, malls and gas stations. Expect transaction fees in addition to charges from your home bank.

CASH
Most people don't carry around much cash these days, but it's handy to have some small bills for tipping valet-parking attendants or bellhops.

CURRENCY

US dollar ($)

HOW MUCH FOR A...

matcha latte
$6

pint of beer
$8

burrito
$12

OCCUPANCY FEES California's hotel tax (aka Transient Occupancy Tax) varies by county and city, but expect to pay roughly 10% to 14% tax on accommodations rates. Hotels in denser cities often charge extra for parking.

BARGAINING
Bargaining or haggling happen sonly at outdoor markets or with individual street vendors. Small mom-and-pop stores might offer you special deals, but otherwise prices are as posted.

SALES TAX
California state sales tax is 7.25%, but cities and counties often tack on variable additional local taxes, adding up to roughly 10%. The US does not offer value-added tax (VAT) refunds.

DISCOUNTS & SAVINGS

Southern California CityPASS For families or anyone planning visits to SoCal theme parks, like Disneyland, Legoland and San Diego Zoo Safari Park, this pass (citypass.com/southern-california) saves money on park tickets and allows you to skip the long ticket lines.

America the Beautiful This interagency pass (store.usgs.gov/pass/index.html; annual $80) grants entry to all US National Parks – 28 of which are in California – plus national wildlife refuges, Bureau of Land Management (BLM) lands and other US parklands.

TIPPING Tipping is not optional except in cases of truly terrible service. Generally, tipping 20% on any service is a good rule of thumb.

Restaurant servers 20%

Bartenders or baristas At least $1 per drink

Hotel housekeeping $2–$5 per day

Taxis or ride-app drivers 10%–20%

UNIQUE & LOCAL WAYS TO STAY

With its multitude of beautiful destinations and innovative spirit, California has hundreds of cool, unique accommodations to check into. Find solitude at a desert campsite or feed all your desires with decadent city luxury. Aside from the usual motels and hotels, the state is full of offbeat options too.

HOW MUCH FOR A...

state park campsite
$20-30

small-town boutique motel
$150

urban boutique hotel
$200

ESTATE WINERIES

Immerse yourself in a Wine Country retreat with views of vineyard rows. Go big at a high-end chateau, complete with spa treatments and south-of-France ambience, or choose from a wide range of more low-key winery digs.

California's wine regions aren't limited to Napa and Sonoma Counties (try Mendocino, San Luis Obispo and Santa Barbara for a start) and accommodation styles can be as individual as their winegrowers and makers. From farmhouse B&Bs to contemporary shipping-container cottages, their features and amenities reflect their local cultures.

BOUTIQUE MOTELS

The humble motel has experienced some revitalization over the last few years, with many tired models receiving makeovers that have given them a second act. Designed with an eye to the mid-century aesthetic and consciously addressing contemporary needs, these roadside spots are hot little properties that can be stylish but affordable options.

CAMPING

There are many flavors of camping in California, be it dispersed camping on Bureau of Land Management land (following Leave No Trace principles), tent camping at established sites in parklands, or car camping at state parks. Popular sites must sometimes be booked a year in advance, while others are first-come, first-served.

GLAMPING

California may not have invented glamping, but what perfect backdrops and set pieces she has for it. National parks and private entities alike have placed canvas tents and yurts in gorgeous settings like Yosemite, Kings Canyon and Big Sur. Much of the state maintains a temperate climate for most of the year, making glamping a realistic accommodation option almost everywhere.

Trailer parks No need to bring your own – this breed of trailer park revamps vintage trailers, setting them up like boho-chic cabins around a communal area usually outfitted with showers and kitchen, plus maybe firepit, pool and/or lounge. They're not necessarily cheap, but you're bound to meet like-minded travelers in cool locations like Ojai, Russian River and Joshua Tree.

Safari tents and yurts From lone yurts on private land to national-park complexes, these lightweight structures make roughing it not so rough. The magical natural environments surrounding them make them desirable stays.

Treehouses Treehouses, human-sized nests and birdhouse-clad pods make up the wilder-feeling luxury aeries you can settle into for the night. Some meet the definition of shelter better than others, so check details, weather report and your comfort zone before committing.

BOOKING

Book as far ahead as possible for high season (June through August) and weekends, and potentially a year in advance for sought-after national- and state-park campsites. It's possible to roll into town and find somewhere to stay midweek, but holidays, weekends and local festivals can sometimes mean zero availability and/or significantly higher prices in popular destinations.

Airbnb (airbnb.com) As everywhere, independent hosts offer accommodations as unique as they are.

VRBO (vrbo.com) Private vacation rentals of all kinds and for a range of budgets.

HipCamp (hipcamp.com) Vetted private camping spots for a variety of tastes and comfort levels – options can be bare-bones and isolated or supersocial glamping scenarios.

Reserve America (reserveamerica.com) The official site for national- and state-park campgrounds. If you haven't booked far in advance, keep checking on desired locations as last-minute cancellations open up.

Farm Stay USA (farmstayus.com) Live out your farm-life fantasies (or be disabused of them).

FARM STAYS

Farm stays are a great way to slow down and get to know a place, especially for children. California's agricultural areas span the state, and hosts offer experiences from overnight lodging to Farm Life 101.

ON THE ROAD

Calculate your carbon footprint. You can find many carbon calculators online, most of which offer the opportunity to offset your footprint per trip.

Rent an electric or hybrid car if available. Charging stations are available in many cities and even along long stretches of highway for longer road trips.

Base your travels in one area, taking day trips and exploring more deeply on a local level.

Take the train between long-distance destinations and rent vehicles to get around locally.

Refill your water bottle. Tap water is safe to drink throughout California; if you forget your reusable water bottle, pick one up as a souvenir.

Avoid single-use plastic. Reusable cutlery, straws and bags are lightweight and easy to throw into your day bag. It can be challenging to reduce consumption of single-use plastic while traveling, but every resuable bottle or bag you use makes a difference.

GIVE BACK

Support Black-owned and green businesses to benefit local communities' diversity and environmental health. Check out Support Black-Owned (supportblackowned.com/states/ca) and the California Green Business Network (greenbusinessca.org) directories.

Donate to a regional California Conservation Corps (CCC; ccc. ca.gov) chapter, which gives young adults work experience in conservation projects all over the Golden State.

Volunteer at a local food bank or soup kitchen if you have a couple of spare hours; idealist.org matches volunteers with organizations in need.

Coastal Cleanup Day can be any day at the beach if you collect trash while there. You'll not only clean up that particular beach but will help reduce the amount of microplastics and other debris in our collective oceans.

DOS & DON'TS

Do keep wildlife wild by enjoying it at a distance, alluring as it may be to approach. Both humans and wildlife remain safer that way.

Don't cause fires. Fire season is year-round in California. Always stub out and dispose of cigarette butts in the trash. Where campfires are allowed, make 100% sure you've extinguished them completely.

LEAVE A SMALL FOOTPRINT

Camp only at established campsites, reducing impact on the surrounding environment.

Stay on trails when hiking to prevent erosion and reduce impact on the local ecosystem; drive on established roads.

Leave campgrounds and hiking trails cleaner than you found them – pick up stray trash you find along the way; coastal storm gutters drain into the ocean.

Use non-nano, mineral sunscreen, which won't harm the marine environment.

Rent a bike or e-bike to explore some of your destinations; many California cities are very bike friendly.

STEVE MARTIN/SHUTTERSTOCK ©

SUPPORT LOCAL

Eat seasonally. Many independent restaurants specialize in using local, seasonal ingredients. With so much produced and harvested in California, it can be easy to eat seasonally without really trying.

Shop locally when you can, circulating your tourist dollars into the local economy. Pop-up markets and indie shops often carry locally made gift items and regional specialty treats you can't find elsewhere.

CLIMATE CHANGE & TRAVEL

It's impossible to ignore the impact we have when traveling, and the importance of making changes where we can. Lonely Planet urges all travelers to engage with their travel carbon footprint. There are many carbon calculators online that allow travellers to estimate the carbon emissions generated by their journey; try resurgence.org/resources/carbon-calculator.html. Many airlines and booking sites offer travelers the option of offsetting the impact of greenhouse gas emissions by contributing to climate-friendly initiatives around the world. We continue to offset the carbon footprint of all Lonely Planet staff travel, while recognising this is a mitigation more than a solution.

RESOURCES

lnt.org
happycow.net
visitcalifornia.com
greenbusinessca.org
supportblackowned.com/states/ca

CALIFORNIA RESPONSIBLE TRAVEL

ESSENTIAL NUTS-AND-BOLTS

PUBLIC HOLIDAYS

There are about a dozen public holidays in the US, when banks, government offices and schools are closed (on Mondays if the holiday falls on a weekend).

BORDER CROSSING

Crossing into Mexico from California is pretty straightforward, but driving into California can take significantly longer, especially at the Tijuana border crossing.

EMERGENCIES

Call 911. For non-life-threatening medical assistance, urgent-care clinics are faster and less costly than emergency rooms.

FAST FACTS

Time Zone
PST/PDT
(GMT-7/-8)

Country Code
+1

Electricity
110-120V/60Hz

GOOD TO KNOW

Travelers from countries with ESTA approval (esta.cbp.dhs.gov) can apply for a visa waiver.

Visitors from many countries may enter the US for stays of 90 days or fewer.

If there's no clear queue when ordering at a counter, find out where to take a number.

On multi-use paths, pedestrians always have right-of-way – bikes, skateboards and horses should yield.

Learning a few words in Spanish can enhance your day-to-day interactions.

ACCESSIBLE TRAVEL

The Americans with Disabilities Act requires that newer public buildings must be wheelchair-accessible, including restrooms. This does not apply to older private buildings; be sure to call ahead.

Hotels and motels built after 1993 must have at least one accessible room; ask about availability when booking.

Call 711 for telephone relay operators who can facilitate calls for the hard of hearing.

National and state parks often have at least one wheelchair-navigable trail or boardwalk for exploring the park. Specialized guides or accommodations are available with prior notice.

Download our free Accessible Travel guide at shop.lonelyplanet.com/products/accessible-travel-online-resources.

Explore wheelchair-accessible destinations at wheelchairtraveling.com.

NAVIGATION
GPS is helpful for navigating city streets and complicated freeway systems; don't rely on it in remote areas.

PUBLIC TOILETS
Where public toilets are not plentiful, gas stations or fast-food restaurants are your best option.

MARIJUANA
Weed is legal for 21-and-overs in California, but consuming in public or driving under the influence is not.

FAMILY TRAVEL

Hotels and motels Kids stay for free at some hotels and motels. Most also offer rollaway beds.

Restaurants and cafes High chairs and kids' menus are usually available at most casual-dining establishments.

Car travel Car seats are required for children under the age of six or weighing less than 60lbs; book ahead when renting a car.

Sights and attractions Children's discounts are usually offered at museums, zoos, amusement parks and theaters.

SMOKING Smoking is prohibited inside most buildings, and in some of California's cities and counties, it is illegal within a certain distance outside of public buildings. The legal age to buy cigarettes is 21. The same laws apply for vaping (smoking e-cigarettes).

ETIQUETTE
Californians tend to be a relaxed bunch and the culture is decidedly casual, but basic etiquette includes returning greetings, tipping your server and maintaining empathy for the state's visible unhoused population. When driving, strive to use your turn signal and not cut off other drivers.

LGBTIQ+ TRAVELERS
Inclusivity tends to be the norm in California, but it is a large and diverse state in terms of demographics and culture. Though largely progressive, attitudes vary from region to region. To grossly generalize, the further from the coast, the less tolerant.

Queer meccas include San Francisco's Castro District, West Hollywood and Palm Springs.

San Francisco Pride, with the largest Pride parade in the US, is celebrated the last weekend in June.

Same-sex marriage is legal in California.

Index

'The Tar Pits are the best. That smell just makes you realize how much history is beneath the LA pavement.'
SHAWN FORNO

'Early morning amongst the towering trees of Sequoia National Park is sublime. You can feel their majesty in the quiet before the day's visitors fill the park and trails.'
RYAN VER BERKMOES

'Channel Island foxes don't see humans as a threat, so keep your camping provisions locked down. I've seen bold little foxes steal away from campsites with unattended deli turkey and dirty diapers alike.'
WENDY YANAGIHARA

'I'll never forget waking up on a misty morning on the Lost Coast and sticking my head out of the tent to find an entire herd of elk grazing around me.'
ALEXIS AVERBUCK

'My first day in Palm Springs, I bumped into a stranger rocking a rainbow caftan – and I assumed they'd lost their way to the pool. A week later, I was the one strutting in a rainbow caftan. In Palm Springs, all paths lead to a pool eventually.'
ALISON BING

THIS BOOK

Design development
Lauren Egan, Tina García, Fergal Condon

Content development
Anne Mason

Cartography development
Wayne Murphy, Katerina Pavkova

Production development
Mario D'Arco, Dan Moore, Sandie Kestell, Virginia Moreno, Juan Winata

Series development leadership Liz Heynes, Darren O'Connell, Piers Pickard, Chris Zeiher

Commissioning editor
Daniel Bolger

Product editor James Appleton

Cartographer Alison Lyall

Book designer Fergal Condon

Coordinating editor
Michelle Bennett

Assisting editors
Mani Ramaswamy, Gabrielle Stefanos, Saralinda Turner

Cover researcher Lauren Egan

Thanks Gwen Cotter, Sandie Kestell, Amy Lynch, Darren O'Connell, John Taufa